METAMORPHOSIS

LESSONS FROM THE FORMATIVE YEARS OF THE CELTIC TIGER, 1979–1993

Con Power

OAK·TREE·PRESS·

Published by
OAK TREE PRESS
19 Rutland Street, Cork, Ireland
www.oaktreepress.com

© 2009 Con Power

A catalogue record of this book is
available from the British Library.

ISBN 978 1 904887 27 0

CONTENTS

Appendices

GRAPHS & TABLES

GRAPHS

TABLES

ACRONYMS

ACC	Agricultural Credit Corporation.
ACCA	Association of Chartered Certified Accountants.
ACCI	Association of Chambers of Commerce in Ireland.
ACE	Active Corps of Executives.
AFF	*An Foras Forbartha*, The National Institute for Physical Planning & Construction Research.
ALMACA	Association of Labour Management Administrators & Consultants on Absenteeism.
AMUE	Association for the Monetary Union of Europe.
AnCO	*An Comhairle Oiliúna*, The Industrial Training Authority.
BIAC	Business & Industry Advisory Committee [to the OECD].
BoR	*Building on Reality 1984-1987*, National Economic Plan, published in October 1984.
BRITE	Business-Related Initiative for Technology-based Enterprises.
BSTAI	Business Studies Teachers' Association of Ireland.
CAP	Common Agricultural Policy.
CBI	Confederation of British Industry.
CCI	Chambers of Commerce of Ireland.
CEEP	European Centre of Enterprises with Public Participation and of Enterprises of General Economic Interest.
CEIF	Council of European Industrial Federations.
CIF	Construction Industry Federation.
CII	Confederation of Irish Industry, which changed its name from FII in March 1970.
CIMA	Chartered Institute of Management Accountants.
CIO	Committee for Industrial Organisation.

CIPD	Chartered Institute of Personnel & Development.
CIPFA	Chartered Institute of Public Finance & Accountancy.
CITI	Chartered Institute of Transport in Ireland.
CORI	Conference of Religious of Ireland.
CPI	Consumer Price Index.
CPSU	Civil & Public Services Union.
CRC	Central Review Committee (of the PNR).
CRO	Companies Registration Office.
CSO	Central Statistics Office.
DevCO	Development Co-operation Organisation.
DIRT	Deposit Interest Retention Tax.
DTI	Dublin Transportation Initiative.
EAP	Employee Assistance Programme.
EBR	Exchequer Borrowing Requirement.
EBRD	European Bank for Reconstruction & Development.
EC	European Community: The executive bodies of the EEC, the ECSC and EURATOM merged in 1967 to form the 'European Community', although the constituent bodies retained their separate legal existence. The term 'European Community' was used more generally after the passing of the Single European Act (SEA) in 1987 and was formally adopted in the Maastricht Treaty in 1992.
ECSC	European Coal & Steel Community: Established under the Treaty of Paris, signed on 18 April 1951, and effective from 23 July 1952.
ECU	European Currency Unit.
EEC	European Economic Community: Established under the Treaty of Rome, signed on 25 March 1957, and effective from 1 January 1958.
EFL	English as a Foreign Language.
EFTA	European Free Trade Area.
EIB	European Investment Bank.
EMF	European Management Forum [later World Management Forum].
EMI	European Monetary Institute.

EMS	European Monetary System.
EMU	Economic & Monetary Union.
EOP	European Orientation Programme, now the Export Orientation Programme.
ERDF	European Regional Development Fund.
ERDO	Eastern Regional Development Organisation.
ERM	Exchange Rate Mechanism (of the EMS).
ESCB	European System of Central Banks.
ESF	European Social Fund.
ESHA	European Secondary Heads Association.
ESR	Export Sales Relief.
ESRI	Economic & Social Research Institute.
ETUC	European Trade Union Confederation.
EU	European Union: The Treaty on European Union, the Maastricht Treaty, was signed on 7 February 1992, and was effective from 1 November 1993.
EURAM	European Academy of Management.
EURATOM	European Atomic Energy Community: Established at the same time as the EEC, under a separate treaty.
FÁS	*Foras Áiseanna Saothair*, The Training & Employment Authority.
FDI	Foreign Direct Investment.
FEIG	Free Enterprise Information Group [of the CEIF].
FEOGA	European Agricultural Guarantee & Guidance Fund.
FIE	Federation of Irish Employers.
FII	Federation of Irish Industry, forerunner to the CII.
FIM	Federation of Irish Manufacturers.
FIS	Family Income Supplement.
FSIA	Financial Services Industry Association, now Financial Services Ireland.
FUE	Federated Union of Employers.
GATT	General Agreement on Tariffs & Trade.
GDP	Gross Domestic Product.
GDR	German Democratic Republic.

GNP	Gross National Product.
IBEC	Irish Business & Employers' Confederation (formerly CII).
ICC	Industrial Credit Corporation.
ICM	Institute of Credit Management.
ICMSA	Irish Creamery Milk Suppliers Association.
ICOS	Irish Co-operative Organisation Society.
ICSA	Institute of Chartered Secretaries & Administrators.
ICTU	Irish Congress of Trade Unions.
IDA	Industrial Development Authority (now IDA Ireland).
IEA	Irish Exporters Association.
IEI	Institution of Engineers in Ireland, now Engineers Ireland.
IFA	Irish Farmers' Association.
IFSC	International Financial Services Centre.
IGC	Institute of Guidance Counsellors.
IIRS	Institute for Industrial Research & Standards.
ILO	International Labour Organisation.
IMF	International Monetary Fund.
IMI	Irish Management Institute.
INOU	Irish National Organisation of the Unemployed.
IPA	Institute of Public Administration.
IPC	Irish Productivity Centre.
IPM	Institute of Personnel Management.
IRL	Irish Rural Link.
ISTA	Irish Science Teachers Association.
ITIC	Irish Tourism Industry Confederation.
JETRO	Japan External Trade Organisation.
LRT	Light Rail Transit, now LUAS.
MCC	Manpower Consultative Committee.
NBST	National Board for Science & Technology.
NCAD	National College of Art & Design.
NCCA	National Council for Curriculum Assessment.

NCEA	National Council for Educational Awards.
NCPP	National Centre for Partnership & Performance.
NESC	National Economic & Social Council.
NESDO	National Economic & Social Development Office.
NESF	National Economic & Social Forum.
NGO	Non-Governmental Organisation.
NIHE	National Institute of Higher Education.
NMS	National Manpower Service.
NRA	National Roads Authority.
NRB	National Rehabilitation Board.
NTMA	National Treasury Management Agency.
NWA	National Wages Agreement.
NWCI	National Women's Council of Ireland.
NYCI	National Youth Council of Ireland.
OECD	Organisation for Economic Co-operation & Development.
OJ	Official Journal [of the European Union].
OPEC	Organisation of the Petroleum Exporting Countries.
PCP	Public Capital Programme.
PCW	*Programme for Competitiveness & Work*, 1994-1996.
PD	Progressive Democrats.
PEE	*Programme for Economic Expansion*, November 1958.
PESP	Programme for Economic & Social Progress.
PFIC	Passive Foreign Investment Company.
PND	*Programme for National Development*, 1979-1981.
PNR	*Programme for National Recovery*, October 1987.
PPP	Public Private Partnership.
PSBR	Public Sector Borrowing Requirement.
R&TD	Research and technical development.
RDO	Regional Development Organisation.
RPT	Residential Property Tax.
RTC	Regional Technical College.
SCORE	Service Corps of Retired Executives.

SEA	Single European Act: Signed on 17 February 1986, at Luxembourg and on 28 February 1986, at The Hague, effective from 1 July 1987.
SFA	Small Firms Association.
SITA	*Societé Internationale de Telecommunication Aeronautique.*
SMEs	Small and medium-sized enterprises.
SPEE	*Second Programme for Economic Expansion*, 1964-1970.
SSIA	Special Saving & Investment Account.
SWIFT	Society for Worldwide International Financial Telecommunication.
TD	Teachta Dála – member of Dáil Éireann.
TPESD	*Third Programme for Economic & Social Development*, 1969-1972.
UCC	University College Cork.
UCD	University College Dublin.
UCG	University College Galway, now the National University of Ireland, Galway.
UCITS	Undertakings for collective investment in transferable securities.
UK	United Kingdom of Great Britain & Northern Ireland.
UN	United Nations.
UNICE	Union of Industrial & Employers' Confederations of Europe (renamed BUSINESSEUROPE: The Confederation of European Business in January 2007).
USA	United States of America.
VPT	Vocation preparation and training.
WEF	World Economic Forum.
YEA	Youth Employment Agency.

ABOUT THE AUTHOR

Con Power was Director, Economic Policy, Irish Business & Employers' Confederation (IBEC), formerly the Confederation of Irish Industry (CII), from 1979 to 1993. More recently, from October 2004 to October 2008, he was the inaugural Chairperson of the Financial Services Ombudsman Council, a statutory body appointed by the Minister for Finance under the *Central Bank & Financial Services Authority of Ireland Act 2004*. As a professional accountant, he serves on the Panel of the Disciplinary and Regulatory Committees of the Association of Chartered Certified Accountants (ACCA), London and is a member of the ACCA Ambassador programme. He also lectures on national economics, including to visiting groups from alumni associations of USA universities.

On two occasions, he was seconded from the CII to the Civil Service, in the Department of the Environment and the Department of the Taoiseach. He played a key role in public policy reforms and national economic initiatives during the formative years of the Celtic Tiger. Prior to that, from 1963 to 1979, he was a civil servant, a College of Technology lecturer, a Research Officer (Unit Leader) with a State institute and Director of the Institute for Technology, Sligo. He authored publications on construction management topics and co-authored research publications on aspects of construction technology. He published some 300 articles, mainly in professional, technical and trade journals, and served on a wide range of governing authorities, commissions and committees in Ireland, the European Union and the Organisation for Economic Co-operation & Development (OECD), in a number of cases as chair. He was one of the inaugural directors of the Institute of European Affairs in 1991.

From 1993 to 2005, Con Power was a consultant economist, with his own economics and public affairs company: DCP Consultants Limited.

He was educated at University College Dublin, where he obtained BComm (Hons) and MEconSc (Hons) degrees. He qualified as a Chartered Secretary (FCIS), Chartered Management Accountant (FCMA) and Chartered Certified Accountant (FCCA). He obtained a PhD in Business Administration from Pacific Western University, with institutional authorisation and degree approval by the State of California, and was admitted a Companion of the Institution of Engineers of Ireland (CompIEI) in recognition of his services to the engineering profession.

ACKNOWLEDGEMENTS

The material in this book is drawn mainly from my years as Director of Economic Policy with the CII from 1979 to 1993, although some aspects are influenced by my earlier career in the public sector and by my later career as an economic consultant.

I am grateful to successive Presidents, members of the Finance & General Purposes Committee, National Executive and National Council, Sectoral and Central Policy chairpersons and the general membership of the CII for giving me the opportunity to serve on many official committees, commissions, working groups and governing authorities in Ireland, the EU and OECD. In particular, I am grateful to my colleague, Liam Connellan, who was Director General for my entire period in the CII. He encouraged me and gave me the freedom to act with great personal flexibility in carrying out my work. I am grateful to Taoisigh, Ministers, party leaders, Opposition spokespersons, TDs, MEPs, Senators, local politicians and civil and public servants and to the representatives of business, trade unions, farmers and other social partnership organisations with whom I worked on official bodies. A number of them are named in the book; others are not, simply because I had to work within constraints of the size of the work.

Some years ago, during my time as an economic consultant, I attempted to begin a book chronicling my years in the CII but, despite the encouragement of my business partner, Mary Hickey, I failed to sustain the effort. Towards the end of 2005, after I retired, my friend and mentor of many years, Professor Vincent McBrierty, guided me to undertake the current project.

My thanks are due to Professor McBrierty and to my good friend of many decades, Myles Tierney, FPRII, PC, for reading drafts and for painstakingly debating issues with me. Without their untiring support, I could not have sustained the effort. My thanks are due to Mary Hickey for her earlier encouragement to get me to write the book, for her sound advice on structure, presentation, layout, for reading sample chapters and for her advice on the selection of the title. Professor Terence Brown gave me invaluable advice on style and presentation, on the realities of publishing and on the constraints of the market for books! Professor Tony Cunningham read a number of sample chapters from an earlier draft. Turlough O'Sullivan, Director General of IBEC read the penultimate draft and kindly gave me valuable feedback, all of which is reflected in the finished work.

Ruairí Quinn TD, who I have known since 1969 and who shared with me many experiences chronicled in the book, forensically read both the penultimate draft and the final draft and gave me detailed feedback. Charlie McCreevy, Member of the European Commission, encouraged me during the years when the book was in gestation, read the final draft and kindly provided the *Foreword*.

Special thanks are due to Joe Tiernan, former President of the Construction Industry Federation (CIF) and long-serving Chairman of HomeBond, the National House Building Guarantee Scheme, for his entrepreneurial view of the potential market for the book and his vote of confidence in supporting its publication.

As Mary Hickey, Vincent McBrierty and Myles Tierney reminded me on many occasions, I had too much material for one book. I was obliged to make choices and omit much of what I originally thought was important. Those hard choices were mine and I apologise if I have omitted material that others consider should have been included or if I failed to mention significant players on the political and economic stage.

Con Power
Dublin
November 2008

FOREWORD

In this book, Con Power has distilled a lifetime's experience as an influential participant in the development of Ireland's social and economic policy. He has provided an insightful and authoritative overview of the State's economic fortunes since its foundation in 1922.

As a young nation, Ireland set out to earn its place among the nations of the world. Growth was slow in the early years. The international depression of the 1930s, the 'economic war' between Britain and Ireland and the 'national emergency' during World War II led to isolationist policies that resulted in economic stagnation and high emigration.

The failure of economic policies in those early decades is chronicled in the watershed Lemass *Programme for Economic Expansion* of 1958, which opened the door for foreign direct investment and heralded a period of industrial development and growth as a prelude to Ireland's decision to join the then EEC in 1973. Growth continued at a more modest level up to 1980, with a focus on diversification of international trade and reduced dependence on the UK market.

National and international factors led to a dramatic downturn, with zero growth between 1981 and 1986. The early 1980s saw political instability, when governments did not give economic leadership and tried, in vain, to stimulate growth through flawed public policy decisions, based upon unsustainably high borrowing, excessive taxation on income and capital and unsustainable levels of public expenditure. The seeds of disaster, thus sown, led to a debt / GDP ratio that, by 1986, virtually put national economic sovereignty at risk.

A turning point came with acceptance of the urgent need to address the problems with the public finances, as State borrowing reached unsustainable levels. The *Programme for National Recovery* of 1987, agreed between the Government and the social partners, signalled a profound attitudinal change in the approach to economic and social development.

The sustained, very rapid economic growth that began in the second half of the 1990s undoubtedly was stimulated by the vigorous implementation of policies to reduce taxes on both capital and labour, to lighten regulatory burdens, to stimulate competition in previously protected sectors, and to make risk-taking worthwhile in Ireland for the first time in decades. From 1997 onwards, this more liberal economic approach delivered a decade of unprecedented growth and transformed the economy into the strongest in Europe.

The beneficial alliance between the business and education sectors also contributed to laying the foundation for Ireland's continuing cutting-edge leadership in the rapidly-growing global knowledge economy. Equally important was the initiative to foster the early development of Ireland's international financial services industry and the promotion of a range of internationally-traded professional and knowledge-based services.

Access to the huge European Union market and a low corporate and direct tax regime were, and remain, essential ingredients in attracting foreign direct investment. In the current period of global economic and financial turbulence, we can learn from Ireland's experience in managing change successfully in times of adversity: Con Power's analysis, in effect, constitutes a self-help manual for business inputs to the process of national economic and social policy formulation. The emphasis on economic realism has an enduring relevance. So too have the policies involving the incentivisation of human endeavour, of risk-taking, and of capital investment through low taxation, light-touch regulation and open and flexible markets that have been a consistent feature of public policy since 1997 and must remain so.

Charlie McCreevy
Member of the European Commission
Brussels

INTRODUCTION

When Con Power set out to write this book, the world was a very different place to what it is now. As he discussed the project with me, over two years ago, I wondered to myself whether there would be much of a readership for the history of macro-economic policy between 1979 and 1993. Since then, the world's economy has encountered the worst global financial crisis since the Great Depression of the 1930s.

Ireland and Spain have their own unique problems because of a burst property bubble. For Ireland, the construction industry and the housing market have had a very hard landing, instead of the soft landing that had been predicted by many economists.

In January 2009, the Irish Government is grappling with our national economic crisis. In September 2008, the Government announced that it was bringing forward the 2009 Budget by seven weeks. However, the public accounts out-turn for 2008 has made the Budget effectively defunct. New plans are being prepared as the Government attempts to obtain social partnership agreement to what will be a painful readjustment of public expenditure. This is not an easy task, and there is no guarantee of success.

It is not the first time that Ireland has been confronted by a major crisis that appeared overwhelming and without a solution. Con Power tells the tale, in a most interesting and comprehensive way, of how it was done before. He is uniquely qualified because he lived through many of the events. He was a player, in his role as Director of Economic Affairs within the Irish Business & Employers Confederation (IBEC), and formerly the Confederation of Irish Industry (CII), from 1979 to 1993.

He has an extensive archive of papers, press releases and commentaries from his time with the CII and IBEC. Con's earlier career as an educationalist richly informs the retelling of the socio-economic and political history of Ireland since our Independence. It was a hard journey, which recent prosperity has obscured.

Ireland is an old nation and a young State. With the partition of the island in 1921, the new independent State found itself cut off from the comparatively rich industrial North-East of Northern Ireland. The 1920s was not the best of times to establish a fledging, predominantly agricultural, democratic State on the periphery of Europe.

The Treaty of Versailles created many new nation states and dismembered two European empires – Austro-Hungary and Germany. Such was the economic and political turbulence across Europe that only three of the new States – Czechoslovakia, Finland and Ireland – remained democratic until the outbreak of the Second World War in 1939.

It takes generations of free citizens to learn how to manage the institutions of the State so as to develop and prosper in a democracy. Countries like Britain, France, Denmark and the Netherlands have been doing it for centuries. None of them would claim that they have been continuously successful.

Creating a civic society that tolerates difference, enshrines the rule of law and provides the comprehensive framework for an enterprise economy is not an easy task. One only has to look at some of the new member States of the European Union that emerged from the Communist empire of the now defunct Soviet Union. Here in Ireland, we take for granted an impartial judiciary and a non-corrupt, politically neutral civil service.

Con Power's work traces the period of recovery from the disastrous General Election of 1977. Presented with a seductive manifesto by Jack Lynch's Fianna Fáil, the Irish people allowed themselves to be conned into thinking that the nation could spend its way into prosperity with borrowed money. The inevitable burst followed the short-lived boom.

We had to learn the lessons of managing a new national currency in a period of constant fluctuation and, consequently, high interest rates and inflation. When I became Minister for Finance in 1994, the goal of the euro was on the distant horizon. Getting into the secure harbour of low inflation with a hard currency, available at low interest rates, was the overwhelming priority.

When we did so, our economy prospered dramatically but we failed to learn the new disciplines of the situation. We carried on as before. As one economic commentator put it: "after we joined the Euro, instead of learning how to become Germans, we continued to behave as if we were Italians"!

This book has arrived at a very appropriate moment. Most Irish people under the age of 40 have no experience of a recession, let alone a depression. Those that do may understand that some of the old solutions to our problems in the past, like interest rate adjustments and devaluation, are no longer available to us now. We have the strength of the euro as a hard currency that has not fallen in value like so many others. This is not a bad thing, as the people of bankrupt Iceland now realise. However, it does mean that we have to develop new policy instruments to resolve our problems within the context of a very changed global world to the one that existed in the last century.

We should not be despondent, as economic recovery and success have been achieved before in difficult times and with fewer resources. This book is a good place to start learning from our successful past.

We are indebted to the author for his scholarship and vision.

Ruairi Quinn, TD
Leader of the Labour Party 1997 to 2002
Minister for Finance 1994 - 1997
Minister for Enterprise and Employment 1993 – 1994
Minister for Labour 1983 – 1987
Minister for the Pubic Service 1985 – 1987
Minister of State for the Environment 1982 – 1983

CHAPTER 1
THE CONTEXT

THE CELTIC TIGER YEARS

The Irish economy was the showcase of the European Union (EU) and of the Organisation for Economic Co-operation & Development (OECD) for more than a decade from 1994. Success was marked particularly by the high level of employment, low unemployment, high living standards, population growth, high inward migration and prudent management of the public finances. By 2006, Irish Gross Domestic Product (GDP) *per capita*, at €34,000, was almost 140% of the average of the EU 27 Member States and was the second highest in the EU, after Luxembourg.[1] In 2007, GDP *per capita* was about €36,200 or 147% of the EU 27 average, remaining second after Luxembourg. Unemployment was around 4.3%, having been stable at that level, or slightly less, for five years and even below 4% in 2001. The number of persons at work increased by over 46% in the decade from 1997 and was more than 2 million in 2006. Economic growth, including employment growth, was greatly facilitated by the creation of an environment supportive of enterprise, including better management of Exchequer finances and a reduced level of National Debt.[1] Economic issues are examined in **Chapter 3**, *The Economy: Warts and All!* The contrast between Ireland in 2006 and Ireland of the early 1980s was dramatic!

One of the most obvious manifestations of success has been population growth, coupled with strong inward migration from 1996. The 2006

---

[1]   GDP is the total value of all goods and traded services produced in the State during any given period, usually a year. Gross National Product (GNP) is the total value of all goods and traded services that accrue to the residents of the State. The difference between the two figures is the net flows into and out of the State, such as the net profit repatriation by multinational enterprises, emigrants' and immigrants' remittances, and interest on the foreign element of the National Debt. In most OECD countries, there is little difference between GDP and GNP. In Ireland's case, however, there is a major difference, mainly because of the large number of USA multinationals here. As an illustration, the Irish GDP of €174.7 billion in 2006 (*per capita* €41,205) was reduced by over 14.3% to get the Irish GNP of €149.1 billion (*per capita* €35,173). [CSO, *National Accounts 2006*]. On a GNP *per capita* basis, Ireland was 5th in terms of the EU 27 average, after Luxembourg, the Netherlands, Austria and Sweden.

Census recorded a population of almost 4.3 million, the largest since 1861. The following two graphs show population and migration in a historical context and illustrate the recent positive trends. Population fell from over 6.5 million in 1841, the year of the first Census, to 4.4 million in 1861, a fall of almost 33% in 20 years. The rate of decrease was lower after that, but the population continued to fall until it reached 2.8 million in 1961, the lowest level on record. After that, population increased at each Census, with the exception of a small drop of 15,000 persons (0.4%) between the Census of 1986 and that of 1991. The population then increased by over 20% in the 15 years between 1991 and 2006.

Graph 1.1: Census of Population, 1841-2006

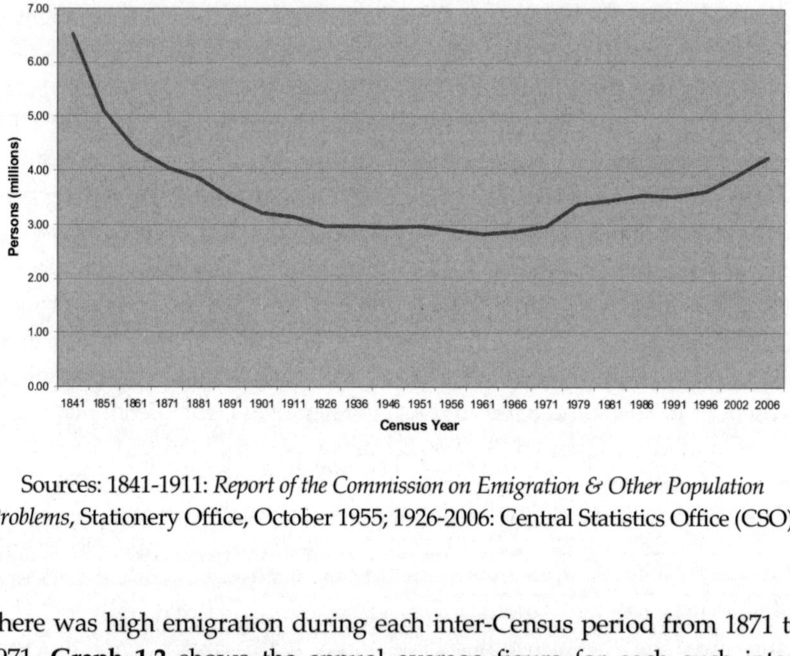

Sources: 1841-1911: *Report of the Commission on Emigration & Other Population Problems*, Stationery Office, October 1955; 1926-2006: Central Statistics Office (CSO).

There was high emigration during each inter-Census period from 1871 to 1971. **Graph 1.2** shows the annual average figure for each such inter-Census period, with the highest level of 59,700 *per annum* recorded in the period 1881-1891. The period 1971 to 1979 showed average annual net inward migration of 13,600, and this was reflected in a population increase of over 13%. Emigration returned in 1980, followed by a small net inward migration in 1981. The graph shows each individual year, rather than inter-Census annual averages, from 1980 to 2006. Emigration resumed in 1982 and continued each year to 1991, reaching a peak for that period of 46,000 in 1989. Small net inward migration in 1992 was followed by the return of low emigration for each of the next three years, 1993-1995. Net inward migration has continued at a sustained level in each year since 1996 and reached almost 70,000 in 2006. The increase in population of 322,645 between the 2002 Census and that of 2006 comprised the natural increase in population of 131,314 and net inward migration of 191,331.

Graph 1.2: Net Migration (000s): 1871-2006

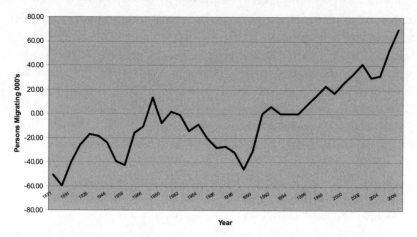

Sources: 1871-1951: *Report of the Commission on Emigration & Other Population Problems*, Stationery Office, Dublin, October 1955; 1956-2006: CSO.

International financial difficulties emerged, however, during 2007 and these adversely affected the Irish economy, most notably the stock exchange, the construction industry and Government finances. There are now grey clouds on the horizon, both within Ireland and on the world stage, which will require Government's re-dedication to prudent national economic management. Inflation was 4.9% *per annum* on average in 2007, as measured by the Consumer Price Index (CPI), about twice the EU average. The economy has been losing competitiveness at a time when there is growing overseas competition in goods, traded services and the attractiveness of business location. At the end of 2006, the Central Bank of Ireland identified a number of external and domestic risks to the Irish economy.[2] The external risks were the correction to the USA current account deficit; the adjustment to the USA housing market; and difficulties in the global oil and commodities markets. The domestic risks were the high dependence on the construction sector; the weakening of our

international competitiveness; high and rising house prices; consumer
spending debt levels; and an inflation rate that was higher than the
Eurozone average. In 2006, the Economic & Social Research Institute
(ESRI) identified three issues that gave rise to concern:[3] the growth in the
deficit on Ireland's external current account balance of payments since
2003; an overly expansionary Budget for 2007; and the possible negative
impact on the Irish economy of events in the USA, including the fall in the
value of the US$. The ESRI concluded that it was vital for Ireland to
maintain international competitiveness. Events in late summer and early
autumn 2007 confirmed the accuracy of the warnings given by the Central
Bank and the ESRI about house prices in Ireland and the possible knock-on
effect of financial turmoil in the USA due to some inappropriate mortgage
lending practices there. The ESRI, in December 2007, recorded that real
GNP growth was estimated at 4.4% in 2007, fuelled in part by
unsustainable components such as the effects of the maturing Special
Saving & Investment Accounts (SSIAs) and the Government's 'highly
stimulatory fiscal stance'.[4] The ESRI forecast GNP growth of 2.3% in 2008,
the lowest since 1992, against a background of continuing uncertainty in
international financial markets and slowdowns in the UK, the USA and the
Eurozone. The ESRI's projection for unemployment in 2008 was 5.8%, with
employment growing by less than 0.5%. In its *Quarterly Economic
Commentary* for Spring 2008, the ESRI reduced its 2008 forecast to 1.6%
GNP growth (the lowest since 1988) and forecast unemployment to reach
6% with no employment growth and a reduction in net inward migration
to 20,000. By the time the *Quarterly Economic Commentary* for Summer 2008
was published, the ESRI forecast a recession in 2008 with both GNP and
GDP reduced by 0.4%, the first recession since 1983. The ESRI also forecast
rising unemployment, a decline in investment, deteriorating Government
finances and a return to net outward migration (emigration) of 20,000 by
2009.

The bleak, but undoubtedly realistic, picture painted by the ESRI
presents a challenge for the Government and for the social partners. Can
Ireland learn any lessons from its immediate past in addressing the
concerns that unfolded in 2006 and 2007 and that gained momentum in
2008? In particular, has Ireland learned the lesson that control of public
finances and of public expenditure is one essential prerequisite to
maintaining the domestic environment for economic stability and growth?

THE POOR RELATION IN EUROPE

The history of the past few decades has been well-documented.[1] Probably one of the bleakest pictures was authoritatively painted in the *Programme for National Recovery* (PNR), agreed by the Government and the social partners in 1987.[5] The PNR acknowledged that the Government and the social partners were conscious of the grave state of Irish economic and social life, and that the principles that should govern its implementation were those contained in the National Economic & Social Council (NESC) Report of November, 1986.[6] The section dealing with the social partnership programmes in **Chapter 5**, *The Turning Point* records the depressing profile of the Irish economy given in the 1987 PNR. The statistics were of low GDP *per capita* relative to the EC average; high levels of National Debt and debt servicing; high annual Exchequer borrowing; high interest rates; high unemployment; high net emigration; and a low level of investment in productive assets.

HOW SUCCESS WAS ACHIEVED

The story of how Ireland succeeded in transforming itself from the bleak situation of 1987 to the success of the Celtic Tiger years has many ingredients, originating domestically, in the EU, and on the world stage. This treatise is an account from the perspective of one insider, based primarily in the Confederation of Irish Industry (CII),[7] a national non-governmental organisation (NGO), who played a key role in national economic initiatives during the critical years of 1979 to 1993.[#]

The CII had campaigned consistently since the beginning of the 1980s for necessary public policy reforms, notably those subsequently contained in the PNR, October 1987. As early as December 1981, the CII signalled to Government that the current budget deficit was at an unsustainably high level. It argued that borrowing to fuel current expenditure starved the Public Capital Programme (PCP) of the ability to provide adequate economic and social infrastructure networks, essential prerequisites to

---

[1] See official publications of the Department of Finance, the National Treasury Management Agency (NTMA), the Central Bank of Ireland, the ESRI, the NESC and numerous other published sources.

[#] See **Appendix I** for a description of the CII and **Appendix II** for Con Power's memberships of governing authorities, commissions and committees in Ireland, the EU and the OECD.

economic growth.[8] The CII strongly criticised the politicians' unwillingness to face economic reality at that time and the resultant erosion of Ireland's international competitiveness, leading to lost export orders, factory closures, redundancies, an alarming deficit of about 14% of national output on Ireland's international current account balance of payments, an inflation rate of about 20% in 1981, and a rate of unemployment that was among the highest in the European Economic Community (EEC).

By the end of 1986, the CII proposed a *Programme for National Recovery* to address the key crisis elements of high unemployment; the unsustainable level of National Debt; and the stagnation in the main productive sectors, as flagged above.[9] In the same submission, the CII suggested a *Plan for Industrial Expansion*, with proposals relative to cost-competitiveness based on the discipline of the European Monetary System (EMS); a reduction in interest rates that would come about as a consequence of correcting the serious imbalance in the public finances; reductions in the costs of the electricity and telecommunications public utilities; and a reduction in liability insurance costs consequent on a change in Court procedures. The CII made recommendations concerning the promotion of industrial investment; investment in the network of national roads; initiatives to recruit additional employees in industry; the restructuring of personal taxation to help overcome the disincentive effect of high marginal tax rates; and the recruitment of a significant number of export marketing trainees.

The CII made an annual pre-Budget submission on the economy to the Government. Preparation of the pre-Budget submission included my informal consultations, as Director of Economic Policy, with Ministers, Opposition spokespersons, and senior civil servants. The 1987 process followed the standard procedure, together with the usual range of formal meetings between a representative delegation of the CII and the Taoiseach, Minister for Finance, other relevant Ministers, and appropriate Opposition spokespersons. Mindful, however, that a General Election was due in 1987, the CII mandated me to discuss directly the seriousness of the national economic situation with Charles J Haughey TD, as Leader of Fianna Fáil, then in Opposition.

My two briefing meetings with Charles J Haughey on behalf of the CII raised issues that, in retrospect, helped to shape Government thinking in a fundamental way as part of the strategy for national economic recovery from 1987 onwards.[10] The first meeting, on an invitation from Mr Haughey, was revealing, to say the least. He was well briefed on CII economic submissions and publications, which he held in a folder labelled

The Power Papers! He sought clarification on many issues therein, given subsequently at the second meeting by way of presentation of a set of CII briefing papers on a variety of economic, fiscal, social and infrastructural issues. Subsequent to that meeting, the CII received copies of the 71-page Fianna Fáil 1987 General Election Manifesto, called *The Programme for National Recovery*,[11] a title that had been taken directly from the CII 1987 Budget submission of November 1986. The Fianna Fáil document contained sections entitled *The Issue is Growth, The Scope for Growth, Improving the National Infrastructure, Caring for Basic Values* and *National Affairs*. The document mirrored many of the issues covered in CII publications and submissions: public finances; the National Debt; personal and corporate taxation; industrial development strategy; science and technology; tourism; energy; traded services; the role of State enterprises; transport infrastructure; environment; and education and training, among other economic and social issues. *Inter alia*, the document proposed to make Ireland a financial centre of international significance and to establish a National Roads Authority with responsibility for the development of an integrated network of national roads, including access to the principal ports and airports. From this, it is clear that the CII representations to the Leader of Fianna Fáil had been successful both in regard to acceptance and to proposed implementation.

ECONOMIC LITERACY: THE KEY

The CII's main target audiences were the Government, Opposition spokespersons, all members of the Oireachtas and relevant public authorities, together with the institutions of the EU, the OECD, and wider international governmental organisations. The major focus was on central policy issues dealing with legislation, regulation, and public administration. The CII focused on core issues of concern to the generality of business and industry, while the individual federations, associations, and groups within the CII dealt with specific sectoral issues important to their own members.

Regular publications of the CII included the weekly *Newsletter, Monthly Economic Trends, Monthly Business Forecast*, sectoral publications, discussion documents, business research publications, the *CII Annual Report*, and the *Annual Reports* of each affiliated organisation. Academic and other experts, commissioned by the CII, prepared many of the discussion documents. Business research publications generally were commissioned from academic staff of the universities, and were intended for use mainly in post-primary schools and higher education institutions. CII publications were widely disseminated, including to member enterprises, members of Dáil Éireann and Seanad Éireann, senior civil servants and to a wide spectrum of policy-forming and other agencies.[1]

The CII Press Office issued media releases and organised press conferences, involving the print media, radio, and television, at national, regional, and local levels. Other functions were the organisation of seminars, the distribution of CII publications, arranging the provision of speakers at functions, and the commissioning and promotion of the use of industrial film and video.

The CII placed a high priority on getting its message across to the general public, as well as to politicians and public authorities. The basic philosophy was that, in a democracy, unless there was a public knowledge and acceptance of a case, there could never be a political willingness to act.

The CII established a close working relationship with the Government, each relevant Minister and Government Department, Opposition spokespersons, and with a wide range of public authorities. These links were established with permanent officials, and with elected representatives and appointed governing authorities. Interaction with Government and with other public authorities was effected through formal and informal meetings, making submissions, distribution of CII publications, news media publicity, and the commissioning of public opinion polls, as well as through membership of the various Governmental and other public authority boards, commissions, and committees.

A structure of regular meetings was established with An Taoiseach, An Tánaiste, Ministers, Opposition spokespersons, TDs, Senators, Members of the European Parliament, groups within political parties, civil servants, local politicians and local authority staff. Periodic submissions were made to Government and to Ministers and their Departments, inputs were made to Green Papers, to White Papers, and to Bills passing through the Oireachtas, and responses were submitted to discussion documents. *Ad hoc* submissions were made on the CII's own initiative, as necessary, on specific issues of concern to business and industry.

---

[1]   Organisations to which CII publications were distributed included the local and other public authorities, Irish Members of the European Parliament, EU and OECD institutions, wider international organisations dealing with trade issues, and to the news media. Additionally, selected publications were distributed to key specific target groups such as county managers, county engineers, educational establishments, and others.

My personal research relied heavily upon the *Parliamentary Reports of Dáil Éireann*, which provided a wealth of authoritative information on public policy and on national economic and social issues. The quality of the contributions on both sides of the House was consistently of the highest level. The *Dáil Reports* demonstrated a depth and breadth of knowledge by politicians of the fundamental nature of the economic malaise in Ireland during the late 1970s and the 1980s, prior to the resumption of social partnership in its more structured format from 1987 onwards, following the short-lived National Understandings of 1979 and 1980. Notwithstanding the political turbulence of the early 1980s, with a series of short-lived Governments, it is surprising that corrective action was not taken earlier by whatever party or parties formed the Government. Could it be that, in a democracy, action by the politicians necessarily had to await the confirmation of widespread public acceptance of economic reality that was implicit in the consensus reached by the representatives of the trade unions, employers, industry and farmers organisations, together with Government appointed members in the NESC's 1986 Report?[12]

POINTERS FOR THE FUTURE & LESSONS THAT OTHERS MIGHT LEARN

There are consistent and recurrent themes throughout the CII campaigns from 1979 to 1993 that remain relevant in Ireland to-day. There is a continuing need for the generation of economic awareness on a broad basis within the community, and for social partnership to unite all stakeholders in the common objective of sustaining growth and ensuring equity in resource distribution. There is a continuing need for vigilance in the management of the public finances, and to guard against community expectations and aspirations outstripping economic reality. Associated with this is the need for vigilance about the level of inflation, especially Government-generated inflation. In relation to promoting an environment for enterprise, there is a need for a balanced approach to business legislation, business taxation, and employee issues, including employee shareholding and participation. Education and training needs to be up-dated constantly in line with, and even ahead of, international best practice. Challenges remain in infrastructure development, balanced regional development, and environmental protection and enhancement. Putting together all of the elements, there is a requirement for a dynamic in identifying national business growth sectors in the light of international developments and of the ongoing international reallocation of product and service specialisations.

Much was learned in Ireland in this regard in the decade and a half prior to the Celtic Tiger era. It is vital that these lessons, then learned the hard way, are not forgotten; they remain relevant not only for Ireland, but for the new and aspirant Member States of the EU and for developing economies throughout the world.

The CII's submissions, published articles, public lectures, and public affairs campaigns during the decade and a half prior to 1993 helped to create the conditions for public acceptance of the steps necessary to achieve national economic renaissance. A study of the CII's campaigns makes the case for a continuing proactive *economic awareness* role for the representatives of business and industry, in both the private and public sectors.

SUMMARY

Major elements of the CII's economic development work during the years 1979 to 1993 contributed significantly to underpinning the Celtic Tiger years, specifically:

◊ Public awareness campaigns and promotion of a public understanding of the economic difficulties that Ireland then faced.

◊ Promotion, facilitation, and direct involvement in business and education linkage initiatives.

◊ Social partnership inputs, notably through the NESC and the National Understandings and social partnership programmes from 1979 onwards.

◊ Submissions to Government regarding public sector management and finances.

◊ Promotion of issues relative to business cost competitiveness.

◊ Promotion of more widespread training within business and industry.

◊ Initiatives relative to infrastructure development, environmental protection, and regional development.

◊ Initiatives relative to the promotion of internationally-traded financial services and of other knowledge-based industries, together with natural resource-based and manufacturing sectors with economic growth potential.

CHAPTER 2
THE EVOLUTION OF
NATIONAL POLICY

THE NEW STATE

Ireland is a young State. The time since the ratification of the Treaty with the UK in 1922 is short enough to warrant brief reference to the early years of national sovereignty, as a background to more recent economic developments. The Articles of Agreement for a Treaty between Britain and Ireland were signed on 6 December 1921, and approved by Dáil Éireann on 7 January 1922.[1] Key issues of governance and public finances contained in the Articles include:

> 'Ireland shall have the same constitutional status in the Community of Nations known as the British Empire as the Dominion of Canada, the Commonwealth of Australia, the Dominion of New Zealand, and the Union of South Africa, with a Parliament having powers to make law for the peace, order and good government of Ireland and an Executive responsible to that Parliament, and shall be styled and known as the Irish Free State.' (Article 1)

> 'The Irish Free State shall assume liability for the service of the Public Debt of the United Kingdom as existing at the date hereof and towards the payment of War Pensions as existing at that date in such proportion as may be fair and equitable, ...' (Article 5)

> 'The Government of the Irish Free State agree to pay fair compensation on terms not less favourable than those accorded by the Act of 1920 (*the Government of Ireland Act 1920*) to judges, officials, members of the Police

---

[1] The Irish Free State, otherwise called *Saorstát Éireann*, was a Constitutional Monarchy with a three-tier Parliament, called the Oireachtas, comprised of the King, Dáil Éireann and Seanad Éireann. Executive authority was vested in the King and was exercised by a Cabinet called the Executive Council, of which the Prime Minister was called the President. The *Constitution of the Irish Free State* (Saorstát Éireann) *Act 1922*, Number 1/1922, was passed and adopted by Dáil Éireann, sitting as a Constituent Assembly of the Provisional Parliament, and by the British Parliament as the *Irish Free State (Constitution) Act 1922*, and it came into operation by Royal Proclamation of His Majesty, King George V, on 6 December 1922.

Forces and other Public Servants who are discharged by it or who retire
in consequence of the change of government effected in pursuance hereof.
... .' (Article 10)

The population in 1921 was 3,096,000. Agriculture was the predominant
industry, and the land tenure system was essentially peasant
proprietorship. Manufacturing industry employed about 13% of the labour
force, which was low relative to Western European standards and, more
particularly, relative to the 40% in Britain and 35% in Northern Ireland.
Irish GDP / GNP *per capita* was estimated at 61% of that of the UK, then the
richest of 23 European countries for which Kennedy gave statistics in his
1988 treatise.[1]

O'Mahony, in 1964, quotes statistics that show that 53% of those at
work in 1926 were in agriculture, forestry and fishing, 10% in
manufacturing and a further 8% in other secondary production, and the
balance of 29% in private and public services. Unemployment was 6.5% of
the labour force.[2]

THE FIRST DECADE

Kennedy and his colleagues describe the first decade as one of establishing
and consolidating the new State.[3] Free trade with the UK continued, with
the national economic policy mainly focused on raising the efficiency of
agriculture.

One of the initial steps taken by Government in the economic sphere
was the establishment of the Fiscal Inquiry Committee in June 1923. The
Committee was charged with examining the fiscal system and reporting
on changes that might be made to foster the development of industry and
agriculture. Its terms of reference required the Committee to have 'due
regard to the interests of the general community and to the economic
relations of the Saorstát (the Irish Free State, otherwise Saorstát Éireann)
with other countries'. The Committee's final report, debated in Dáil
Éireann in January, 1924, recommended a cautious approach to the policy
of State protection of industry.[4] A range of duties were imposed, examples
being the new Customs duties in the *Finance Act 1924*, including *ad valorem*
duties of 10% on candles, 15% on boots and shoes, 33$^{1}/_{3}$% on empty bottles,
and 10% on soap! The Dáil generally supported the introduction of
protective tariffs,[5] with a tendency for extension to other industrial sectors.[6]

In 1926, the Government established the Tariff Commission to report to the Minister for Finance on proposals for the imposition, modification, abolition, or renewal of Customs duties on imports.[7]

The reduction in emigration, and consequent rise in unemployment, was a factor that sharpened the focus on protective tariffs. Emigration, which averaged 33,000 *per annum* in the decade 1921-1931, fell dramatically because of restrictive immigration laws in the USA and the decline in job opportunities, due to the Great Depression. The Irish population, which had fallen in each year since Independence, rose by 11,000 in 1931, with a consequent urgent need to create more jobs. Pressure for protective duties on imports mounted, notably from industrialists. The Government enacted legislation in 1931 to allow the imposition of such protective duties:

> '... to authorise during a limited period the provisional imposition or variation of Customs Duties by the Executive Council (*the Cabinet*), where such imposition or variation appears to be immediately necessary to prevent an expected dumping of goods or other threatened industrial injury, and ... to authorise the reference to the Tariff Commission of questions relating to such Duties,... .'[8]

Relative to public finances generally, the Government did not favour the creation of a large public sector and was anxious to reduce taxation. The Government reduced the standard rate of income tax progressively from 25% in 1924 to 15% in 1927, reflecting the fall in public expenditure consequent on the reduction in the size and cost of the Army after the end of the Civil War. It is of interest to note that, in the mid-1920s, taxes on income equated to only 3% of GNP and that almost 75% of public revenue came from indirect taxes, such as customs and excise duties and local authority rates on property.

PROTECTIONISM & THE ECONOMIC WAR

Because of the Great World Depression of 1929 / 1930 and the early 1930s, many countries abandoned free trade and resorted to protectionism. By November 1931, the Cumann na nGaedheal Government had already taken power to impose tariffs on a wide basis. There was a change in Government following the General Election of 1932. Fianna Fáil, led by Eamon de Valera, took office in March 1932 as a minority Government, with the support of the Labour Party. The new Government immediately took steps to put in place a policy of economic self-sufficiency, including legislation to keep ownership of manufacturing enterprises in the hands of nationals of Saorstát Éireann.[9]

A further factor that impacted on trade was the Government's decision in 1932 to refuse to pay land annuities due to Britain for land purchase loans made by the British Government to Irish tenant farmers prior to 1922. In February 1923, the Government had agreed to collect these sums and to pay them over in full to the British Exchequer. The amount involved was about £3 million (€3.8 million) *per annum*, equating to approximately 2% of GNP. The Irish Government reaffirmed its liability to pay these sums when, in 1925, Saorstát Éireann was released from any other liability for the public debt of the UK. Furthermore, the Irish liability to pay the land annuities was acknowledged in an agreement made, in March 1926, between the Irish Minister for Finance and the British Chancellor of the Exchequer. Following the 1932 refusal to pay the land annuities, the Irish Government suggested arbitration to resolve the issue, as provided in the 1922 Treaty. The British Government rejected arbitration and, on 12 July 1932, imposed an *ad valorem* duty of 20% on imports to Britain of the main Irish agricultural products, thus initiating the 'economic war'. The stated British objective was to raise an amount equal to the £3 million *per annum* land annuity payments withheld by the Irish Government. The duty was increased to 30% in November 1932, and simultaneously the exemption of Irish products from a separate and general import duty of 10% was revoked, thus resulting in a double additional imposition.[10] The Irish Government responded with legislation that allowed the Executive Council to impose, vary, and remove by Order, Customs duties, Excise duties, and Stamp duties.[11] Additional import controls were imposed in 1934 and 1937. [12]

On the wider issue of developing national sovereignty, the Oireachtas enacted the *Constitution (Amendment No. 27) Act 1936*, and the *Executive Authority (External Relations) Act 1936*, in the context of the abdication of His Majesty, King Edward VIII. These enactments significantly diminished the position of the King and of Representatives of the Crown under the Irish Constitution, and provided for the appointment of diplomatic consular representatives of Saorstát Éireann by the Executive Council (*the Cabinet*). The legislation retained a limited role for the King in relation to diplomatic and consular appointments, and international agreements, for so long as Ireland remained associated with Australia, Canada, Great Britain, New Zealand and South Africa. Subsequently, following the *Plebiscite (Draft Constitution) Act* of 2 June 1937, a new Constitution for Ireland was passed by referendum of the people on 1 July 1937, effective from 29 December 1937. It declared Ireland a sovereign State, although Ireland remained within the British Commonwealth, and replaced the earlier Constitution enacted by the *Constitution of the Irish Free State* (Saorstát Éireann) *Act 1922*.

The economic war with Britain ended with the Anglo-Irish Agreement of 29 April 1938. There were three separate elements to the Agreement: satisfaction of the British claim to land annuities by a single payment of £10 million (€12.7 million), the mutual elimination of all recent tariffs in order to promote trade between the two countries, and the withdrawal of Britain from the three Irish ports that it still occupied under Article 7 (a) of the 1922 Treaty.[*] The Government enacted legislation relative to the elimination of tariffs and to the agreement on the land annuities payments.[13]

WORLD WAR II & ITS AFTERMATH

Immediately prior to the declaration of World War II, the Government enacted legislation to confirm certain Orders that had been made under the *Emergency Imposition of Duties Act 1932*.[14] This was followed by the *Emergency Powers Act 1939*, which *inter alia* gave the Government direct control of the economy.[15] The *Emergency Powers Act* was repealed on 2 September 1946. The main aim of public policy during what, in Ireland, was called 'the Emergency' was the security of the State. Kennedy and others deal with economic aspects of the wartime experience and post-war policy.[16]

In terms of sovereignty, Ireland became a Republic in 1949.[¶] During the late 1940s and the 1950s, there was a high level of unemployment, growing emigration, and high balance of payments deficits. Dissatisfaction with the economic situation led eventually to a comprehensive examination by the Department of Finance of all aspects of the economy.

After the War, Ireland benefited from the US Marshall Plan to the extent of US$133 million in grants and low-interest loans,[17] just over 1% of the total US$12.7 billion that was voted by the US Congress in April 1948, to promote European recovery and reconstruction.

In the context of post-War industrialisation, Daniel Morrissey TD, Minister for Industry & Commerce, appointed the first members of the

---

[*]   The three deep water Treaty ports were Berehaven and Cobh in County Cork and Lough Swilly in Donegal.

[¶]   The *Republic of Ireland Act 1948*, No.22 of 1948, was enacted on 21 December 1948. It was effective from 18 April 1949, under the *Republic of Ireland Act 1948 (Commencement) Order 1949*, S.I. 27/1949 dated 4 February 1949.

Industrial Development Authority (IDA – now IDA Ireland) in May 1949 and the legislation to establish the IDA was enacted in 1950.[#]

LEMASS / WHITAKER, 1958

Ireland's economic development, in the modern sense, began with the publication of a White Paper, the *Programme for Economic Expansion* (PEE), laid by the Government before the Houses of the Oireachtas in November 1958.[18] Eamon de Valera was Taoiseach, Dr Jim Ryan was Minister for Finance, Seán Lemass was Tánaiste and Minister for Industry & Commerce, and Kenneth Whitaker was Secretary General of the Department of Finance.[19] Almost 20 months earlier, Ireland's only Nobel Laureate in science, Ernest Walton, in April, 1957, had sent a letter and comprehensive accompanying memorandum to the Taoiseach highlighting the need to promote science research in Ireland and its implications for economic growth. Walton anticipated many issues relative to economic development and to the knowledge economy.[20] Whitaker is generally acknowledged as the main architect of the PEE, although Ryan formally brought Whitaker's proposals to the Cabinet.[¶] Seán Lemass succeeded Eamon de Valera as Taoiseach in June, 1959.

The Introduction to the Programme stated:

> 'Production has not been increasing fast enough to provide employment and acceptable living standards for growing numbers of our people; a high level of unemployment has accompanied large-scale emigration. Emigration will not be checked nor will unemployment be permanently reduced until the rate of increase in national output is greatly accelerated.'

[#]   Daniel Morrissey TD, Minister for Industry & Commerce, by warrant dated 25 May 1949, appointed James Patrick Beddy as Chairman of the IDA, together with the other members, Kevin C McCourt, Luke J Dully and John J Walsh. The *Industrial Development Authority Act 1950* (No.29 of 1950) was enacted on 20 December 1950.

[¶]   Kenneth Whitaker was appointed Secretary of the Department of Finance in 1955 at the age of 39. The appointment, made by the Fine Gael / Labour Party Government of 1954-1957, bypassed the then norm of making such appointments on the basis of seniority, making Whitaker the youngest person to be appointed to that post. John A Costello TD was Taoiseach, William Norton TD was Tánaiste and Minister for Industry & Commerce, and Gerard Sweetman TD was Minister for Finance. A year after his appointment, in 1956, Whitaker began work on the preparation of the policy document *Economic Development*, with the help of Charlie Murray (Department of An Taoiseach), Maurice Doyle and other colleagues in the Department of Finance.

'There is general agreement that productive capital expenditure … must receive a greater priority than at present in the public capital programme.'

'No programme for economic development will be successful unless the people have the will to work and are prepared to accept the living standards to which their efforts entitle them … wage standards must be realistic, having regard to the level of productivity in this country and the need for ensuring competitive costs per unit of output.'

'Fiscal policy also will be guided primarily by the need to encourage production and saving. In particular, the Government's aim is to create conditions permitting as soon as possible of a reduction in direct taxation. This would be a tonic to the economy, a stimulus to personal and corporate saving and an encouragement both to native and foreign enterprise to undertake new projects. High taxation is necessitated by high expenditure and can be reduced only if expenditure is reduced, or if taxable incomes are raised by increased production and the cost of current services is at the same time held rigidly in check.'

Those quotations define the practical economics of the PEE, and the points made are as valid today as when they were first written. It is fascinating, in retrospect, to see that the points made in the 1958 PEE were key issues for the CII throughout the campaigning years of 1979 to 1993, and that the CII's focus on them contributed greatly to establishing the preconditions for the creation of the Celtic Tiger. For that reason, it is useful to emphasise the key points, in summary, when following the CII's public affairs campaign of later years:

♦ It is only by increasing economic output that we create more jobs and earn higher living standards.

♦ Public capital investment in productive infrastructure needs to be given a higher priority.

♦ Unit cost competitiveness is vital to success, including wage levels linked realistically to productivity.

♦ Direct taxation needs to be reduced to stimulate personal and corporate savings, and to encourage enterprise. The reduction in high taxation must necessarily be linked to a reduction in public expenditure and / or to economic growth.

The PEE dealt with agriculture, fisheries, forestry and forest products, industry, capital cost, and available resources. *Industry*, Part V of the Programme, comprised sections on foreign participation, State facilities for industry, State participation in industry, mining, tourism, restrictive practices and the reappraisal of existing policies. The section on the reappraisal of policies included the encouragement of foreign investment, the removal of tariff protection and of restrictive practices and concluded with the statement that:

> 'The need for increased industrial employment is so compelling, however, that the Government will not hesitate to make further changes that may be necessary if it appears that progress is being impeded by any aspect of existing policy.'

The PEE proposed making full use of the provisions of the *Industrial Development (Encouragement of External Investment) Act 1958*, under which the mandate of the IDA was greatly enhanced. This marked a fundamental change in policy of all Irish Governments to date through the formal abandonment of protectionism and the commencement of Ireland's encouragement of foreign direct investment (FDI), from which the country benefited significantly in the following decades and which was one of the principal pillars on which the Celtic Tiger years were built and sustained.

It is instructive to recall the final sentence of paragraph 138, *External Borrowing*, in view of the extent of Government borrowing in later years, including external borrowing. The Programme wisely stated:

> 'As interest and repayment charges on external borrowing impose a strain on the balance of payments, any external borrowing will be confined to the financing of productive projects.'

The final paragraph, 139, in its last sentence may well have prophesied the need for social partnership:

> 'The programme will, therefore, make a significant contribution towards the advancement of national prosperity, but, in the last resort, progress will depend on the determination of the people to prosper, on their capacity for hard work and on their willingness to cooperate in the fulfilment of a comprehensive national programme.'

In hindsight, that statement can be seen as sowing the intellectual seed that led to social partnership in national economic and social planning, through a number of evolutionary stages.

THE GOVERNMENT'S ECONOMIC PROGRAMMES, 1964 – 1972

The *Second Programme for Economic Expansion 1964-1970* (SPEE) was published in two parts. The first part, laid by the Government before the Houses of the Oireachtas and published in August 1963, contained the general objectives of the Programme.[21] The second part, published in July 1964, contained the detailed provisions.[22]

State provision of post-primary education was extended on a universal basis during the period of the SPEE. In that context, the first part of the SPEE included a comprehensive section on *Education & Training*, based on the policy statement that:

> 'Since our wealth lies ultimately in our people, the aim of educational policy must be to enable all individuals to realise their full potential as human persons … Better education and training will support continued economic expansion.'

The Programme went on:

> 'Since, however, changes and improvements in the educational system will yield their fruits only over a long period, measures to rectify what appears to be the greatest weakness in the field of post-primary education have been under consideration.'

The SPEE referred to announcements recently made by the Government regarding the provision of comprehensive post-primary education; parity of status between vocational school courses and courses in secondary schools; provision of career guidance facilities, including in areas of subject choice; establishment of the Technical Schools Leaving Certificate; education of technicians and technologists, who were vital to planned economic expansion; and the provision of an increased number of higher education scholarships. Reference was made to curriculum development, particularly in relation to mathematics, science and languages, and to meeting the continuing in-service training needs of employees and managers.

The SPEE 1964-1970, in addition to covering the sectors that had been included in the PEE of November 1958, included issues relating to energy; physical planning and building and construction; services; education; transport; tourism; State-sponsored bodies; current expenditure and taxation; and the public capital programme.

The negotiation and signing of the Anglo-Irish Free Trade Area Agreement in 1965 was a major development during the period of the

SPEE. The Agreement provided for the abolition of tariffs on Irish exports to the UK from 1966, and for the phasing out over a period of 10 years of all tariffs on goods imported into Ireland from the UK. In that context, the UK was then Ireland's largest trading partner.

The *Third Programme: Economic & Social Development 1969-1972* (TPESD), published in 1968, covered the years immediately prior to Ireland's entry to the EC.[23] The TPESD covered the complete range of economic sectors, including the marine, tourism, research and services. Major social development issues included education and health. An *Annual Review* was published to facilitate sustained monitoring of the Programme: such review was an innovation in public administration.

Included among the structural issues proposed were a general review of the tax system and a major overhaul of the system of local taxation. Other proposals included the publication of estimated future Government expenditure, side-by-side with the traditional format of Budget tables, and the introduction, initially on a pilot basis, of new procedures for programming and analysing public expenditure. A review was also announced of the activities and functions of the County Development Teams, and of the Central Development Committee that co-ordinated the activities of those Teams.

Overlapping the Second and Third Programmes, the Regional Technical Colleges (RTCs) were established in 1969, following the Steering Committee Report of 1967,[24] which responded to an OECD Report on *Technician Education in Ireland*. The principal aim of the RTCs, from the beginning, was to work with the private sector to provide people with the necessary technical skills for the new manufacturing and service industries. In particular, those RTCs outside the Greater Dublin Area worked within the EC imperative of helping to facilitate the movement of young people from agriculture to industry and services, and their retention in employment in regional and rural areas.

THE INITIAL SUCCESS

Following the commencement of the PEE, November 1958, and throughout the period of the SPEE, there was rapid economic growth. During the 1960s and 1970s, Irish living standards more than doubled in real terms. The greatest success was between 1961 and 1973. Annual growth in GNP was 4.3% in real terms, albeit from a low base. The average annual rate of unemployment was 4.7%. Much of the early development drive came about because of the action of the Government led by Seán Lemass, in encouraging the participation of employers, trade unions, and industry in the new process of economic planning. That process included the establishment of the Committee for Industrial Organisation (CIO), on which the FII (Federation of Irish Industry) (which changed its name to the CII in March 1970) had four representatives. Adaptation Councils, which functioned under the umbrella of the CIO, helped to accelerate the restructuring of industrial sectors to the coming era of free trade. Indeed, this was the first time in the history of the State that the Government formally consulted expert interest groups. The Government, in 1962, organised a number of national economic planning meetings, involving representatives of those interest groups, and drawing on European experience, typically that of senior French civil servants involved in planning.

EEC MEMBERSHIP, 1973 & THE ROLE OF THE CII

Ireland, together with Denmark and the UK, joined the EEC on 1 January 1973. The existing EEC Member States were Belgium, the Federal Republic of Germany, France, Italy, Luxembourg and the Netherlands.

Ireland's focus of attention for the transition period of five years was on initial integration into the EEC. No new national Programme was published until 1978.[25] There was, however, a major shift in national attitudes and a growing self-confidence that reflected Ireland's new status as a sovereign State among equals in the EEC. Economically and socially, parochialism diminished and there was the beginning of a reduction in Ireland's economic dependence on the UK market. The benefits of membership of the EEC were apparent from an early date. By the end of the transition period on 31 December 1978, almost all barriers to trade between Ireland and the other eight EEC Member States had been removed. As will be mentioned later, there was significant growth of the knowledge infrastructure, consequent on a major boost in research and development funding from EEC Framework Programmes.

A publication in 1982, describing the first 50 years of the CII, provides useful insights into events leading up to EEC membership and thereafter.[26] The years 1951-1965 are described as the period of adaptation to free trade.[1] In 1968, the then FII (the CII after 1970) published a discussion document on the potential consequences for Irish industry of the free trade that would follow the Anglo-Irish Free Trade Area Agreement of 1965, and the growing possibility of Ireland's membership of the EC. This marked the commencement of the formal adoption of a free trade policy by the FII, a reversal of its previous protectionist policy. The organisation's new dynamic European and world trade view was consolidated with the expansion of the membership base. The CII hosted the Annual Conference of the Council of European Industrial Federations (CEIF) in 1970, thus publicly demonstrating its new European stature and its outward and internationally-competitive perspectives.

The CII was actively involved in preparations for Ireland's membership of the EC. This was the context for a major crisis in the organisation when six senior personnel died tragically on Monday, 18 June 1972. They were on their way to Brussels when their British European Airways Trident aircraft stalled shortly after take-off from Heathrow, and crashed into a nearby field in Staines. All 118 persons on board were killed.[27] Among them was Michael Sweetman, the CII Director of Business Policy, who had been granted a year's leave of absence in July 1971, to become Director of the Irish Council of the European Movement.

The CII, together with the Federated Union of Employers (FUE) and the Association of Chambers of Commerce of Ireland (ACCI), established the Irish Business Bureau in Brussels in November 1972. The aim was to represent the interests of Irish business to the institutions of the EEC, and to provide a focus for institutional involvement in the affairs of the EEC. The Bureau provided information on EEC issues for members of the participating organisations, including information on European legislation, regulation, administration, and proposed initiatives, and assisted members to obtain access to European programmes, financial and otherwise. The CII joined and became an active member of the Union of Industrial & Employers' Confederations of Europe (UNICE, now BUSINESSEUROPE), which provided a forum for my personal input on behalf of the CII at European level.[28]

On 31 December 1972, immediately prior to Ireland's entry to the EEC, the Irish National Debt amounted to €1,588 million, of which only €137 million or 9% was foreign debt.[29] On the same date, the Government's

---

[1]   The 1982 publication gives an authoritative account of the CII, based on archival research, divided into four periods: 1932-1950; 1951-1965; 1966-1972; and 1973-1982.

official external reserves amounted to €483.9 million, so that Ireland was, on balance, a creditor country.

On joining the EEC, Ireland began to benefit immediately from transfers under the Common Agricultural Policy (CAP), both the price guarantees and guidance funds, and the European Social Fund (ESF).[30] Funds began to flow from the European Regional Development Fund (ERDF) from 1975 onwards. In addition, there were grants and subsidies from other EEC sources, together with low-interest loans from the European Investment Bank (EIB) and the European Coal & Steel Community (ECSC).

In higher education, there was a critical boost for research, with major funding from Framework Programmes and opportunities for the establishment of research networks and partnerships across the EEC. This had a direct impact on knowledge-based industrial development and a favourable impact on the attraction to Ireland of significant levels of FDI. In 1973, the first year of Ireland's membership of the EEC, the inflow of European grants and subsidies, net of Ireland's contributions to European institutions, amounted to IR£37.7 million (€47.9 million). This grew rapidly in the early years, and by 1977, year five of EEC membership, net inflows to Ireland from European grants and subsidies amounted to IR£263.7 million (€334.9 million). Aggregate net inflows over the five years, 1973 to 1977, amounted to IR£615.8 million (€781.9 million), and Ireland received low-interest loans from European institutions amounting to IR£146.8 million (€186.4 million).

A TIME OF MORE MODEST GROWTH

Real economic growth, adjusted for inflation, fell to the still relatively high rate of 3.4% *per annum* between 1974 and 1980, but annual average unemployment during the same period, at 8.1%, was significantly higher than during the period 1961 to 1973.[1] Unemployment was about 5% of the labour force in 1961 and remained in the range of about 4.7% to 5.3% throughout the 1960s. It rose at the beginning of the 1970s and was about 6.4% in 1972, the year before Ireland's EEC membership. The 1970s saw a cessation of emigration for the first time since the foundation of the State, and the flow of population turned to net immigration. By early 1979, the impact of sustained economic growth resulted in shortages of key

---

[1]   In a talk I gave in 1982, I mentioned that, during the 1970s, Irish industrial output grew by 5% *per annum* on average, and total employment in that decade grew by about 10%.

technological skills and, in at least five of the 26 counties, the unemployment rate had fallen to between 3% and 5%.[31] Towards the end of the period, the Government became concerned about wage inflation and the rise in unit wage costs.[32]

The years 1976 to 1981 saw some notable achievements in the industrial sector. The annual average compound growth rate in industrial production was just over 4.5%, the highest such growth rate in the EEC during that period. This contrasted with zero industrial growth in the United Kingdom and just over 1.6% *per annum* in the Federal Republic of Germany. During the same period, Ireland achieved the highest annual average OECD growth rate of 11% in the chemicals industry. Similarly, in the capital goods industries, Ireland achieved the third highest growth rate in the world in the period 1976 to 1981, after Portugal and Japan.[33] Albeit, the high levels of Ireland's industrial growth were from a low base but the levels achieved in high technology sectors reflected the growing internationalisation of Irish industry and the success of the IDA's programme to attract quality inward investment.

From the end of the Third Programme, 1969-1972, until 1978, there was no formal national economic programme, and social partnership programmes had not yet begun. That was a period of international economic turbulence and currency fluctuations following the first of the two Organisation of Petroleum Exporting Countries (OPEC) oil price shocks of the 1970s. The *White Paper* of January 1978, was published in the wake of an international economic recovery and there followed a good year for the Irish economy.[34] Growth in national output was about 7%, which was almost three times the average rate of 2.5% achieved in the EEC. Irish inflation fell from an average of 13.6% in 1977 to an average of 7.6% in 1978. The number of new jobs created was an all-time record high since the foundation of the State, the number of people at work increasing by a net 17,000. These positive indicators were the background to my talk delivered to the North-West Region of the Irish Management Institute (IMI) in Sligo in May 1979.[35] The only significant negative factor, at that stage, was the deteriorating industrial relations climate, including the large number of days lost through industrial disputes.

National Wages Agreements (NWAs) constituted a centralised system of pay determination in Ireland and, between 1970 and 1978, there were seven NWAs negotiated between the Irish Congress of Trade Unions (ICTU) and the employers' organisations, through the Employer-Labour Conference, established in 1970. As an economic representative body, the CII was not involved in the NWAs, having no mandate in the area of industrial relations negotiations. The Government was involved in the NWAs solely as the public sector employer. Between 1975 and 1978, the Government began to make wider informal inputs so that the outcome of wage negotiations would be broadly in line with national economic and social policy objectives. This process was formalised in the National Understandings of 1979 and 1980, which included a number of broader economic and social issues, as well as pay.

SUMMARY

◊ On the eve of the 1980s, there were still some remnants in Ireland of the post-1922 protectionist tendencies, as it was only 20 years since the dramatic reversal of earlier policies heralded in the *Programme for Economic Expansion*, 1958.

◊ Notwithstanding any remaining protectionist tendencies at the end of the period, Ireland of the 1960s and 1970s had a new, more open, economic vision, reflected in strong growth, albeit from a low base.

◊ There were some dark clouds, including difficulties in Northern Ireland, especially since 1968. The conflict in Northern Ireland imposed a drain on the public purse of the Republic of Ireland through additional expenditure on the Defence Forces, the Garda Síochána and the Prison Service. The conflict was also a major cause of political disruption that impacted negatively on the previous socio-economic consensus. The negative image abroad of instability on the island of Ireland called for extensive international promotional initiatives aimed at sustaining a flow of quality inward investment.

◊ In spite of the difficulties, there was phenomenal progress, aided significantly, in terms of both economic and social interventions, by membership of the EEC from the beginning of 1973.

CHAPTER 3
THE ECONOMY: WARTS & ALL!

THE BROAD ECONOMIC PICTURE

Graph 3.1 puts the period of economic crisis – 1981-1986 – in a broad historical context by showing Irish GNP volume growth in each year from 1960 to 2007, using 1960 as the base (1960 = 100). By 1960, implementation of the 1958 *Programme for Economic Expansion* had begun to benefit the economy demonstrably.

Graph 3.1: GNP Volume Growth Index, 1961-2007

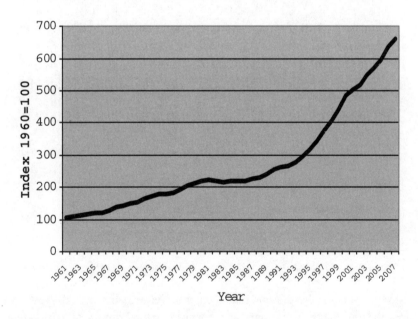

Key points illustrated by the graph include:

♦ GNP volume doubled over the 18 years from 1960 to 1978.

♦ GNP growth ceased in 1981, was negative in each of the two years, 1982 and 1983, and was zero in aggregate for the six year period from 1981 to 1986.

♦ After GNP growth resumed in 1987, it took a further nine years to 1995 before the GNP volume reached three times that of 1960.

♦ GNP volume reached four times that of 1960 in 1998, five times in 2001, and six times in 2006.

The period 1981 to 1986 is put into focus in **Graph 3.2**, which shows annual GNP volume growth as a percentage of the previous year for each of the years 1960 to 2007.

Graph 3.2: Annual GNP Volume Growth, % on previous year, 1961-2007

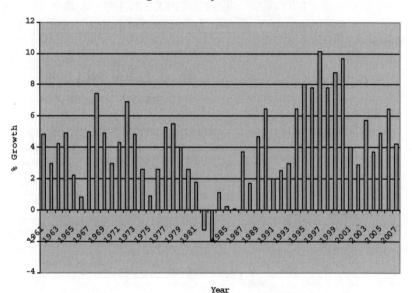

THE YEAR OF CRISIS, 1986

In terms of national economic management, 1986 was Ireland's darkest year since the foundation of the State, as evidenced by the grim statistics presented in the PNR negotiated between Government and the social partners in October 1987 (see **Chapter 5**).[1] The many challenges and difficulties before 1986 had climaxed in high net emigration, high unemployment, low living standards relative to the EC average, imprudently high Government borrowing, a high National Debt and debt servicing, among other national economic problems. An article in *The Irish Times* in November 1986, raised the serious concern that foreign lenders might soon begin to question Ireland's capacity to service and repay the debts.[2]

Such was the background against which the CII signalled the plight of industry in its pre-Budget submission to Government for 1987.[3] [#] The submission stated:

> 'It is against this background that 1986 can be seen as a year of crisis in industry. Output has stopped growing, investment is stagnant, and employment in industry is falling. The crisis in industry reflects the deeper malaise in the national economy ... The very serious situation in industry is, in large part, a reflection of the persistent and increasing high deficit in the public finances ... The inability of successive Governments to halt the rising spiral of Government debt is a matter of grave concern to industry, since the confidence of investors will not be restored until the public debt is brought under control, and moves are set in train to reduce it steadily to the level obtaining in other EEC countries. The primary prerequisite for recovery in industry must be control of the public finances ... The Irish economy is in a state of crisis, with very high unemployment, a level of National Debt, which is unsustainable, and stagnation in the main productive sectors. Unless these factors are recognised, and successfully addressed, the overall indebtedness will continue to rise sharply. The rising burden of debt servicing would continue to usurp an ever increasing amount of economic effort, and consequently increase unemployment further.'

The CII supported the views of the NESC that the immediate objective must be to stop the rising spiral of National Debt.[4]

THE SEEDS OF DISASTER, 1972

The crisis of National Debt had its roots in 1972. The then Minister for Finance, George Colley TD, noted in his 1972 Budget Speech that the volume of national production had expanded by 3% in 1971, and despite being somewhat higher than the 2.5% achieved in 1970, the performance could not be regarded as satisfactory.[5] The Minister spoke about 'a continuing reflationary stimulus', which he said was 'clearly necessary for

---

[#] Under the heading, *A Crisis in Industry*, the CII pointed out that manufacturing output recorded zero growth in 1986, and that there was a fall of about 9,000 in manufacturing employment between mid-1986 and mid-1987. More worrying still was that manufacturing investment had stagnated, having expanded at an annual average rate of 7% over the previous 20 years, from 1965 to 1985.

the economy this year'. What this meant in layman's terms was that the Minister intended to inject spending power into the economy artificially by borrowing to pay for some of the Government's current expenditure programmes. He hoped that the additional spending power would result in increased output of goods and traded services. His goal was to benefit the unemployed, who then numbered 71,000 or 6.4% of the workforce. Unemployment had risen from 56,000 on average in 1969, or just under 5% of the work force, to 65,000 on average in 1970 and 1971, or just under 6% of the work force.

The Minister identified three factors that contributed to the rise in unemployment: sluggish industrial production due to an absence of buoyancy in demand; an increase in numbers entering the labour market; and a sharp reduction in emigration.

The Government's response was to resort to deficit financing in an effort to stimulate the economy in terms of employment and spending power. The Minister for Finance acknowledged in his Budget Speech that the Government was aware of the economic risks inherent in such an approach:

> 'In opting for growth, as against stability, through a budget deficit, I am, indeed, taking a calculated risk – a risk that I may be fuelling the fire of inflation rather than the engine of growth. It is essential, therefore, that there should be a widespread acceptance of the need to redouble our efforts to check price and cost inflation.'

However, the budget deficit was used mainly to fund current public expenditure programmes and, thus, the seeds of economic destruction were sown!

COUNTDOWN TO CRISIS, 1981–1986

The CII's pre-Budget submission for 1987, in addition to labelling 1986 as a year of crisis in industry, gave a number of key economic statistics for each year from 1981 to 1986, in terms of public borrowing and the accumulation of National Debt. The resultant stark reality was that, between 1981 and 1986, there was zero economic growth in aggregate and there was a continuous economic deterioration in each of the six years. The number of persons at work fell by about 6.2% in those six years, from 1.146 million to 1.075 million. The situation was relatively worse in manufacturing industry, with a reduction in the number employed of 16.8%, from 234,200 to 194,900.[6] The number unemployed increased by 80.2% from 126,000 to 227,000.

The CII, furthermore, was unhappy with Government's response, notably with regard to the 1986 Budget, which it viewed as having had an adverse impact on the climate for investment, allowing the main problems of the economy to remain.[7] The CII based its conclusions on the following key economic trends in public finances over each of the six years, 1981 to 1986:

♦ Government spending was increasing persistently, boosted by current expenditure which had risen from IR£4,400 million (€5,587 million) in 1981 to IR£8,000 million (€10,158 million) in 1986. The increased current expenditure had squeezed out capital spending which, at IR£1,800 million (€2,285 million) in 1986, had fallen from the IR£2,000 million (€2,529 million) reached in 1982.

♦ Government spending as a percentage of GNP had remained virtually unchanged at 60% throughout the period. However, the composition changed, in that current spending had risen from 42% of GNP to 49%, while capital spending had been squeezed from 18% of GNP to 11%.

♦ Increased spending was fuelled by the ever-growing demands of personal, corporate, indirect and capital taxation. Tax revenue increased from IR£3,300 million (€4,190 million) in 1981 to IR£6,100 million (€7,745 million) in 1986, rising from 31.5% of GNP to 37%, with serious adverse affects on society at large.

♦ Growing tax revenue was not sufficient to pay for Government expenditure programmes and little progress was made in containing Government borrowing. In 1986, Government borrowing amounted to IR£2,000 million (€2,539 million), compared with IR£1,700 million (€2,159 million) in 1981.

♦ Government borrowing as a percentage of GNP had been reduced from 16.4% in 1981 to just over 12% in 1986, but this had been achieved almost entirely by reducing capital borrowing, thus squeezing out expenditure on productive infrastructure such as the national roads network.

♦ The split between current and capital borrowing by Government had changed dramatically. In 1981, capital borrowing accounted for over 53% of total Government borrowing; in 1986, it accounted for less than 38%. In well-managed economies, Government borrowing is primarily for capital purposes, designed to yield a positive economic and social return on investment. This was not the case in Ireland in the first half of the 1980s.

It must be acknowledged that the three General Elections in 18 months – June 1981, February 1982 and November 1982 – created the most politically unstable period in the history of the State since the end of the Civil War in 1923!

The CII viewed the deteriorating situation in industry as, in a large part, a reflection of the persistent and increasingly high deficit in the public finances. The National Debt increased by a factor of 2.7 during the six years 1981 to 1986, from just over IR£10,000 million (€12,697 million) at the end of 1980 to over IR£27,000 million (€34,283 million) at the end of 1986.[8] The sharp escalation in Government borrowing, and in the accumulation of National Debt, between 1985 and 1986 reinforced the CII's claim that the essential prerequisite for recovery in industry was control of public finances.

BORROWING LIKE THERE WAS NO TOMORROW

The CII campaign urging Government to bring order to the public finances gained momentum in its 1982 pre-Budget submission.[9] [¶] The submission warned that the Government faced a serious problem with current spending, and that the current budget deficit was at an unsustainably high level. Two international factors to which the Irish economy was unable to respond adequately were highlighted: the oil crisis of 1979/1980, which had exacerbated, but not caused, Ireland's economic problems; and the implications for Ireland of joining the EMS. The CII claimed that these two international factors were compounded by the Government's 'unwillingness to face economic reality at home'. In particular, the CII emphasised the 'massive increases in the cost of funding the public sector' that had 'resulted in higher taxation and an unsustainable Government current budget deficit'. As a direct consequence, high pay increases had been 'demanded from industry, with little regard to the adverse effect on international competitiveness, and to the implications of membership of the EMS'.

The CII observed that the net result of the erosion of international competitiveness was 'manifested in lost export orders, factory closures, and redundancies', and emphasised that there was no scope for Government action that would stimulate the economy generally. The CII considered that 'the primary concern of Government should be to take action which will create the conditions for sustained economic recovery',

---

[¶]   This was published in December, 1981, and was the first of 12 such annual submissions that I drafted.

and it defined those conditions as including 'a lower rate of inflation, a reduced rate of Government current spending, and less Government reliance on borrowing.'

The economic situation, however, continued to deteriorate as shown in **Table 3.1**. The CII pre-Budget submission for 1983 again emphasised, as the root cause of Ireland's economic problems, the 'serious imbalance in the Government's finances – the overwhelming magnitude of Government expenditure and the total impossibility of raising matching revenue through taxation'.[10]

Table 3.1: Exchequer Borrowing, 1977 - 1982

Year	Current Budget Deficit	Exchequer Borrowing Requirement*
	% of GNP	% of GNP
1977	3.6	10.0
1978	5.9	12.6
1979	7.1	13.6
1980	6.4	14.2
1981	7.9	16.8
1982	7.5	16.0

*   Total Exchequer Borrowing comprised the current budget deficit and the Public Capital Programme.

Table 3.2: Exchequer Borrowing & National Debt, % of GNP, 1981-1986

Year	Current Budget Deficit	Exchequer Borrowing Requirement	National Debt
1981*	7.6	15.9	94
1982*	8.0	15.8	103
1983	7.1	13.0	118
1984	7.1	12.5	128
1985	8.4	13.2	134
1986	8.8	13.6	145

* Note: The 1981 and 1982 figures that were used in the CII 1987 pre-Budget submission were revised from those used in the 1983 pre-Budget submission in the light of more recent published official Exchequer returns. The Department of Finance, *Budget & Economic Statistics 2007*, gives revised figures for the National Debt / GNP ratio: 1981 (85.7%), 1982 (84.8%), 1983 (95.8%), 1984 (103.3%), 1985 (106%), 1986 (115.1%), and 1987 (117.6%).

The thrust of the 1983 pre-Budget submission was that a substantial cut in Government spending would reduce the Government's borrowing requirement.

The real effects of the substantial growth in the Government's current budget deficit, from 3.6% of GNP to 7.5%, and in the Exchequer Borrowing Requirement (EBR), from 10% of GNP to 16%, were an increase in the rate of inflation; a decline in international competitiveness; a decline in profitability and investment; a large and unsustainable growth in the deficit on Ireland's current account international balance of payments; and mounting unemployment.

Alan Dukes TD, Minister for Finance, in his Budget Speech in February 1983, recognised these economic realities: the CII agreed with the Minister's analysis.[11] The Minister traced the stable self-sustained growth in the 1960s and spoke of the shock of the massive oil price rise in 1973, the transfer of real resources to the oil-producing countries and the fact that Ireland ignored reality and decided to maintain living standards through international borrowing. The Minister referenced the second oil shock of 1979-1980 and the fact that Ireland continued in the delusion that living standards could be maintained by international borrowing. He concluded that borrowing merely bought time for Ireland in the face of world recession, but the cost of repayment and of debt servicing pre-empted resources for the future. In essence, the Minister acknowledged that there had been an injudicious approach to public borrowing. His perceptive analysis at last injected a dose of realism into the political debate.

Matters had not improved, however, by the time the CII pre-Budget submission for 1984 was published.[12] Under the two headings of *Encourage Enterprise* and *National Economic Management*, the CII again called for a reduction in the public sector borrowing requirement, and the elimination of the Government's current budget deficit by 1987. The CII believed at that stage that there was widespread acceptance among all sectors of the community of the economic difficulties that needed to be overcome, and was confident that the resources existed in Ireland with which to commence the work of economic recovery, *provided dynamic economic leadership was given* by the Government within a budgetary framework supportive of enterprise.

The Fine Gael / Labour Party Government's National Economic Plan *Building on Reality 1984-1987* was published in October 1984. The CII's 1985 pre-Budget submission contained a response to that Plan.[13] Despite a general welcome for the Plan as providing a stable framework in which industry could plan over the following three years, the CII recommended a number of changes in emphasis. In the light of the buoyancy of international trade, growing Irish exports, and rising industrial output, the CII was concerned that the elimination of the Government's current budget deficit by 1987 had not been proposed. Rather, the Plan aimed to reduce the public sector borrowing requirement by almost 6% of GNP by 1987, with a planned current budget deficit of 5% of GNP.

The CII's pre-Budget submission for 1986 noted the Government's projection of an Exchequer Borrowing Requirement (EBR) of over 13% of GNP and a National Debt close to IR£20,000 million (€25,395 million), over 130% of GNP, by far the highest such ratio in the EC.[14] Government expenditure in 1985 would increase by 9%, in contrast to the projected average rate of inflation of about 5.5%. The CII argued for a current public spending increase of not more than 3% in nominal terms for 1986, with redeployment of public expenditure under a number of headings. The CII further argued trenchantly for a reduction of 2% of GNP in the current budget deficit, so that the Government's planned target of a 5% of GNP current budget deficit by 1987 could be achieved.

The CII's pre-Budget submission for 1987 dealt with Government borrowing and debt in the context of advocating control of public finances as the key prerequisite for recovery in industry.[15] The Government's budget deficit had escalated sharply in 1986 and, by the end of September 1986, the National Debt had reached a staggering 145% of GNP, compared to 134% at the end of December 1985.[¶]

By the end of 1986, the projected current deficit for that year was IR£1,250 million (€1,587 million) and public borrowing had emerged as the most serious threat to employment and living standards.[16] The Government, having started in the 1972 Budget on the road of current budget deficit financing to 'stimulate' growth, continued to borrow, with the result that, on 30 September 1986, the National Debt amounted to IR£23,290 million (€29,572 million), about 145% of the 1986 GNP.[#] The cost of debt servicing in 1986 was about one-third of the Exchequer's total tax revenue.

[¶]   The figures for National Debt and related statistics used by the CII were the most up-to-date and contemporaneously accurate figures available from public sources such as the Department of Finance and the Central Bank of Ireland. In subsequent years, the public authorities in Ireland and in the EU reviewed those figures and published updates. In some cases, definitions evolved, and new requirements were introduced, such as the practice of using the General Government Debt / GDP Ratio for comparative purposes, as defined in the European System of Integrated Economic Accounts, ESA 95, in use since 1990. The up-to-date figures are published annually in the *Budget Statistics & Tables* of the Department of Finance, and in *Annual Reports* and other publications of the NTMA.

[#]   The 1987 National Debt is shown as €30,085 million in the Department of Finance *Budget & Economic Statistics 2007*, and the National Debt / GNP ratio is 117.6%, still the

The National Debt in 1986 was IR£23,290 million (€29,572 million) compared to IR£1,251 million (€1,588 million) in March, 1972. The source of Ireland's public borrowing presented an even more serious complication. In 1972, IR£1,143 million (€1,451 million) was borrowed on the Irish markets, and only IR£108 million (€137 million), or 8.5%, was borrowed overseas but, by the end of 1986, the overseas borrowing amounted to 42% of the National Debt. An analysis of the National Debt at the end of 1986 showed that 60% was denominated in US$ and DM, almost an equal amount in each of those two major international currencies. A further 10% each was denominated in Swiss francs, Japanese yen, and Sterling. By the end of 1986, Ireland had risen to fourth place among all 135 debtor nations of the world on a foreign debt *per capita* basis, topped only by the United Arab Emirates, Israel, and Kuwait. John Bruton TD, Minister for Finance, noted that Ireland was sending significantly more than IR£700 million (€889 million) abroad each year in interest payments on foreign debt, funds that had to be earned by Irish sales of goods and services on foreign markets and which could have been better used for job creation at home.[17] Such a high level of foreign interest payment was another example of the way in which high Government borrowing compromised national sovereignty. The CII yet again reiterated that foreign borrowing should only be undertaken for projects that, directly or indirectly, generated additional foreign currency earnings, sufficient both to service and to repay the foreign debt incurred.

INDISCRIMINATE SPENDING

The NESC in 1981 examined a range of social expenditure problems.[18] The conclusion, endorsed by the representatives of the trade unions, employers, farmers, and industry, and the independent members that comprised the Council, was that, rather than being progressive, many of the major social policy schemes were socially regressive, as illustrated in the following quotations from its report:

> 'Education benefits higher income groups more than proportionately because of higher relative participation at the more advanced level.'

> 'Housing benefits are not directed to those most in need.'

> 'Health involves a regressive subsidy to higher income groups.'

---

highest on record. The National Debt and the National Debt / GNP ratio for 1986 are €27,440 million and 115.1%, respectively.

Regarding perceptions of the public at large, my presentation to the Kilkenny Rotary Club in October 1982, emphasising the indiscriminate nature of State spending, was widely reported in local and national newspapers, and in a subsequent *CII Newsletter*.[19] The analysis therein caught the public's attention and generated further media debate, notably in the *Sligo Champion* towards the end of October 1982. The message was stark: the absence of a clear focus in Irish social policy had generated aggregate indiscriminate social spending, which had grown out of all proportion to the economy's resources, and to key social needs. The article warned that, without major changes in national economic policies, Ireland was confronted with the prospect of declining living standards and rising unemployment. The article further reiterated the CII's concern that society must seek to protect those members of the community least able to provide for themselves. In this regard, the CII made three key points:

♦ In the context of effective use of the taxpayers' scarce resources, Ireland needed to establish a realistic working criterion that would concentrate aid on alleviating actual hardship. By 1982 international standards, Irish living standards were then such that 80% of the world's population would have been below the Irish poverty line.

♦ During the 20 years prior to 1982, Ireland had enjoyed unprecedented economic growth that averaged a compound rate of 3.5% *per annum*. In the same 20 years, Government spending on social services increased at a compound rate of 6.5% *per annum* in real terms, adjusted for inflation.

♦ In 1982, Government expenditure on public programmes amounted to over IR£95 (€120.63) each week for every person at work in the nation. In addition, nearly IR£23 (€29.20) per week per person at work was spent on servicing the National Debt, accumulated mainly by fuelling Government current expenditure in the previous short few years. Thus, between Government current expenditure programmes and interest on the National Debt, the Government spent a staggering IR£118 (€149.83) per week per person at work or a total of about IR£6,136 (€7,791) *per annum* per person at work in the full year 1982. This was almost 57% of the GNP of IR£10,837 (€13,760) per person at work!

The follow-up *CII Newsletter*, after the Kilkenny presentation, analysed Government spending under each of eight major headings that, between them, accounted for 92% of expenditure on all current public programmes. The CII concluded that Government spending on those programmes was wasteful for two reasons. First, the same people on whom the taxation was levied in the first instance consumed the vast majority of Government services. Collection of taxation and administration of the services inevitably involved a real cost to the taxpayer, while the high level of personal taxation diminished the incentive for additional work effort throughout the economy, as proven by the PAYE tax protest of 1983. Individuals could not escape taxation, and therefore were penalised whether or not they consumed a particular public service. This gave rise to the second reason why some public expenditure programmes were wasteful, namely, that there was no incentive on the part of individuals to curtail consumption. Hence, paradoxically, many of the public expenditure programmes were designed to encourage over-consumption by the individual, thus entailing a significant waste of resources to the community at large.

SEDUCED BY 'BIG GOVERNMENT'

The other side of the high taxation coin was that Government expenditure in Ireland, as a proportion of national output, was astronomically high, both in absolute terms and relative to international comparisons. Expenditure, both current and capital, comprised transfer payments, public infrastructure provision and maintenance, the provision of administrative, legislative, and regulatory services, and the funding of all other public expenditure programmes. Public expenditure consumed 30% of GNP in 1961, the year in which Ireland's drive towards high technology industrialisation had gathered momentum following the 1958 Lemass / Whitaker initiatives. Twelve years later, in 1973, when Ireland joined the EEC, the figure had increased to 42% each of GDP and GNP.[20] Figures published by the Department of Finance showed that a further 12 years on, in 1985, Government expenditure, current and capital, consumed 66.9% of GDP, and 75.6% of GNP.[21] In effect, 'Big Government' had seduced Ireland.[¶]

It was pointless for the Government or for any interest group to claim justification by making comparisons on a current basis between Ireland and then richer countries, such as Sweden, where total outlays of Government as a proportion of GNP were, in the mid-1980s, almost as

---

[¶]   These figures, originally published by the Department of Finance in 1987, were subsequently revised on a number of occasions and *per* the *2003 Revised Estimates for Public Services & Public Capital Programme*, total Government expenditure peaked at 62.2% of GNP in 1983. The revised figures are used in **Graph 3.3**.

high as in Ireland, but where real income per head of population was double or more that of Ireland. Similarly, a current comparison with Denmark in the mid-1980s was invalid, because real income per head of population there was about one and three-quarters that of Ireland.

My presentations to the Institute of Chartered Secretaries & Administrators (ICSA), Republic of Ireland Region, in September 1985, and to the CII Mid-West Region in Limerick in November 1985 emphasised the need for 'like with like' international comparisons. The topic was developed in a *CII Newsletter* of December 1985, giving international comparisons of the extent to which Government was involved in the economy in each of the OECD countries for the years from 1950 to 1983, the latter being the latest year for which OECD published statistics were then available.[22]

To make valid international comparisons, it was necessary to calculate the year in which each of the other OECD countries had a GNP *per capita* in purchasing power terms equal to Ireland's GNP *per capita* in the early 1980s. The calculation revealed, for example, that public expenditure in Switzerland in 1950, when Switzerland earned a GNP *per capita* in purchasing power terms equal to Ireland's GNP *per capita* in 1983, amounted to 16% of national output. The Swiss figure was the lowest of any OECD country at Ireland's 1983 level of economic development. Austria, with 40% in 1971, was second to Ireland in the percentage of national output consumed by Government expenditure. All other OECD countries that in the early 1980s earned a real GNP per head of population higher than Ireland had Government expenditure within the range of 16% to 40% of national output and the average for all OECD countries at Ireland's 1983 level of economic development was 31%.

To analyse trends and draw conclusions, the December 1985 *Newsletter* made a comparison between the average rate of growth in real incomes per head of population, and the level of Government spending, in each of the OECD countries for each of the four periods between 1960 and 1983. The analysis revealed that countries with levels of Government spending of less than 25% of national output earned average annual *per capita* growth rates of 5.6%. When Government spending was between 25% and 50% of national output, the growth rate was about 3%. For those countries where Government spending was more than 50% of national output, the growth rate was around 0.5%.

Relative to the experience of all OECD countries from 1960 to 1983, it was clear why Ireland had zero aggregate economic growth between 1980 and 1986. The conclusion, drawn objectively from the analysis, was that development prospects for the Irish economy depended critically on reducing Government spending to a level appropriate to Ireland's 1983 level of economic development. Unless Ireland could roll back public expenditure to manageable proportions, Ireland would be condemned inevitably to a continuation of low growth, or no growth, and even to a fall in national output and living standards. **Table 3.3** shows a summary of GNP volume growth from 1961 to 1986.

Table 3.3: Annual % GNP Volume Growth, 1961-1986

Year(s)	%
Average 1961-1973	+ 4.3
Average 1974-1980	+ 3.4
1981	+ 1.8
1982	- 1.3
1983	- 1.9
1984	+ 1.1
1985	+ 0.2
1986	+ 0.1

In 1972, the year in which the Government first borrowed to sustain day-to-day spending, current Government expenditure amounted to 29% of GNP, and investment in the PCP amounted to 11% of GNP. Total Government expenditure, current and capital, was, therefore, 40% of GNP. The Central Bank of Ireland's *Annual Report 1972-1973* stated that real public expenditure, current and capital, was 30% of GNP in 1961, and increased to 44% in 1973. The Central Bank issued the following warning:

> 'If recent trends were to continue, it would lead to a situation where public expenditure would amount to over 60% of GNP in the early 1980s. Both the level of taxation and the level of borrowing that would be found necessary to finance such a level of public expenditure would, of course, be inordinate by present standards.'

The position outlined by Alan Dukes TD, Minister for Finance, in his 1986 Budget speech was that current Government expenditure was expected to be 59% of GNP that year, and the PCP would take a further 11% of GNP.[23] The Minister projected that total Exchequer spending, current and capital, would amount to 70% of GNP. The figure for public expenditure would have been even higher if the incremental expenditure of local authorities and other State bodies, net of Exchequer transfer payments, were added.

A delegation from the Electrical All-Island Committee of the CII meeting with
Alan Dukes TD, Minister for Finance (seated second from left). The
delegation included (seated, left to right): Alan Lawless, Vice President, Radio
& TV Retailing Association of Ireland; Peter Webster, Chairman, Electrical
All-Island Committee; Edward Johnston, Director FEII; (standing, left to
right): Ron Winfield, Managing Director, RTV National Vision; Tadhg
Sugrue, Irish TV Renters Association; and Albert Brooks, Chairman, Radio &
TV Setmakers & Distributors Group.

Judging by news media reports of the time, there seemed to have been a
myth among some politicians, some interest groups, and some sections of
the community that Government itself had unlimited resources that the
community did not need to earn. The general view seemed to have been
that Government could 'create' jobs, provide services and maintain living
standards to an unlimited extent. The political process had largely fostered
this myth, although in the years immediately prior to 1986, some
politicians had begun to criticise the 'politics of promise'.

Graph 3.3 demonstrates the negative correlation between total
Government expenditure as a percentage of GNP and annual GNP
volume growth. The graph shows that the years 1994 to 2000, inclusive,
when total Government expenditure as a percentage of GNP fell
continuously from 46.1% to 34.8%, were years of high GNP volume
growth, ranging between 6.5% in 1994 and the peak of 10.1% in 1997. The
rise in Government expenditure to 36.8% in 2001 was accompanied by a
fall in real GNP growth to 4%, from 9.7% in the previous year. After the
year 2000, growth did not return to the 1994 level of 6.5% until 2006.

Graph 3.3: Government Expenditure, Economic Growth & Exchequer Balance, % of GNP, 1980-2007

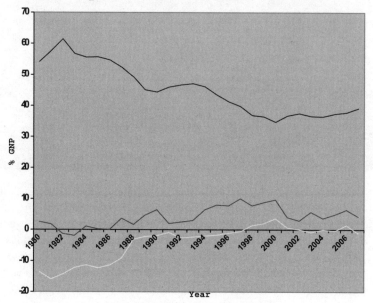

Source: Department of Finance, *Revised Estimates for Public Services,
2003* for years 1980-1982, and *Revised Estimates for Public Services,
2007* for 1983 onwards.

Graph 3.3 also demonstrates a similar negative correlation between the annual Exchequer balance and annual GNP volume growth.

THE TAX REVOLT

The significant increases in the burden of PAYE income tax, including very high marginal rates, and in PRSI, provoked a sharp adverse reaction from individuals in the early 1980s. The introduction to the CII's 1982 pre-Budget submission referred to higher taxation as one of the consequences of the massive increase in the cost of funding the National Debt, accumulated over the previous few years mainly because of the unsustainable current Budget deficits. The top rate of income tax in 1980 / 1981 was 60%, and, as a temporary measure, this was increased to 65% in each of the two years 1983/1984 and 1984/1985. It was not until 1985 / 1986 that the process of reducing the rates of income tax began.

By April 1983, the situation was so serious that the *Sunday Press*, in a report headlined 'Countdown to the City's Tax March', claimed that more pressure than had ever been exerted on any Government was being applied by the PAYE sector for reforms to at least spread more equitably some of the tax burden.[24] [¶] The issue of a more equitable spread of the tax burden was important against the background of a widespread perception of an undue burden on the PAYE sector and of significant tax evasion in other sectors. The latter perception was confirmed in the late 1990s and early 2000s in the Deposit Interest Retention Tax (DIRT) Enquiry undertaken by the Oireachtas Public Accounts Committee, evidence before the Moriarty Tribunal, and investigations by the Revenue Commissioners. The tax march took place on Wednesday, 13 April 1983.

The focus of the introduction to the CII's 1983 pre-Budget submission once again was that the serious imbalance in the Government's finances, the overwhelming magnitude of Government expenditure and the total impossibility of raising matching revenue through taxation were the root causes of the Irish economic problems at the time.

In early April 1983, I was invited by the *Irish Independent* to write a News Analysis column on the tax debate.[25] The article argued that the PAYE tax revolt brought the true nature of Ireland's economic problems into sharp focus. It was understandable and valid that the mantle of the PAYE tax protest was taken up by some trade unions, but it was equally important to point out that trade unions did not exclusively represent all who paid income tax through the PAYE system. In 1982, PAYE taxpayers numbered two-thirds of the entire labour force, employer, employee, and self-employed, in both the public and the private sectors, and in every area of economic activity. The number of people within the scope of the PAYE system was 792,000, in a total labour force of 1,200,000, which included every managing director, every executive director, and every senior manager, all of whom by law came within the PAYE system. The number of company directors was over 30,000, and the PAYE system covered about half of the 80,000 self-employed in sectors outside of agriculture. The CII view was that, if a proportion as high as two-thirds of the nation's labour force protested against the impact of taxation, Government was obliged to listen and respond. In that context, something had gone seriously and fundamentally wrong with the tax system, direct and indirect: it was time to look at fundamentals. The debate on the almost

---

[¶] In the article, I was cited as being strongly critical of the introduction of taxes that adversely impacted on economic output and employment.

universally accepted need for tax reform in Ireland in 1983 was
complicated by the fact that it was taking place against a background of
national and international recession. National recession was further
intensified by the financial crisis facing the Government, which had
evolved over a period of a decade or more.

A second invited article on taxation in the *Irish Independent* in April
1983, put industry's view of high taxation in perspective, with the
following background statement[26]:

> 'The rapid growth in public expenditure for consumption purposes and
> for capital projects, has been financed by foreign borrowing, and has
> increased inflation by increasing consumer demand beyond the supply
> capacity of the productive sectors of the economy. This has resulted in a
> cost and price spiral, which has made Ireland the highest inflation country
> on average in the EEC over the past four years. The result has been a
> massive erosion of competitiveness both on home and overseas markets.'

Additionally, in May 1983, *The Irish Times* published a similar article with
the following introduction: [27]

> 'There is a grave danger that social unrest could be caused by the
> current spread of misinformation regarding taxation, according to Con
> Power, Director of Economic Policy, Confederation of Irish Industry,
> who in this article presents the views of the CII on taxation.'

The CII's 1984 pre-Budget submission showed that, while wages and
salaries had increased by 14.2% *per annum* on average over the four years
1980 to 1983, inclusive, the income tax burden increased by 19.7% *per
annum* on average. There was significant erosion of take-home pay due to
high taxation. The pressure of the increasing tax burden on wages and
salaries led to demands for higher remuneration, and generated a
disincentive to work. Neither characteristic was conducive to the efficient
performance of the economy. As such, the CII concluded that tax increases
did not represent a viable option in solving the Government's financial
crisis. Despite that, the Government significantly increased both direct and
indirect taxes in the 1983 Budget.

In its 1984 Budget submission, the CII raised the growing concern
among enterprises at the disincentive effect of high taxation on all PAYE
taxpayers. The narrowing of the tax bands in the 1982 Budget, the higher
rate of 65% announced in the 1983 Budget, and the 2% additional levies on
total income, had a dramatic effect in reducing the take-home pay of
employees. The CII urged the Government to recognise the disincentive
effect of narrow tax bands and high marginal rates of personal taxation,

and urged the Government to restore the tax bands in real terms, inflation-adjusted, to those that prevailed prior to the 1982 Budget.

When making its 1984 pre-Budget submission, it was a matter of serious concern to the CII, in terms of the disincentive offered to the taxpayer, that a single person then earning less than IR£12,000 (€15,237) *per annum*, with taxable income of just over IR£10,000 (€12,697) after basic allowances, could be subject to the highest marginal tax rate. The submission recorded the contrast with the United Kingdom, where the highest tax rate was 60% and where entry to that band did not occur until the taxable income threshold of £36,000 sterling was exceeded. The CII was particularly concerned that the most highly skilled persons in the economy were being forced to look abroad to obtain a greater financial reward for their efforts. During the previous year, the CII had received numerous complaints from member enterprises of difficulties experienced in retaining key internationally-mobile executives, who were liable to punitively high levels of personal taxation in Ireland.

The CII's 1984 pre-Budget submission showed that real earnings, adjusted for inflation, for a taxpayer on the average industrial wage over the five year period 1979 to 1983, inclusive, had fallen by 19%. Real earnings, adjusted for inflation, for a taxpayer on twice the average industrial wage over the same five year period had fallen by 21%. Real earnings, adjusted for inflation, for a taxpayer on four times the average industrial wage had fallen by 30% over the same period. Those calculations were based on a taxpayer with a dependent spouse not working, and with two dependent children. Earnings were shown net of income tax, PRSI, and levies, and, for the purposes of calculation, it was assumed that personal reliefs and allowances only were due to the taxpayer. No wonder taxpayers were revolting!

The CII's 1985 pre-Budget submission was also a response to the National Economic Plan, *Building on Reality 1984-1987*, (BoR) published in October 1984. The CII emphasised that the very high level of personal taxation was causing major difficulties for industry in recruiting, retaining, and motivating key staff. The exceptionally high rates of taxation impacted on pay negotiations, employees' willingness to accept promotion and to work overtime, and increased the attraction of the black economy. The CII noted that BoR committed the Government to halting the increase in the burden of taxation as a percentage of GNP, notably by increasing income tax bands and thresholds with a view to halting, and to some small degree reducing, the PAYE burden during the ensuing three year period. In that context, the CII recommended the removal of the 65% marginal tax rate that had been introduced as a temporary measure in 1983 / 1984, and this was done for 1985 / 1986.

The serious detrimental effects of high personal taxation were revisited in the CII's 1986 pre-Budget submission. The CII recommended that the focus of any alleviation of the income tax burden should be primarily on widening the 35% and 48% tax bands, preferably by expanding the base of taxation in accordance with recommendations of the Reports of the Commission on Taxation.[28] The point was made in the CII's 1986 pre-Budget submission that the level of taxation in Ireland was as high as the European average, and that it was much higher in the case of PAYE. The CII again recommended that there was no scope for increasing taxation, and that the tax system should be restructured by widening the base, broadly along lines recommended by the Commission on Taxation.

SUMMARY

◊ From 1981 onwards, the CII argued trenchantly that unsustainably high current Government borrowing was the gravest contributory factor to the continuous national economic deterioration in each of the years from 1981 to 1986, inclusive.

◊ Borrowing fuelled indiscriminate public expenditure and resulted in Government programmes consuming proportionately more of national output than in any other OECD country at Ireland's level of economic development.

◊ The high level of borrowing was exacerbated by inordinately high personal taxation that led to protest marches organised by the trade union movement, which also highlighted issues of tax inequities.

◊ The period was marked by the absence of a shared analysis of the problems and of the potential solutions. The economic debate was isolated from the parallel political debates and trade union debates. The employers refused to enter national talks on pay issues.

◊ Eventually, the social partners, through the NESC, agreed an economic and social agenda that included bringing order to the public finances and they accepted the immediate objective to stop the rising spiral of National Debt. The agreement set the scene for the negotiation of the PNR, endorsed by Government and the social partners in October 1987. Implementation of the

PNR and of subsequent programmes helped to pave the way for national economic success.

CHAPTER 4
FAILED 'SOLUTIONS'

THE DECADE OF UNCERTAINTY, 1977–1987

The period of uncertainty, in my view, was from the second Government of Jack Lynch, who took office on 5 July 1977, to the third Government of Charles J Haughey, who took office on 10 March 1987. This was a period of turbulence in politics, marked by frequent changes in Government.[1] For much of the time, the uncertainty facing politicians meant that they had little opportunity to formulate and implement long-term programmes. Nevertheless, some of programmes that were introduced provided a valuable backdrop and a testing ground for policies that ultimately succeeded. Politicians, and, indeed, the nation, learned from their mistakes. Successive Governments correctly diagnosed the economic and social problems but were unable to work effectively towards a solution. The decade saw the first tentative steps towards social partnership in Ireland in the form of the National Understandings of 1979 and 1980 and saw the seeds of co-operation on both sides of the Oireachtas in Dr Garret FitzGerald's congratulations on Charles J Haughey's election as Taoiseach in March 1982.

LYNCH / O'DONOGHUE, 1977

The Fianna Fáil Manifesto for the General Election of June 1977 marked a new departure in Irish politics. In retrospect, it is seen as ushering in 'the politics of promise', and it generated widespread public expectations and aspirations, not matched by economic reality. Fianna Fáil, with 84 of the then 148 seats in the Dáil, achieved the largest majority of a single Party since the foundation of the State.[1] Fine Gael and the Labour Party, which had formed the outgoing Coalition Government since March 1973, fought

---

[1]   The outcome of the 1977 General Election was Fianna Fáil 84, Fine Gael 43, Labour Party 17, Independent Fianna Fáil 1, and Others 3, for a total of 148 seats.

the campaign on their record in Government. In contrast, Fianna Fáil, under Jack Lynch, conducted a presidential-style campaign and issued a detailed *General Election Manifesto*. Professor Martin O'Donoghue is generally credited as the main architect of the Manifesto, which contained many financial, economic, and social undertakings. The Manifesto is popularly remembered for promises such as the abolition of rates on domestic dwellings and the abolition of the annual motorcar registration tax. In national economic terms, the aim of the expansionary proposals was to reduce unemployment quickly to below 100,000. The Manifesto also contained social proposals, including one on gender equality.

THE PROGRAMME FOR NATIONAL DEVELOPMENT, 1978

Professor Martin O'Donoghue TD was appointed Minister in the newly-created Department of Economic Planning & Development on his first day in Dáil Éireann. A Government *White Paper* was published in January 1978, drafted by his Department,[2] which formalised much of what had been contained in the Fianna Fáil General Election Manifesto. Specific targets were set for each year to 1980, including a 25,000 annual average reduction in the numbers unemployed, a 7% *per annum* growth in GNP, a reduction in inflation to 5% by 1980, and a reduction in Exchequer borrowing to 8% of GNP.

The Government believed that changes in policy were needed to achieve these targets, and the Department of Economic Planning & Development was tasked with identifying the required actions. The result was a *Green Paper* published in June 1978, which gave *indicative options* for the *directly-productive sectors*, including agriculture, industry and private services.[3] Emphasis was placed on enhancing the national capacity in marketing and in research and development. The primary focus of the *Green Paper* was to establish the basis for reaching full employment and ending unemployment within five years.

The *Green Paper* recognised that:

> 'We will not meet the challenge unless there is a fundamental change in attitudes . . . There is a natural reluctance to face difficult decisions and to adopt painful courses of action, but that reluctance must be overcome.'

The Government acknowledged that the *White Paper* of January 1978, and the *Green Paper* of June 1978, formed only the initial steps in the planning cycle. Consultations followed with various interest groups, including the CII, and a further *White Paper* was published in January 1979.[4] Publication of the 1979 *White Paper* was against the background of GDP growth of about 7% in 1978, which was almost three times the 2.5% average growth rate achieved in the EEC. Irish inflation fell from 13.6% in 1977 to 7.6% in 1978. The White Paper stated that the number of new jobs created had been an all-time record since the foundation of the State, and, net of redundancies and other job losses, the number of people at work increased by about 17,000. Those indicators seemed to augur well for Ireland's prospects in the 1980s, although employment creation in the public sector was increasing rapidly, with implications for future public expenditure.[1] Additionally, the *White Paper* acknowledged that the output growth of 7% achieved in 1978 was associated with a rapid increase in consumer spending and that '… it would not be possible to sustain such increases in later years'. In particular, the *White Paper* warned of the dangers associated with 'the growing proportion of personal spending devoted to imports' and stated that such spending was 'one illustration of the trend which would require corrective action …'. Basic increases negotiated under the National Pay Agreement in 1978 exceeded what Government considered desirable and these increases were augmented in many cases by large supplementary awards. The *White Paper* cautioned that '… it is unfortunate that the degree of pay moderation and of industrial relations harmony required to ensure success in the fields of employment and inflation was not forthcoming, especially having regard to the tax reliefs afforded by the 1978 Budget'.

The CII's view, in the summer of 1979, was that the economic achievements of 1978 could be repeated and that the targets set in the *Programme for National Development 1979-1981* (PND) could be met if broadly-based community consensus was reached, based on economic awareness.[5] In particular, it was necessary to foster in the schools an attitude conducive to entrepreneurship. The climate of industrial relations required significant improvement. In the light of the worldwide energy crisis, a renewed effort was needed to develop Ireland's indigenous energy resources, both through exploration and through the development of

---

[1]   According to the then Department of the Public Service, full-time public service employment increased from 250,100 in 1976, to 266,200 in 1978, 284,900 in 1980, and 301,200 in 1982, when it stabilised. The increase in public service employment between 1976 and 1982 was over 20%, whereas the increase in the total number of people at work in the State was only 7.7%.

renewable energy sources. Finally, Ireland needed to embrace fully the disciplines of monetary stability implicit in membership of the EMS.

The CII pointed out that, as 1978 was the first year of Ireland's full membership of the EEC, following the transition period of five years since entry on 1 January 1973, Ireland now faced free trade within the EEC and would have to obey all external trade rules of the Community. The CII saw the need for Ireland to prepare for the new challenges and the opportunities presented by the proposed enlargement of the EEC, with Greece joining on 1 January 1981, and with negotiations with Portugal and Spain at an advanced stage. The CII emphasised that the task of preparation was a tripartite one involving Government, employers and industry, and the trade unions, thus publicly supporting the first tentative formal steps taken by Government during April and May 1979 to develop broadly-based social partnership.

THE NATIONAL
UNDERSTANDINGS, 1979 & 1980

Against the background of criticism by the Government of pay developments in 1978, the Department of Economic Planning & Development met informally with ICTU and the representative bodies of employers and industry to discuss the possibility of *tripartite discussions* as a basis for economic and social planning. The basis for a tripartite approach already existed in some policy areas at Community level within the EEC since the Treaty of Rome 1957, but it was not as broad in scope or as deep in character as that proposed by the Department of Economic Planning & Development.[1] The CII's Director General and I attended an exploratory meeting with the Department on 6 April 1979. This was CII's first involvement in social partnership. In a landmark announcement on 2

---

[1]   The ESF, the oldest of the four EU Structural Funds, was established under the Treaty of Rome in 1957. It is assisted by the Committee of the European Social Fund, structured on a tripartite basis with representatives of Governments, employers' organisations and trade unions. The Rules for the Committee were published in EEC *Official Journal* 1201/60 and an amendment was published in *Official Journal* L 291/107 of 1979. The Economic & Social Committee of the EEC, also established under the Treaty of Rome, includes representatives of employers' organisations and of trade unions. The Standing Committee on Employment was established by EEC Council Decision 70/532/EEC of 24 December 1970 (*Official Journal* L273), in response to a wish expressed by the representatives of employers' and workers' organisations at a conference on employment problems held in Luxembourg in April 1970. The 1970 structure was amended by Council Decision 75/62/EEC of 20 January 1975 (*Official Journal* L21) and was further reformed in 1999.

May 1979, the Taoiseach, Jack Lynch TD, in answer to a Parliamentary Question from Michael O'Leary TD, Deputy Leader of the Labour Party, stated that agreement was reached on 24 April 1979 between the Government, representatives of ICTU, and of employer and industry organisations on proposals for a *National Understanding for Economic & Social Development*, including pay policy. The Taoiseach laid the agreed proposals before the Dáil and Seanad on 25 April 1979.

Not surprisingly, in the light of the specific comments on pay in the *White Paper* of January 1979, the Taoiseach stressed that implementation of the National Understanding would be conditional on ratification of the pay provisions. The Taoiseach added that the Understanding represented a new approach by the participating organisations to employment, economic growth, industrial relations, pay, social welfare and related matters. The Taoiseach said that the National Understanding could bring about a new sense of national purpose and commitment, and could offer the prospect of a new unity, a new stability, and a new attitude, which would focus on co-operation rather than confrontation.

The discussions between the organisations continued through a Central Policy Committee, which met between April and July 1979. The proposed *National Understanding for Economic & Social Development* was accepted by a national delegate conference of ICTU, and also by the members of the employer and industry organisations. The National Understanding included clauses relating to personal taxation, the maintenance of social welfare allowances in real terms, employee involvement, and education and training initiatives.

The establishment of the Employment Guarantee Fund, financed jointly by Government and the employers, was an innovative approach to economic development and job-creation under the National Understanding. The employers' contribution was by way of a surcharge on the employers' social security payment for the tax year 1980-1981. The Fund, formally established under the *Employment Guarantee Fund Act 1980*, supported 33 projects, with 2,800 whole-time equivalent jobs. The projects were assessed by representatives of the social partners, as well as by officials of the relevant Government Departments.[1]

Charles J Haughey TD succeeded Jack Lynch as Leader of Fianna Fáil and Taoiseach on 11 December 1979. A *Second National Understanding for Economic*

---

[1]   The late Ruaidhrí Roberts, General Secretary of ICTU, 1967-1981, and Con Power formed the Committee that assessed the grant applications successfully made by Waterford Regional Airport and Sligo Regional Airport.

& Social Development was negotiated in 1980. This time, there was direct involvement by the Department of the Taoiseach, as the Taoiseach abolished the Department of Economic Planning & Development early in 1980. The *Second National Understanding* was wider in scope than the first, demonstrating Haughey's view of the holistic nature of the issues. It covered issues such as employment creation; construction and infrastructure development; social and economic legislation; health; social welfare; education and training; housing; and employee involvement. The CII was to the forefront in promoting the need to widen the scope of the National Understanding.

When the Second National Understanding expired, talks between ICTU and the employers' organisations, under the Employer-Labour Conference, failed to bring about a new agreement on pay, mainly because the employers' organisations refused to enter into national pay negotiations. The CII, which was not party to the pay negotiations, advocated the desirability of a further National Understanding, exclusive of pay and industrial relations, but that issue was not taken up by the Government, ICTU, or by the employers' organisations. There followed a period of decentralised pay bargaining from 1981 to 1987. Outside of the pay negotiations framework, the CII continued to advocate economic and social developments in areas including reduced personal taxation; employee shareholding; employee information and consultation; education and training; and employment-related social issues, with a focus on the national need for policy formation to generate higher economic growth and increased employment.

'THE WAY FORWARD', 1982

A Fine Gael / Labour Party Government with Dr Garret FitzGerald TD, Leader of Fine Gael, as Taoiseach and Michael O'Leary TD, Leader of the Labour Party, as Tánaiste, was formed in June 1981. This was succeeded nine months later by a minority Fianna Fáil Government, with Charles J Haughey TD as Taoiseach, and with the support of The Workers' Party and of Tony Gregory TD, Independent. Ray MacSharry TD was Tánaiste and Minister for Finance from 9 March 1982 until Alan Dukes TD of Fine Gael succeeded him on 14 December 1982 in a new Fine Gael / Labour Party Government.[1] Dr FitzGerald, in offering congratulations to Haughey on his nomination as Taoiseach in March, 1982, stated:[6]

---

[1] Ray MacSharry TD became Minister for Finance (and the Public Service) for a second period in another Government led by Charles J Haughey TD from 10 March 1987 to 24 November 1988, when he became the Irish Member of the European Commission.

'After the past eight months, I am in no doubt as to the difficulties which face him on the economic front. We shall offer constructive opposition and will support all reasonable measures that may be necessary to maintain the real underlying level of borrowing and the current deficit in the amount set by us and accepted in principle by Deputy Haughey and his party. We believe that this must be the new Government's priority if they are to have the possibility of securing existing employment, maintaining the value of our currency necessary to protect the living standards of our workers and retaining the freedom to promote the expansion of our economy and the creation of jobs. We shall facilitate the passage of all measures that are in the national interest.'

The Fianna Fáil Government produced an economic and social programme, *The Way Forward*, following consultation with interest groups, including the CII. The programme focussed on bringing order to the public finances, and proposed *inter alia* the elimination of the current budget deficit by 1986. It was debated in the Dáil in November 1982, when The Workers' Party and Tony Gregory TD withdrew their support because of the massive public spending cuts proposed. A vote of confidence in the Government, proposed by the Taoiseach, was defeated, and a General Election followed. A Fine Gael / Labour Party Government with Dr FitzGerald as Taoiseach and with Dick Spring TD as Tánaiste was returned to office in December 1982. Dick Spring TD had been elected Leader of the Labour Party after the resignation in 1982 of Michael O'Leary TD, who joined Fine Gael.

'BUILDING ON REALITY', 1984

Two years later, the Fine Gael / Labour Party Government produced a National Economic Plan, *Building on Reality 1984-1987*, after consultation with the interest groups, including the CII.[7] The CII's response to the Plan comprised its pre-Budget submission for 1985.[8] While it welcomed BoR as providing a stable framework for industry to plan over the three-year period, there were some points of difference in emphasis. Changes recommended were in areas of management of the public finances, industrial policy, cost competitiveness, and the creation of a climate that would reward work, initiative and investment. Of particular concern to industry was the 65% of GNP consumed by Government programmes, compared with the EEC average of 45%. Additionally, the Government failed to propose the elimination of the current budget deficit by 1987.

SUMMARY

◊   The decade 1977 to 1987 was one of uncertainty in Irish politics
    and the period 1981 to 1986 was one of turbulence.

◊   The Fianna Fáil *General Election Manifesto* of 1977 ushered in a
    period of the 'politics of promise' and, while some short-term
    economic gains were made, these were quickly lost again.

◊   The short-lived *National Understandings for Economic & Social
    Development* of 1979 and 1980 represented Ireland's first formal
    attempt at social partnership along lines somewhat similar to
    those that were put in place for some EEC institutions under
    the Treaty of Rome in 1957 and subsequently. The experiment
    failed mainly because, after 1980, the employers' organisations
    declined to enter into national pay agreements, and that
    remained the position until the aftermath of the NESC Report
    of 1986, followed by the PNR, published in 1987.[9]

◊   The correct diagnosis of economic ills was made, but not acted
    upon, by successive Governments during the period 1981-1986.

CHAPTER 5
THE TURNING POINT

THE CII ANNUAL CONFERENCE, 1986

The CII Annual Conference for 1986 was held in the Royal Hospital, Kilmainham on Friday, 21 February. An Taoiseach, Dr Garret FitzGerald TD was the guest speaker at the Conference Dinner. Extensive extracts from his address were published by the CII, together with the address of the CII President, Leo O'Donnell, on the theme of *The European Challenge.*[1]

An Taoiseach, Dr Garret FitzGerald TD, being welcomed to the 1986 CII Conference Dinner by Leo O'Donnell (right), CII President, and Liam Connellan, CII Director General.

Dr FitzGerald stated, in reference to the NESC and the social partners:

'In speaking to some of you in a different forum, the National Economic & Social Council, last November *(1985)*, I asked whether there were any feasible proposals in the short-term for specific improvements in the environment for job creation and job protection which the social partners could jointly recommend. I also asked if, beyond the 1986 Budget, the National Economic & Social Council could bring forward agreed views on development policies – in particular, policies that would have a strong impact on employment – that would have a longer-term implementation and results time-scale.

I have to say that so far the response has been disappointing. I believe that we are now moving out of the low growth environment of the early 1980s … But, we will not reap the full benefits of this more favourable environment unless there are changes in attitudes and a willingness to transcend sectional interests with the broader objectives of developing our country and, especially, of generating employment. Can I, therefore, use tonight's forum to ask again for a new spirit of co-operation in Ireland such that we can have the required agreed proposals?'

Some days later, I responded to the Taoiseach's request and gave the CII's view on development policies in a talk to a Fine Gael meeting in South Dublin on Tuesday 25 February, on the topic *Strategy for Economic Development*. I outlined an indicative 10-point plan, based on published CII policy documents and submissions to Government.[2] The points included:

- The adoption of a national political objective for five years to foster the creation of more jobs and higher living standards, closer to at least the EC average.

- A plea for social partnership, industrial peace and employee involvement, including broadly-based structured employee shareholding.

- Elimination of the Government's current budget deficit, with a consequential reduction in interest rates.

- The need to focus the public capital programme more sharply on productive infrastructure, including national roads, the natural gas grid and telecommunications, together with a focus on joint venture and shared equity housing.

- A reduction in the level of total Government expenditure over a five-year period from about 70% of GNP to about 40% of GNP to release more national resources for the generation of goods and traded services, with consequential viable job creation.

- The need to analyse all public expenditure programmes on a 'zero-base justification' basis.

- An increased emphasis on internationally-traded services, including financial services, tourism and labour-intensive, high added-value, highly-skilled professional services, as well as increased emphasis on high technology, knowledge-based manufacturing industries, indigenous and multinational.

♦ Redeployment of public service personnel to the greatest extent appropriate in areas related to economic development, enforcement of public revenue collection, the elimination of abuses in public expenditure programmes and the elimination of the black economy.

♦ The creation of a better climate for enterprise, commercial risk-taking, and individual and corporate economic effort through lifting the burden of administrative and regulatory costs and through reduction of the personal tax burden.

♦ The promotion, through political leadership, of a widespread economic literacy programme.

The points were discussed at a meeting between An Taoiseach, Dr Garret FitzGerald TD and CII representatives, of whom I was one, on 20 May 1986, and were pursued separately with relevant Ministers and Opposition spokespersons, as recorded in various Chapters of this book. Many of the points were further expanded in position papers submitted to the NESC through the CII representatives thereon and most points were reflected in the November 1986 NESC Report.

THE VOICE OF REASON

Since 1980, the NESC had published an annual economic and social report. As was mentioned at the end of the last chapter, the 1986 report was important in its contribution to establishing the preconditions for the Celtic Tiger. As requested by An Taoiseach, Dr Garret FitzGerald TD, in November 1985, the report was significantly different from the preceding ones, which had tended to be *pro forma*. In the 1986 Report, the approach was more comprehensive, and addressed a medium-term, rather than an annual, framework. The Council, in its Preface, stated that it was 'concerned at the evolution of the economic and social situation over the first half of the 1980s' and 'was apprehensive at the implications of a continuation of present policies'. The Council stated that, as its report was being finalised, 'the overall economic and social situation deteriorated seriously in a number of important respects'. In the Council's view, the deterioration underlined the necessity for immediate remedial action in the form of an integrated strategy, placed firmly in a medium-term context. The Council added that:

> 'The fact that the various interests have been able to agree on the major
> elements of an integrated strategy and on the general policies for the
> major sectors of the economy should be a substantial help to
> Government.'

The broad consensus achieved in private dialogue at Council by the various interest groups represented on the NESC, as contained in the November 1986 Report,[3] was based on four main planks of agreement. These were: control of public expenditure, tax equity, development policies and the removal of social inequities. However, the agreement achieved at the NESC, and contained in the 1986 Report, was not always as clearly articulated in public utterances by the participating organisations!

Pádraig Ó hUiginn, as Secretary General of the Department of the Taoiseach, was Chairman of the NESC and played a major part in the achievement of the broad consensus between the representatives of the social partners. He had been a participant in many aspects of the evolving social partnership and in other National Programmes, dating from the early days of the first National Understanding of 1979 when he was on the staff of the Department of Economic Planning & Development. Subsequent to the publication of the NESC Report in November 1986, Pádraig Ó hUiginn was centrally involved in the social partnership programmes until he retired at the end of April 1993.

THE ZEAL OF THE CONVERT

Hastings, Sheehan & Yeates, in their 2007 work, recorded what happened following the NESC publication of November 1986:[4]

> 'The unanimity of the social partners gave the 1986 NESC strategy
> report an important moral authority. The incoming minority Fianna Fáil
> Government also endorsed it, and then used it as the basis for
> negotiating an agreement for which there could be widespread support.
> Even before the NESC report was published, however, the opposition
> Fianna Fáil party and its leader Charles Haughey and labour
> spokesman Bertie Ahern, building on long established contacts and
> relationships, had been making overtures to the trade unions.'

As part of his discussions with representatives of the social partners following the NESC Report, Charles J Haughey TD invited me to give him the CII's views on public finances, the National Debt, and economic development policies at two meetings with him for that purpose, on 28

October and 1 November 1986. The agenda, at Haughey's request, included CII publications and public lectures on national economics; monetary and fiscal policy; public finances; public borrowing; taxation; physical planning; regional development; development of the network of national roads through a proposed National Roads Authority; the work of the Financial Services Industry Association (FSIA), established within the CII in 1984; promotion of internationally-traded financial and professional services with Ireland as a base; education and training for a knowledge-based economy; industrial sectors with growth potential; the role of State commercial enterprises; and social partnership.

The CII's 1987 pre-Budget submission was prepared subsequent to the NESC Report of November 1986, in which the CII was an active participant.[5] The submission welcomed the internal consensus within the NESC, representing the combined interests of employers, farmers, trade unions, and industry. The CII expressed the hope for a similar consensus between the political parties, but, in retrospect, this was not achieved and had virtually no prospect of achievement due to the public campaign against aspects of the Government's attempt to control public expenditure. Indeed, some industrialists on the CII National Council expressed the fear that a Fianna Fáil Government, if returned at the next General Election, might not continue and intensify efforts to control public expenditure. Consequently, the CII's 1987 pre-Budget submission focussed on national policy issues, rather than issues specific to industry, due to the serious problems caused by the rapid growth in the National Debt, zero economic growth and the stagnation of industrial output. After detailing the crisis in industry, the CII submission was divided into two main sections, *Programme for National Recovery* and *Plan for Industrial Expansion*. The latter covered issues such as cost competitiveness, investment, employment, a reduction in the burden of personal taxation and export promotion. Industry was strongly of the view that action was needed to correct the serious imbalance in the national finances, and to restore the confidence of investors in projects with viable productive employment. The CII consistently had given that view to successive Governments from 1981 onwards, in spite of the unwillingness or inability of Governments to face economic reality. The CII's pre-Budget meeting with John Bruton TD, Minister for Finance, took place on 8 January 1987, and a pre-Budget meeting was held with Charles J Haughey TD, Leader of Fianna Fáil, and members of his Front Bench on the same day. Haughey invited the CII to nominate a representative to speak at a Fianna Fáil National Business Conference in the Burlington Hotel on Sunday, 18 January 1987. The CII nominated me and I gave a talk reiterating the key points in the CII's pre-Budget submission, both in relation to the *Programme for National Recovery* and *Plan for Industrial Expansion.*[6]

A CII delegation meeting with Charles J Haughey, Leader of the Opposition, and members of the Fianna Fáil Front Bench at Leinster House for discussions on the CII's 1987 pre-Budget submission. Pictured (from left) are: Tom Hardiman, CII National Executive; Leo O'Donnell, CII Past President; Con Power, CII Director of Economic Policy; Liam Connellan, CII Director General; Terry Larkin, CII President; Charles J Haughey TD; Vincent Brady TD, Fianna Fáil Chief Whip; Brian Lenihan TD, Deputy Leader; and Ray Burke TD, spokesman on the Environment.

The deficit in public finances had escalated sharply in 1986, and the National Debt was 145% of GNP at the end of September 1986, in contrast to 134% at the end of 1985.[¶] The CII recommended that the stabilisation of the National Debt be achieved over a two-year period, and estimated that this would require the public sector deficit to be reduced by about 2.5% of GNP or IR£400 million (€508 million) *per annum* compared with the 1986 out-turn. An adjustment of a similar magnitude had been made in Denmark from a deficit of over 9% of GNP in 1982 to a surplus of almost 3% of GNP in 1986. While the adjustment was being made in the public finances, employment in the Danish economy had increased by almost 2% *per annum*.

¶   *Budget & Economic Statistics 2007*, Department of Finance, published revised figures for National Debt and the National Debt / GNP ratio for various years. The figures, in € millions, for the relevant years are 1985, €23,493 (106.0%); 1986, €27,440 (115.1%); and 1987, €30,085 (117.6%).

The Fine Gael / Labour Party Government did not introduce a Budget in 1987. The Labour Party withdrew from Government on 20 January 1987, because it disagreed with Budget proposals. The subsequent General Election that was held on 17 February 1987, was the fourth in the 1980s.

The Fianna Fáil *General Election Manifesto 1987* comprised a 71-page document, entitled the *Programme for National Recovery*, which was effectively a strategic policy response to the NESC Report of November 1986, to the CII's 1987 pre-Budget submission and to other central policy and sectoral submissions.

Because of the link with the NESC Report, with the CII's published submissions and the subsequent negotiation of the social partnership programme, which was also called the *Programme for National Recovery*, it is interesting, in retrospect, to note the comprehensive nature of the Fianna Fáil document:

♦ Restoration of national confidence, in the context of taxation and interest rates then at an all-time high, significant emigration, high national debt, and record high Government current budget deficits.

♦ The need to use additional wealth created during economic recovery to reduce the burden of national debt, in the first instance.

♦ Management of the public finances in a prudent economic and social manner.

♦ Progressive reductions in tax levels, including personal taxation, and management of the tax system on a just and equitable basis.

♦ Creation of industrial consensus, and the establishment of a forum in which the social partners could negotiate the terms of a national plan for recovery, based on agreed medium-term objectives.

♦ Growth proposals relating to creating enterprise in trade and industry, together with specific sectoral programmes in science and technology, tourism, energy, agriculture and food, horticulture, forestry, marine, inland fisheries, services, financial services (including the development of a strong international financial services centre), and the entertainment industry.

♦ Improving the national infrastructure including training for employment, the civil service, State enterprises, transport, broadcasting, decentralisation and regionalisation (including decentralisation of sections of Government Departments outside Dublin, a comprehensive reorganisation of local government structures, and reform of local government finances), and natural and built environment issues (including the establishment of a National Roads Authority, county roads, housing, rented accommodation, environmental amenities, planning and development, and urban renewal).

♦ Caring for basic values in terms of social welfare, health, education, justice, women's affairs, youth, An Gaeilge, the Arts, and heritage and conservation.

♦ National affairs in terms of Northern Ireland, foreign affairs, and defence.

When the Dáil met on 10 March 1987, Charles J Haughey TD was elected Taoiseach on the casting vote of the Ceann Comhairle. The outcome of the General Election was a minority Fianna Fáil Government, with 82 seats out of 166.

Dr Garret FitzGerald TD, Leader of Fine Gael and outgoing Taoiseach, stated in his congratulations to Charles J Haughey:[7]

> 'Deputy Haughey will be aware that there exists in this House a clear and decisive majority in favour of decisive action in the economic sphere. I refer to the action necessary to create conditions favouring increased employment and a lasting cut in the tax burden achieved by means, which do not add further to the share of public revenue, pre-empted by interest payments, which, indeed, it would be desirable to reduce as soon as possible. The action necessary to achieve these objectives will in present circumstances necessarily involve decisions that will not find favour with sections of the community. The new Government will require the necessary support in this House to carry them through. In so far as the incoming Government introduce budgetary measures, which correspond to the objectives, which I have just mentioned …, my party will not oppose such measures or legislative action required to implement the necessary budgetary provisions. It is important that the Dáil and public opinion generally understand that this is the situation.'

Alan Dukes TD succeeded Dr Garret FitzGerald as Leader of Fine Gael on 21 March 1987. Subsequently, as a personal initiative on 2 September 1987, in a talk to the then Tallaght Chamber of Commerce, he gave a public undertaking that, for so long as the minority Government led by Charles J Haughey followed a responsible economic path, Fine Gael would not oppose the Government. Duke's talk was widely reported at the time, and became known as the *Tallaght Strategy*. The fact that Fine Gael under Alan Dukes honoured that commitment had a profound impact on national economic policy.[8] History records that Dukes did not extract a single piece of political gain for his action, taken in the national interest. In 1990, John

Bruton TD, who held the post until 2001, replaced Dukes as Leader of Fine Gael.

SOCIAL PARTNERSHIP PROGRAMMES, 1987–2015

The PNR was negotiated between the minority Fianna Fáil Government (1987-1989) and the social partners during the summer of 1987, and was signed and published in October 1987.[9] The social partners then were ICTU, FUE, CII, the Construction Industry Federation (CIF), the Irish Farmers' Association (IFA), Macra na Feirme, and the Irish Co-operative Organisation Society (ICOS). The Programme covered the period to the end of 1990.

The first paragraph of the PNR read as follows:

> 'The Government, the ICTU, the FUE, the CII, the CIF, the IFA, Macra na Feirme and the ICOS, conscious of the grave state of our economic and social life, have agreed on this Programme to seek to regenerate our economy and improve the social equity of our society through their combined efforts. The principles that should govern such efforts were set out in the NESC study, *A Strategy for Development 1986-1990*.'

The approach was more advanced in its structure than developments in social dialogue that commenced in the EC in 1985 on the initiative of Commission President Jacques Delors.[¶]

In addition to the broadly-based consensus of the social partners, the Government obtained the consensus of the majority in both Dáil and Seanad, including, as mentioned earlier, through the *Tallaght Strategy* of Fine Gael under its leader, Alan Dukes TD.

[¶]   In January, 1985, President Delors invited the Chairpersons and General Secretaries / Directors General of all the national organisations affiliated to UNICE, the European Centre of Enterprises with Public Participation and of Enterprises of General Economic Interest (CEEP) and the European Trade Union Confederation (ETUC) to meet at the Castle of Val Duchesse outside Brussels to discuss furthering the European Social Dialogue. Some 'joint opinions' were subsequently concluded on a bilateral basis. European Social Dialogue was formally recognised in the *Single European Act 1986*, which came into force in 1987. A Protocol & Agreement on Social Policy, adopted by 11 of the then 12 Member States (excluding the United Kingdom), was attached to the Treaty of Maastricht, signed in 1992 and entered into force on 1 November 1993. The Treaty of Amsterdam, June 1997, included the Agreement on Social Policy as part of the Social Chapter of the EC Treaty. By the end of 2007, the European social partners had agreed some 300 joint texts and signed a number of important agreements.

The four main objectives of the Programme were:

♦ Creation of a fiscal, exchange rate, and monetary climate conducive to economic growth.

♦ Movement towards greater equity and fairness in the tax system.

♦ Diminishing or removing social inequities in society.

♦ Intensification of practical measures to generate increased job opportunities on a sectoral basis.

The PNR recognised the extent of the difficulties that faced the Irish economy under each of the following headings:

♦ GDP *per capita* at only 64% of the then EEC average, in purchasing power terms.

♦ National Debt amounting to IR£25 billion (€31.7 billion), or 150% plus of GNP (subsequently recalculated by the Department of Finance as 117.6%), with debt servicing amounting to one-third of total Exchequer tax revenue.

♦ Exchequer borrowing at 10.7% of GNP in 1987.

♦ High interest rates.

♦ 18.5% unemployment (subsequently recalculated by the CSO as 17.5%).

♦ Agricultural employment in decline at twice the EEC average rate.

♦ Net emigration amounting to 30,000 *per annum*.

♦ No volume increase in investment in equipment over five years, despite a 20% increase in aggregate in the then EEC.

The PNR addressed these issues:

♦ EC dimension.

♦ Macroeconomic policies, including stabilisation of the National Debt / GNP ratio, reduction in Exchequer borrowing and control of public expenditure.

♦ Tax reform.

♦ Greater social equity.

♦ Employment in specific sectors, including international financial services.

♦ Labour legislation.

♦ Mechanisms for the monitoring and review of the Programme.

♦ Proposals for the development of State enterprises.

Much of the detailed economic analysis of the PNR was in accord with the policies on national development and on the management of the public finances, including tax reform, proposed by the CII to Government, inputs made by the social partners to the NESC Report and inputs made by the social partners during the course of the negotiations for the Programme.

The PNR established the basis for the development of the International Financial Services Centre (IFSC) at the Custom House Docks site; measures to reduce certain business costs, including liability insurance premiums; development of industries based on natural resources such as agriculture, horticulture, forestry, the marine and tourism; development proposals for State commercial enterprises and for a major increase in science-based developments, in areas such as information technology, biotechnology, engineering, and mariculture.

Since the PNR did not include the establishment of the National Roads Authority (NRA), which had been specifically promised in the Fianna Fáil 1987 *General Election Manifesto*, the CII continued to press for the early establishment of a authority for national roads.

A draft *Agreement on Pay & Conditions* between ICTU and employers' organisations was negotiated and published as a separate document.

As one of the CII negotiators for the PNR, I served on the Central Review Committee (CRC), established to monitor and review the implementation of the Programme, including the achievement of targets and objectives. Additionally, I served on the Secretariat Group of the CRC, on the Education Centre Working Party established in June 1989, and on the Working Group on State Companies established in May 1990.

During the period from March 1987 to May 1989, Alan Dukes TD, Leader of Fine Gael, allowed the minority Fianna Fáil Government to pursue its economic policies without opposition, provided they were in the national interest, in a manner that represented a new departure in Irish politics. Despite this support from Fine Gael, the Taoiseach, Charles J Haughey TD, on 25 May 1989, advised the President to dissolve the Dáil. The context was the defeat of the Government on a motion to establish a trust fund for the benefit of HIV-infected haemophiliacs. The motion in the name of Dick Spring TD, Brendan Howlin TD, and other members of the Labour Party was carried on 26 April 1989, and a Government amendment was lost.[10] Opinion polls suggested the possibility of an overall majority for Fianna Fáil. Cuts in the funding of health services dominated the General Election campaign. In the event, Fianna Fáil lost four seats and the formation of a Government proved very difficult. Fine Gael refused to continue its support for any Fianna Fáil minority Government that might emerge. A Government was not formed when the incoming Dáil met on 29 June, as scheduled. Fianna Fáil was obliged to enter into a coalition Government for the first time in the party's history. Subsequently, on 12 July 1989, Charles J Haughey TD was elected Taoiseach of a Fianna Fáil / Progressive Democrats (PD) Coalition Government (1989-1992). By way of postscript, within the life of the same Dáil (the 25th), Albert Reynolds TD became Taoiseach on 11 February 1992, on a change in leadership of Fianna Fáil.

In succession to the PNR, the Government, the ICTU, the Federation of Irish Employers (FIE), the CII, the CIF, the IFA, the Irish Creamery Milk Suppliers Association (ICMSA), the ICOS, and Macra na Feirme negotiated the *Programme for Economic & Social Progress* (PESP), published in January 1991.[11] The CII and the FIE merged to form the Irish Business & Employers' Confederation (IBEC) in 1993, prior to the termination of the PESP.

The PESP dealt with the strategy for the 1990s, including macroeconomic stability, tax reform, social reform, employment and training, agricultural development, area-based response to long-term unemployment, European Community dimension, labour, company and related legislation, and institutional developments. A detailed section was included on State enterprises. There were sections on aspects of infrastructure development, together with social issues embracing education, housing, justice, equality, and disability.

The PESP included two appendices, a *Draft Agreement on Pay & Conditions between ICTU and Employers' Organisations*, and a *Memorandum of Understanding in relation to Surplus Staff & Age Limits in the Public Service*.

The PESP provided continuity for the progress made under the PNR, and built on and refined the various initiatives. I was a member of the CRC for the PESP from January 1991, and was the CII representative on the Secretariat Group of the CRC, as I had been for the PNR. I was seconded to the Department of the Taoiseach as Special Economic Development Officer, at the request of An Taoiseach, Albert Reynolds TD, made to my employers, then the CII, in March 1992, until I resigned from IBEC in April 1993. Senior officials of the IDA previously had held this public service post, created in 1987 to provide an industrial development input to the PNR secretariat. Following my resignation from IBEC, I continued on a consultancy basis as Chairman of each of three Working Groups of the CRC – Ireland as an International Education Centre; State Companies & SME Linkages; and Telemarketing & Direct Marketing – and to complete other development projects then in process, until the end of 1993.

A FRAMEWORK FOR THE
CELTIC TIGER

Because of their importance in helping to facilitate the restoration of order to the public finances and to the successful establishment of a framework for the emergence of the Celtic Tiger, a very brief overview follows of the social partnership programmes after 1993.

In addition to these programmes, new institutions were established and the scope of involvement was extended beyond the original seven social partnership organisations of the trade unions, employers and industry, and agricultural interests. A significant development in 1993 was the establishment of the National Economic & Social Forum (NESF) to provide advice on policies to achieve greater equality and social inclusion in the context of social partnership arrangements and to facilitate public consultation on policy issues referred by Government to the Forum. One policy reason for the establishment of the NESF was a perceived democratic deficit in policy formulation due to the narrow base of social partnership, as originally constituted. Membership of the NESF comprises four broad strands, namely:

◆ Members of Dáil Éireann and Seanad Éireann.

◆ Representatives of employers and business organisations, trade unions, and farming organisations.

◆ Representatives of voluntary and community organisations.

◆ Representatives of central and local government entities, together with independent members.

The first programme that followed on the conclusion of the PESP in 1993 was the *Programme for Competitiveness & Work* (PCW), which covered the period 1994-1996 (during the Fine Gael, Labour Party, and Democratic Left Government of 1994-1997), with certain elements of the pay agreement extending to include a wage increase due on 1 June 1996. The main focus of the PCW was on tax reform, further development of the partnership approach, social equity, and macroeconomic stability. There was an emphasis on agriculture, food, forestry, and rural development. Economic development issues included export promotion, inward investment, and development of service industries, as well as financial services, and ancillary industrial issues.

Partnership 2000 for Inclusion, Employment & Competitiveness 1997-2000 came next (during the Fianna Fáil / Progressive Democrats Government of 1997-2002). It stated that:

> 'The key objectives of the strategy are the continued development of an efficient modern economy capable of high and sustainable economic and employment growth, and operating within the constraints of international competitiveness, ensuring that Irish society becomes more inclusive, that long-term unemployment is substantially reduced, and that the benefits of growth are more equally distributed.'

On the recommendation of the NESC and the NESF, the Government extended social partnership to include the Irish National Organisation of the Unemployed (INOU), the Congress Centres for the Unemployed, the Community Platform, the Conference of Religious of Ireland (CORI), the National Women's Council of Ireland (NWCI), the National Youth Council of Ireland (NYCI), the Society of Saint Vincent de Paul, Protestant Aid, the Small Firms Association (SFA), the Irish Exporters' Association (IEA), the Irish Tourist Industry Confederation (ITIC), and the Chambers of Commerce of Ireland (CCI).

Two discussion documents were issued to the participating organisations. These were the NESC Report, *Strategy into the 21ˢᵗ Century*, and an NESF Report entitled *Post-PCW Negotiations: A New Deal?*. All 19 organisations – the seven organisations that participated with Government in the PCW and the 12 additional organisations above – made presentations at the opening discussions held in Dublin Castle on 23 October 1996.

Partnership 2000 dealt with the challenges facing the economy, the macroeconomic framework, living standards (pay, personal taxation, and social welfare), greater social inclusion, a new focus on equality, promotion of enterprise and jobs, small business, development of agriculture food and forestry, partnership within enterprises, modernisation of the public service, and partnership and monitoring. A draft agreement on pay and conditions of employment was provided by way of an Appendix, and a public service pay agreement was contained in an Annex.

Since 1997, the 19 organisations that participated in *Partnership 2000* have been grouped into four 'Pillars' – employers and business, farming, community and voluntary, and trade union – with a view to streamlining the initial consideration of sectoral issues. Each Pillar comprises the relevant interest groups from among the 19. Plenary meetings comprise representatives of all participating organisations, and of Government, and a Steering Group looks after points of structure and of detail.

Negotiations for the *Programme for Prosperity & Fairness 2000-2002* were launched on 9 November 1999, during the Fianna Fáil / Progressive Democrats Government of 1997-2002. The NESC Report *Opportunities, Challenges & Capacities for Choice* provided the background for those negotiations. All 19 organisations were parties to the negotiations, together with the Government.

The Programme recognised that Ireland faced three challenges:

♦ Ensuring that everyone could benefit from social partnership, in a context where, for many people, poverty and social exclusion were still a stark reality.

♦ Bringing about tangible improvements in living standards, not only in terms of income, but also in terms of quality of life issues, such as housing and transport.

♦ Mastering the challenges posed by the information revolution, including globalisation and the enlargement of the European Union.

In addition to the 19 organisations previously involved, the Irish Rural Link (IRL) was granted social partnership status within the Community & Voluntary Pillar from 2002.

Sustaining Progress 2003-2005, negotiated during the Fianna Fáil / Progressive Democrats Government of 1997-2002, included 10 initiatives of a community nature, in addition to agreeing new mechanisms for engagement, and updating the focus on a range of economic and social issues.

Early in the life of *Sustaining Progress*, in 2001, the Government established the National Centre for Partnership & Performance (NCPP) under the chairmanship of Peter Cassells, former Secretary General of ICTU. NCPP's mission is to lead and support change and innovation in the workplace. Its Council comprises representatives of IBEC, ICTU and Government Departments, together with independent experts from industry and academia.

In the Foreword to the document, *Towards 2016, Ten-Year Framework Social Partnership Agreement 2006-2015*, during the Fianna Fáil / Progressive Democrats Government of 2002-2007, the Taoiseach, Bertie Ahern TD, acknowledged that social partnership had helped to maintain a strategic focus on key national priorities, and had created and sustained the conditions for high employment growth, fiscal stability, restructuring the economy to respond to new challenges and opportunities, dramatic improvement in living standards, lower taxation, lower inflation, and a culture of dialogue.

Towards 2016 includes a new framework to focus on the needs of children, young adults, people of working age, older people, and people with disabilities. Restructuring public services around individuals and their needs, rather than administrative boundaries and definitions, is a stated focus.

The *National Economic & Social Development Act 2006* established the National Economic & Social Development Office (NESDO), which comprises and co-ordinates the work of the NESC, NESF, and NCPP. Its main function is to advise the Taoiseach on all strategic matters relevant to economic and social developments.

EMPLOYERS & TRADE UNIONS

The CII, while it existed as a separate entity, was involved in all non-pay elements of social partnership, but, not being an employers' organisation, it had no role in pay negotiations or in industrial relations. In my view, however, social partnership would not have been possible without pay bargaining and the accompanying enthusiastic and active involvement of the trade unions and employers' organisations. That involvement brought about industrial peace, with a reduction in the number of strikes from 152 with over 1.4 million days lost in 1979, the peak year, to 32 with 24,000 days lost in 1994. There had been serious incidents of strikes in the 1960s, with some reduction in the early 1970s and a return to high numbers of strikes of longer duration in the late 1970s and early 1980s. Private sector strikes fell significantly in number and duration throughout the 1960s, 1970s and 1980s, while the incidence of public sector strikes increased. The industrial peace that accompanied social partnership allowed Government the flexibility to address the fundamental economic issues of public borrowing, National Debt and public expenditure. Strikes and related employer / trade union issues are examined in the 2007 publication, *Saving the Future*, which records *inter alia* the work of the former Taoiseach, Bertie Ahern TD, in negotiations with the trade unions, ICTU, and employers' organisations in each of his roles over the years as Minister for Labour, Minister for Finance, and Taoiseach.[12] *Saving the Future* makes reference to Ahern's role as it covered all except two-and-a-half years of the 20 years of social partnership up to 2007, and was then still continuing. Noel Treacy TD, Minister of State, speaking in Dáil Éireann in 2005, also referenced Ahern's long involvement in the social partnership process, with special reference to his negotiating skills.[13]

FÁS Consultation with CII, FUE and ICTU on training and development
initiatives partly financed by the ESF, Barrettstown Castle, 8 December 1989:
(seated, left to right) Brendan Leahy, Director General, FÁS; John Dunne,
Director General, FUE; John Lynch, Chairman, FÁS; Bertie Ahern, TD, Minister
for Labour; Liam Connellan, Director General, CII; John Keogh, Group Finance
Director, AIB; Tom Toner, Managing Director, Brooks Watson Group; Gerry
Grogan, President, FUE; (standing, left to right) Con Power, Director of
Economic Policy, CII; Jim O'Brien, Divisional Director, FUE; Manus O'Riordan,
Research Officer, ITGWU; Billy Attley, General Secretary, FWUI; Kevin Duffy,
Assistant General Secretary, ICTU; Peter Cassells, General Secretary, ICTU;
Paul Tansey, Consultant Economist; Frank Roche, UCD; Michael Jacob,
Managing Director, Premier Dairies; Finbar Flood, Personnel Director, Arthur
Guinness, Son & Co. Ltd; Brendan Moreland, Managing Director, Donnelly
Mirrors Ltd; Donal Byrne, Managing Director, Cadbury Ireland Ltd; Peter
Webster, Divisional Managing Director (Packaging), Smurfit Group; Diarmuid
Quirke, Managing Director, Irish Cement Ltd; Ray Bowman, Secretary,
Manpower Policy Committee, CII; Henry Murdoch, Assistant Director
General, FÁS.

As Taoiseach, speaking at the World Economic Forum (WEF) Annual
Meeting in 2007, Ahern gave his own view of the process when he said:[14]

> 'But perhaps most significant of all has been our strong, perhaps unique,
> system of social partnership. Since 1987, innovative three-year
> agreements between Government, unions and employers, have
> delivered wage moderation underpinned by tax policy, coupled with a
> commitment to industrial stability. This combination gave the economy
> the stimulus it needed. The overall impact was so convincing that new
> agreements have been negotiated at regular intervals without
> interruption since.'

Ahern equally could have mentioned the National Understandings of 1979 and 1980 (see **Chapter 4**) and the work of the NESC since its establishment in November, 1973. Broadly-based social partnership in Ireland had its roots long prior to 1987.

Later in 2007, Ahern, speaking to the Chartered Institute of Public Finance & Accountancy (CIPFA) on issues related to the management of the economy, said:[15]

> 'One of the key strategies underpinning this *(prudent management of the economy and key strategic decisions)* has been our system of social partnership, which is unique in Ireland. This has allowed Government, business, the trade unions and all the social partners to maximise the scope of their shared agendas and to engage in creative problem-solving. The stability provided by social partnership has played a large part in allowing the Irish economy to go from strength to strength.'

LABOUR MARKET POLICY

Returning to the pre-social partnership days in Ireland, in the late 1970s and early 1980s, the rise in unemployment in the EEC generally gave a sense of urgency to the task of improving the operation of the labour market. The European Commission considered the functions of labour market policy, and the steps necessary to improve the operation of labour market policy within the Community.

The European Commission sent a Communication to the Council of Ministers in May, 1980, proposing guidelines for a Community labour market policy 'designed essentially to facilitate adjustments, both in time and space, on the labour market'.[16] On 27 June 1980, the Council of Ministers for Labour adopted a Resolution based on the Commission's Communication, but more limited in scope. The Oireachtas Joint Committee on the Secondary Legislation of the European Communities examined the documentation, early in 1981, and issued a report.

The areas for action suggested in the EEC Council's Resolution were:

♦ The need for better knowledge and information on the labour market, in order to have qualitative as well as quantitative data.

♦ Initiatives for improved vocational guidance, training, and retraining.

♦ Initiatives for better placement services (e.g. more experienced officials) to act as effective intermediaries between labour supply and demand.

- Promotion of a forward-looking approach on education and information by the appropriate authorities, by management, and by the workers themselves.
- Proposals for special measures for specific categories of workers (e.g. young people, women, the elderly, migrants, and the handicapped).
- Regional and sectoral measures.

The Joint Committee studied the position in Ireland in each of those areas, and examined the potential for improvement. Written submissions were made by the Department of Labour, Department of Education, and CII. In addition, representatives from the Department of Labour, CII, and ICTU gave oral evidence before the Joint Committee.

In 1981, the CII commissioned and published a background study of the labour market in Ireland, entitled *Jobs & the Workforce*.[17] The study examined inefficiencies and imperfections in the functioning of the labour market that threatened to constrain economic growth. The study included an examination of the difficulties in filling some job vacancies, which occurred in the wake of the recession of 1975-1976. This was an attempt to assist the CII in formulating proposals to ensure that, during the next upswing in economic activity, industrial growth would not be constrained by skill shortages and other mismatches between jobs and the persons available to fill them. The issue arose, because, during the latter half of 1978 and into 1979, the CII / ESRI *Survey of Industry* revealed a sharp rise in the proportion of enterprises that were constrained by labour shortages, as the Irish industrial sector experienced difficulties in filling vacancies requiring special skills, especially those with engineering qualifications at craft, technician, and degree levels.

The study further examined the causes of the then recent trend towards a growth in the Irish labour force. It put Ireland's high unemployment in perspective, given the major restructuring of the economy over the previous twenty years, and the substantial increase in unemployment in all other countries of the EEC in the 1970s. Emigration had fallen, and, for the first time since Irish Census records began in 1841, there was net immigration of 13,600 *per annum* on average between the Census of 1971 and that of 1979. This added over 100,000 to the population's natural increase of 281,000, a population increase of over 390,000 between those two Census dates! Emigrants numbered about 8,000 in 1980, there was net immigration of about 2,000 in 1981, and net emigration then returned in each year from 1982 to 1991.

The likely demand for labour and the implications of technical progress were also assessed. The experience of the Irish economy, since 1974-1975, indicated that growth rates above those of the main industrialised countries were attainable, given the appropriate public policies. Ways of achieving full employment, in the context of labour market efficiency, were also explored.

A specific opportunity for CII to collaborate in a labour market initiative arose during the term of the Fine Gael / Labour Party Government led by Dr Garret FitzGerald and Dick Spring when Ruairí Quinn TD, Minister for Labour, announced the establishment of the Enterprise Allowance Scheme on 19 December 1983, and the first participants entered the Scheme from 1 January 1984. Under the Scheme, which still continues, people who are unemployed for more than three months can obtain an allowance if they became self-employed.

The CII welcomed the establishment of the Enterprise Allowance Scheme, and collaborated with the National Manpower Service (NMS), both nationally and locally, from its inception,[18] in seeking ways in which the business community could assist.[19] It soon become apparent to the members of the staff of the NMS, that many of the participants needed advice, much of which could only be given by people with practical business experience. The main areas in which advice was required were identified by the NMS as financial planning and control; commercial and trading activities; insurance and legal affairs; and manufacturing methods and technology.

I approached the Department of Labour and the NMS during early summer 1984 and discussed ways for the business and industry community, together with various professional and trade organisations, to provide a mechanism for advising participants in the Enterprise Allowance Scheme on a voluntary basis. I suggested a mechanism similar to that operating in the USA, where the Service Corps of Retired Executives (SCORE) and the Active Corps of Executives (ACE) offered an advisory service on a voluntary basis. In order to get the idea off the ground in Ireland, I co-ordinated arrangements between the CII, the Department of Labour, and the National Director of the NMS to organise a pilot project in Sligo, where I had been Principal of the RTC from 1972 to 1979. The CII contacted a wide range of people in Sligo, including members of the CII, the Sligo Chamber of Commerce, education and training authorities, and a range of clubs and societies with community interests. Following two meetings in Sligo, an *ad hoc* committee was elected to draft the terms of reference for a Business & Industry Panel of Advisers.

This was done, and about 50 people joined the Panel. The *ad hoc* committee, including representatives of the CII and the NMS, agreed to be the Board of Management for one year. While the Sligo project was a success, the profile did not lend itself to replication on a national basis and was discontinued in favour of alternative arrangements made by the NMS. The CII as a national membership representative body did not have staff located throughout the country to assist in organising on-going operational services of this nature and the NMS did not see a direct role for itself in organising voluntary inputs by business people.

In 1984, the Government decided to implement a Social Guarantee for young people, and the Youth Employment Agency (YEA) issued a consultative document. The CII made a submission to the YEA welcoming the focus on young people who left the post-primary schools, either without qualifications or with a low level of qualifications.[20] Points covered by the CII included induction of young people into the labour market; the financing of new basic vocational training courses by the ESF; addressing the problems of young disadvantaged people within their families and communities from a very early age; and the provision of community education to tackle the root causes of disadvantage. Other issues included the enhancement of career guidance provision in schools as part of a wider counselling function; the involvement of business and industry in the design of the new vocational training courses; and the provision of structured work experience as part of those courses.

The CII supported the recommendations in the Government's *White Paper on Manpower Policy*, aimed at improving the policy-making functions in the manpower area.[21] The White Paper also proposed the integration of the NMS, YEA and AnCO into what ultimately became FÁS in January 1988, under the *Labour Services Act 1987*. The CII viewed the Levy / Grant Scheme in general as having been successful in achieving its objective of structuring and improving in-company training, but the task of the Scheme was now completed. Industrial training had changed radically, and for the better, since the enactment of the *Industrial Training Act 1967*. The CII believed that the Department of Labour should discuss with all interested parties the replacement of the Levy / Grant Scheme by a system that would more effectively meet the needs of business and industry. The electronics industry, for example, had made proposals for the replacement of Levy / Grant in that industry, and the proposals were accepted by AnCO and the Department of Labour, to operate for a trial period on a pilot basis. The *White Paper on Manpower Policy* accepted that wider changes were needed to ensure more effective targeting of resources and to encourage the development of training in small firms. The CII believed, however, that there was a continuing role for the Industrial Training Committees in the establishment of criteria for training and in quality assurance.

The CII supported the *White Paper*'s proposal that operational links between the NMS and the Employment Exchanges be strengthened. The CII made a similar, but more broadly-based, recommendation in a submission to Government in July 1986.[22] The recommendation was that every member of the workforce – employee, self-employed, and unemployed – should have one unique reference number for PAYE, PRSI, Live Register, and NMS purposes, and for training programmes. Such a system would help to eliminate abuses in public expenditure programmes, and would help ensure more effective delivery of services to the unemployed.

The CII welcomed the main recommendations of the Commission on Social Welfare 1986, having made a submission to the Commission in December 1983, but warned that full implementation necessarily depended on a marked improvement in the public finances or on recommendations being self-financing.[¶] In response to an invitation from the Minister for Social Welfare, Gemma Hussey TD, the CII commented on and agreed with key recommendations of the Commission.[23] Areas of agreement included that the self-employed should be brought within the scope of social insurance and of long-term benefits, on condition of self-funding on an actuarial basis. Agreed also was that, for the future, all public service recruits should be within the scope of standard-rate PRSI, being entitled to benefits accordingly. These employment-related recommendations were subsequently implemented.

The Commission on Social Welfare referred to 'a single comprehensive insurance system', that industry believed should be self-funding, with premiums being paid by as wide a spectrum of the population as possible. The Commission also argued that a social welfare system should have explicit underlying principles and that 'the sense of entitlement to payment is an important aspect of a social welfare system'. The CII agreed with that

---

¶   The CII commented on the payment structure, social insurance, social assistance, finance, housing support, and the unemployed. The areas of agreement with the Commission were on strategies for Social Welfare; the payment structure; social assistance; financing; child income support; housing benefit; one-parent families; complementarity of the functions of the Department of Health and the Department of Social Welfare; the appeals system; the delivery process; and policy formulation. The CII supported the recommendation that social welfare payments be adjusted annually, and agreed that short-term social welfare benefits should be treated as part of total income and be assessable to income tax, where such a liability arose.

sentiment, and believed that stigmatisation would be removed only when the codes of income tax and social welfare were fully integrated for all members of the workforce, whether employed, self-employed or unemployed.

The CII was invited by the National Rehabilitation Board (NRB) to make a submission, on a report of a Working Party of the Board, regarding a possible quota scheme for the employment of disabled persons in the public and private sectors.[24] It was in agreement with the NRB Working Party that a compulsory quota system in the private sector would be counterproductive in promoting the employment of disabled persons. Consequently, the CII favoured a voluntary approach in both the private and the State-commercial sectors, while acknowledging that it could be legitimate for the Government to impose a quota system in the non-commercial public sector.

The CII agreed with the NRB Working Party that all of the then existing employment incentive schemes, operated by the NMS and the YEA, should be used to the greatest possible extent in achieving equal employment opportunity for the disabled. However, it opposed the proposal for a statutory requirement, on companies above a certain size, to publish information in their annual reports concerning company policy on recruitment of disabled workers. It believed that such a requirement would be counterproductive to the real interests of the disabled and was convinced that the focus should be on preparing the disabled for full open employment where no stigma would attach to them.

Ireland's membership of the EEC from 1973 onwards impacted directly on many aspects of labour market policy of an employer / employee nature. For example, one of the earliest pieces of Irish legislation enacted in response to EEC membership was the *Anti-Discrimination (Pay) Act 1974*, which ensured equal treatment, in relation to certain terms and conditions of employment, between men and women employed on like work.

The following two graphs show in summary format the outcome of economic and labour market policies, set in the timeframe from the beginning of modern Irish industrialisation in 1960 to the end of 2007.

The number of persons at work was 1.05 million in 1961, and did not exceed 1.10 million until 1978, when it remained at, or slightly above or slightly below, that figure until 1993. Numbers at work exceeded 1.2 million for the first time in 1994. From that point onwards, numbers at work increased rapidly, moving to over 1.5 million in 1999, over 1.75 million in 2002 and over 2.0 million in 2006. Overall, numbers at work almost doubled from 1.09 million when the *Programme for National Recovery* commenced in 1987 to almost 2.1 million at the end of 2007.

Graph 5.1: Numbers at Work (000s), 1961-2007

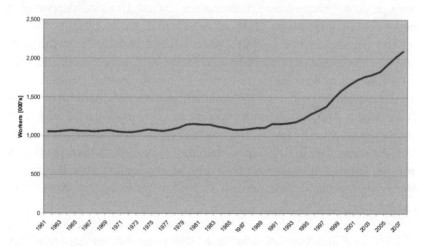

Sources: Central Statistics Office (CSO) and *Budget & Economic
Statistics*, Department of Finance, various years.

A marked improvement in the unemployment situation accompanied the
significant increase in the number of persons at work, as shown by **Graph 5.2.**

Graph 5.2: Annual % Unemployed, 1961-2007

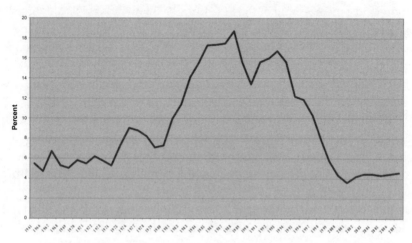

Sources: 1961-1984: *Manpower Policy in Ireland*, NESC Report No.82,
December 1985; 1967-1969 and 1985-2007: *Administration Yearbook &
Diary*, Institute of Public Administration, various years.

Unemployment was 4.7% in 1966 and increased to 9.9% by 1981, with an average of 6.75% over the intervening 16 years. During that period, it never again fell below 5%. The figure rose to 11.4% in 1982 and, for the next 16 years to the end of 1997, it never fell to under 10%. For 10 of those 16 years, unemployment was above 15%. The average for the period 1982-1997 was just marginally below 15%, with a peak of 18.7% in 1988 and a low of 10.3% in 1997, the last year of that period. Unemployment fell sharply after 1997, to 7.8% in 1998, 5.7% in 1999, and below 4.5% in each year thereafter, until it again returned to 4.5% in 2007. The lowest figure was 2.6% in 2001. In line with other projections of a slowdown in the economy, the ESRI's *Quarterly Economic Commentary*, Spring 2008, forecast 6% unemployment in 2008.

EMPLOYEE INVOLVEMENT

The CII was to the fore in promoting the concept and the practice of employee shareholding, and discussed the issue with John Bruton TD, Minister for Finance, prior to his 1982 Budget, which introduced Ireland's first scheme of tax-based employee shareholding.

February 1982: The Minister for Finance, John Bruton TD (centre), receiving a CII delegation for discussion on the CII's 1982 Budget submission. The delegation included (left to right): Liam Connellan, Director General; Michael Meagher, Chairman, Economics & Taxation Policy Committee; Tom Hardiman, Vice President; and Con Power, Director of Economic Policy.

The legislation allowed for the establishment of a trust, and the allocation of funds by a company to the trustees to purchase and hold shares for the benefit of employees, without giving rise to an immediate tax liability. The

1982 scheme was improved in the *Finance Act 1984*. Following its implementation, it emerged that the complexity of the regulations led to few enterprises introducing an Employee Shareholding Scheme, and, therefore, the CII negotiated a Standard Trust Deed with the Revenue Commissioners that simplified the process and reduced the administrative cost of introducing a Scheme. The CII Standard Trust Deed was widely distributed to companies in April 1985, and was subsequently revised to reflect improvements introduced in the *Finance Act 1986*.

In its pre-Budget submission for 1986, the CII sought, and obtained, further changes to encourage more enterprises to introduce employee shareholding and employee share option schemes.[25] The improvements obtained by the CII in the *Finance Act 1986* were that Capital Gains Tax would only be assessed when a share option was exercised, and that the retention period of seven years for approved profit-sharing schemes be reduced to five years. The CII achieved the introduction of a formula for the calculation of the taxable benefit conferred by the share option, where restrictions had been placed on the shares, and the introduction of two new tax incentive schemes for share options that did not give rise to income tax and where Capital Gains Tax applied only when the shares were sold. The Minister for Finance also introduced a number of improvements to the Business Expansion Scheme, based on CII's proposals.

The Irish Productivity Centre (IPC) published a booklet on employee information and consultation systems in 1980.[26] The booklet made an important point:

> 'The generally accepted purpose of communication is to create understanding. Few would dispute the need for employees to understand the objectives of the firm for which they are working. Understanding generates commitment. It is difficult to imagine an employee giving full commitment to decisions and policies which he cannot or does not understand.'

The CII agreed with this and, because the situation in each enterprise is different, the CII favoured a framework approach to the issue, with responsibility for implementation resting on negotiations in the workplace.

In 1980, an EEC Council Directive on procedures for informing and consulting employees, subsequently known as the Vredeling Directive, began its life as a company law issue. The proposal was widened in scope in 1983, but the main emphasis until 1984 was on procedures relating to enterprises with a complex structure, and particularly to multinational enterprises. The issues involved were, however, of a more fundamental nature. The position in 1984 was pointing more towards a proposal for an EEC Directive that would be of a social policy nature rather than a company law nature, and the debate was led by Henk Vredeling, the Dutch Commissioner with responsibility for social affairs. What was proposed was consultation and information about major structural changes affecting the workforce, before any change occurred. A point of general relevance was that the European Commission considered the Vredeling proposal in the context of other European Labour Law and Company Law Directives. The Fourth and Seventh European Company Law Directives were relevant, as was the draft Fifth Directive and the draft Regulation for a European Company Statute. It was desirable that the European Commission rationalise its own position and set down in a single memorandum the various inter-related enactments, drafts, and proposals with a view to eliminating overlap and even contradictions.

Early in 1984, Ruairí Quinn TD, Minister for Labour, referred to the need for a continuous flow of information between management and workers at enterprise level, as a means of increasing communication and promoting greater harmony in industrial relations. The Minister stressed this as a priority issue.

The CII responded to Minister Quinn by advocating and supporting a voluntary approach to this important issue, comprising a *Code of Practice* adopted and implemented by business and industry, rather than one imposed by legislation. The President of the CII, Dr TP Hardiman, in his President's Statement in the *CII Annual Report 1983*, issued subsequent to the request by the Minister for Labour, stated that:

'A particular responsibility rests with Irish management to improve the information flow about performance within the individual company, and to provide regular opportunities for ensuring that the information is discussed and understood. A characteristic of a successful company is the ability and willingness of management to communicate effectively within the company, to think fast, and to stay ahead of the economic, social, political, and technological changes in the environment in which it operates.'

The CII believed that the objectives outlined by the Minister could best be achieved by agreement, at local level, between employers and employees, and viewed the sharing of information, consultation, and employee participation as part of good industrial relations practice.

The ensuing news media reports, while accurately recording the CII's emphasis on management's responsibility to provide 'appropriate and relevant' information to employees, and on the institution of agreed consultation procedures, headlined as a *negative* the CII's preference for negotiated agreements at enterprise level rather than imposition by EEC legislation.[27]

A different approach was taken under the Irish Presidency of the EEC during the second half of 1984 and it adopted, as its starting point, the right of the employee to receive information, rather than the duty of the employer to give the information. The proposed Directive then would be seen more clearly as an aspect of social policy, albeit with economic development dimensions. The CII's view was that it would be important to emphasise that any such right necessarily had a counterbalancing obligation. The new emphasis was on the principle of co-operation between employers and employees' representatives, and was not seen as solely employee-oriented. The Irish Presidency brokered important amendments, aimed at achieving progress in the face of some deep-rooted objections to any Directive of that nature, including the outright opposition of the then British Government to the very principle of the proposed Vredeling Directive.

The CII recognised that, from an economic development viewpoint, the importance of achieving a climate of co-operation in business and industry could not be overestimated. I maintained this stance at a talk to the Rotary Club of Cork in October 1984,[28] and subsequently at a seminar organised by the Institute of Personnel Management (IPM) and the IPC in Dublin in December 1984.[29] The seminar was widely reported, emphasising both the CII's opposition to a legislative approach[30] and the CII's guidelines for a voluntary code, based on management's responsibility to improve the flow of information to employees in a climate of consultation and co-operation at enterprise level.[31]

The basis for a voluntary approach to employee information and consultation existed as far back as 1967[32] in a recommendation of the International Labour Organisation (ILO), adopted almost unanimously by Government, employer, and trade union representatives:

> 'An effective policy of communication should ensure that information is given and that consultation takes place between the parties concerned before decisions on matters of major interest are taken by management, in so far as disclosure of the information will not cause damage to either party.'

During 1984, the CII issued broad guidelines for a voluntary *Code of Practice* at enterprise level. In January, 1985, my talk entitled *Reporting to Employees*, at a conference of professional bodies, covered employee shareholding as well as employee information and consultation systems.[33] The message was that Ireland could no longer dissipate its energy on unproductive conflict; the threats to our wellbeing were far too damaging, and co-operation needed to extend to the workplace as well as to every other facet of society.[34]

Later in 1985, I presented evidence before the Joint Oireachtas Committee on the Secondary Legislation of the EEC in its examination of the proposed EEC Directive on Employee Information & Consultation (Vredeling). The Joint Committee 'welcomed the stated support of the CII for a voluntary code of practice'.[35] The view of the Joint Committee was that 'there is undoubtedly an imbalance in the Draft Directive between the interests of the employers and employees, in that obligations under the Draft Directive are placed on employers only without comparable duties on the part of employee representatives except in relation to "secret" information … The Joint Committee urges that every step be taken to bridge the chasm that exists between the protagonists in this debate'.[36]

Work on the Vredeling proposal was suspended in 1986, initially for a period of three years, but was never resumed. The Vredeling initiative resulted in a narrower European Community Company Law Directive.[37] In Ireland, the principle of voluntarism prevailed over legislative direction and the issues of employee information and consultation, as well as other employee participation issues, including employee shareholding, were subsumed into the wider issues of social partnership. Ireland's flexible labour market, underpinned by social partnership, provides safeguards for workers together with maximum management discretion for structural change.

SUMMARY

◊ The work of the NESC was the voice of reason, focussing the combined views of trade unions, farmers, employers, and industry, to influence Government on national social and economic development. The NESC Report *A Strategy for Development 1986-1990*, November 1986, followed on the continuing crisis of the early and mid-1980s.

◊ The NESC Report directly paved the way for the PNR, adopted by Government and the social partners in October 1987, based on the four main planks of agreement of control of public

expenditure; tax equity; development policies; and the removal
of social inequities.

◊ Successive social partnership programmes, up to the present,
   have been a major factor in underpinning economic success
   and achieving social progress.

◊ Important issues in this Chapter also embraced equality of
   access to the labour market, including for the disabled;
   employee information and consultation; employee assistance
   programmes; and employee shareholding.

CHAPTER 6
ROOM FOR IMPROVEMENT

BALANCE THE BUDGET!

The PNR, published in October 1987, was one of the turning points in the fortunes of the Irish economy.[1] However, the PNR did not end the CII's campaign to achieve an environment supportive of investment, economic growth and sustainable job creation. That campaign continued during the years of the improving economy from 1987 to 1993.

The CII's 1988 pre-Budget submission followed the Government's decision to reduce the annual deficit on public finances by about 2.5% of GNP *per annum* through expenditure reductions.[2] Industry accepted that it would have to bear its share of the spending cuts. The CII made its submission with the aim of reinforcing the emerging climate of national confidence and to create conditions for more rapid industrial growth, which would lead to higher employment. The submission recommended that the EBR should be reduced by 2.5% of GNP, from 10.7% in 1987 to 8.2% in 1988. Such a reduction implied the stabilisation of the National Debt / GNP ratio by the end of 1989, thus completing the most difficult phase of the fiscal correction.

My paper at the Fifth Annual Irish Corporate Finance Conference in November 1988, acknowledged that the Government, with the unique support of Fine Gael under their Leader, Alan Dukes TD, took a correct fiscal stance in the Budgets of 1987 and 1988 and continued on a thorough and consistent path to bring the public finances under control.[3]

There was a tax amnesty in 1988 and the consequential non-recurring windfall to the Exchequer reduced the EBR to about 5% of GNP. In its 1989 pre-Budget submission, the CII recommended that the EBR for 1989 not exceed 5% of GNP, in order to stabilise the National Debt to GNP ratio in that year and the cost of debt servicing.[4] In a post-Budget press release in January 1989, the CII welcomed the overall thrust of the Budget in continuing progress to reduce public borrowing, and welcomed measures to improve employment and to improve both the income tax and social welfare systems.[5]

The CII's 1990 pre-Budget submission noted the progress made in the financial management of the economy since 1986.[6] The CII urged the Government to reduce the EBR to about 1.5% of GNP in 1990, this reduction being less than the average annual reduction achieved by the Government over the previous three years. The ESRI's suggestion was for an EBR of 1.3% of GNP in 1990 and its estimate was that the Exchequer would go into surplus from 1991 onwards, based on continuity of current Government policies.[7] A favourable commentary on Ireland, published by the OECD in 1989 was:[8]

> 'The significant improvement in macroeconomic performance and prospects achieved over the last two years provides an excellent opportunity for making further progress in the various areas which still hold back Ireland's development. The necessary changes may be politically less difficult to implement in periods of relatively stronger growth and low inflation. The present positive international and domestic economic climate should be capitalised on by stepping up efforts to reduce the excessive debt / GNP ratio, to restructure the tax system, and to promote microeconomic reform.'

Manufacturing growth was 12% in each of the two years 1987 and 1988, and 12.5% in 1989. Strong economic growth, coupled with low inflation, allowed the Government to intensify efforts to reduce the high level of National Debt and consequential debt servicing.[9] In 1989, borrowing by the Exchequer was 2.4% of GNP, a significant improvement on the Budget target. The Exchequer was still borrowing, although the National Debt / GNP ratio stabilised at 131% in 1988 and fell to 123.5% in 1989.[¶] Debt servicing in 1990 consumed almost 11% of GNP, about 29% of total tax revenue or almost the entire proceeds of PAYE tax. Debt servicing consumed funds that could otherwise have been used to reduce the level of personal taxation and / or to provide enhanced public services. Exchequer borrowing was a form of deferred double taxation; not only would the capital borrowed have to be repaid from taxation at some future date, but, meanwhile, annual interest payments would have to be made from taxation.

The CII's 1991 pre-Budget submission acknowledged the progress made under the PNR in terms of strong economic growth; low inflation

---

[¶]   *Budget & Economic Statistics 2007*, Department of Finance, show revised figures for the National Debt and the National Debt / GNP ratio for 1988 (116.2%), down from the peak of 117.6% in 1987, and 1989 (106.8%). Thereafter, the ratio fell in each year from 99.4% in 1990 to 24.1% in 2006.

relative to the EC average and to Ireland's main trading partners; greater control of public expenditure; a significant reduction in the EBR; some reduction in personal taxation and a modest reduction in indirect taxes.[10] The CII recommended that the EBR be reduced from the expected out-turn of 1.75% of GNP in 1990 to zero in 1991. It noted the twin objectives of continuing the process of reducing the National Debt / GNP ratio and the burden of interest payments that still in 1990 amounted to over IR£2 billion (€2.5 billion) or about 9.5% of GNP. My talk to the Foundation for Fiscal Studies in Dublin in January 1991 emphasised the need for Budget initiatives to promote economic growth and outlined priorities under the four headings of economic and monetary policy; public expenditure; taxation policy; and business development.[11]

The international recession, particularly in the United Kingdom, had a knock-on effect in Ireland that directly contributed to the worsening of Exchequer finances in 1991. Notwithstanding the failure to achieve the desired zero EBR in 1991, the National Debt / GNP ratio showed a modest improvement, due mainly to the proceeds from the sale of some State assets.# The CII, in its pre-Budget submission, recommended an EBR of 1.5% of GNP in 1992, with a target of a zero EBR to be achieved as quickly as possible.[12] The urgency to achieve a zero EBR arose because the National Debt still amounted to about IR£26 billion (€33 billion) or 109% of GNP, and debt servicing consumed about IR£2.4 billion (€3 billion) or over 21.5% of gross current Exchequer payments.

The 1992 submission was the last that I drafted, because of my secondment to the Department of the Taoiseach from April 1992. It is interesting to note, however, the view of the 1993 Budget published by IBEC:[13]

> 'Business looked to Budget '93 for strong and convincing evidence that the Government recognised the need to restore competitiveness to the economy. It sought a budget for business that would boost confidence, investment and employment. The Government had that opportunity on Ash Wednesday but, in many respects, it produced a budget of missed opportunities.'

The Minister for Finance, Bertie Ahern TD, in his first Budget in 1993 set the EBR at 2.9% of GNP, somewhat lower than most commentators

---

The Department of Finance revised the basis for GNP calculation in 1990, reducing the National (Exchequer) Debt as a % of GNP from 104.3% to 99.4%. The ratio was reduced to 95.9% of GNP in 1991, inclusive of €434 million from the flotation of Irish Life plc and €80 million received from the sale of shares in Greencore.

expected, thus showing that the Minister recognised the imperative to continue firm control over the public finances. IBEC regretted, however, that the figure was achieved, not by trimming costs in the economy as recommended by IBEC, but by increasing Government revenue and expenditure as a percentage of GNP.

Ruairí Quinn TD, Minister for Finance, ultimately balanced the Government's current budget in 1996. A current budget surplus of IR£292 million (€370.7 million) was achieved against a planned deficit of IR£82 million (€104 million) or 0.2% of GNP. Minister Quinn went on to achieve a planned current budget surplus in 1997, and projected a surplus for the following two years, 1998 and 1999.[14]

Budget Day, 1996: Ruairí Quinn TD achieved a balanced Budget in out-turn for the first time since 1972.

VALUE FOR MONEY

In addition to control of public expenditure and public borrowing, the Department of Finance consistently pursued the objective of getting value for public money. The Analysis Section of the Department initiated a scheme for the formal training of analysts as far back as 1972. The training lasted two years, after which the analyst was assigned to a Government Department. The first year of training was spent carrying out a number of analytical studies under supervision, and the second led to a M.Sc. degree at the University of Dublin, Trinity College. One requirement for the degree was the preparation of a minor thesis based on an analytical study. I was the academic supervisor for one such thesis in 1981 / 1982, involving a policy evaluation of a Government Department's construction programme and the cost-effectiveness of the programme. My involvement in that project as a member of the staff of the CII was innovative and synergistic, and served to demonstrate to the CII member enterprises the quality and relevance of the work done by the Analysis Section of the Department of Finance.

Alan Dukes TD, Minister for Finance, in his Budget speech 1983, announced his intention to publish the results of a pilot exercise undertaken by the Department of Finance, aimed at a new, comprehensive presentation of public expenditure by programme.[15] In the light of the reaction to the pilot presentation, the Minister would consider extending the approach to the whole range of public expenditure. The results of the pilot exercise were published in July 1983.[16]

The need for in-depth analysis of public expenditure, to ensure value for money for taxpayers' funds, was the theme of my article in January 1984.[17] Two factors had increased the need for an analytical approach to public expenditure in the 1980s. They were the critical state of public finances and the need for administrative reforms within the public service. My article described the work of the Analysis Section of the Department of Finance, expressed support for that work and urged that the in-depth approach to analysis of public expenditure programmes be further developed, as an integral and mainstream part of public administration. The article recommended the following actions to Government to support and disseminate the results of analytical work:

♦ Publication of analytical reports, where appropriate.

♦ Circulation of reports for attention in a political context, perhaps for examination by an appropriate Oireachtas Committee.

♦ Establishment by the Department of Finance of a formal mechanism to follow-up all analytical studies to ensure that the best value was obtained from the carrying out of those studies.

The January 1984 article contained the CII response to the Government's July 1983 document, *Comprehensive Public Expenditure Programmes,* which it viewed as directly related to the work of the Analysis Section of the Department of Finance. The CII welcomed the publication of the document, as it brought together in one place a substantial amount of information regarding a variety of State agencies and the programmes undertaken by them. Industry's view was that the focus should be on improving the quality of judgement and of decision-making, with a view to ensuring value for money for public expenditure. The analysis should relate not only to the use of investment appraisal techniques for capital projects, but also to the periodic review of the justification for, and performance of, each current and capital programme. The analysis should include taking a view of the national economy, as well as looking at the narrower focus of Government or public sector expenditure.

One of the fundamental questions that needed to be addressed was the role of Government in both economic and social affairs. The validity of involvement by Government needed to be clearly demonstrated for each public expenditure programme, together with its cost-effectiveness. In order to justify the use of taxpayers' funds, a clear statement was required as to why a particular programme should be undertaken by the State, and an assessment made of the benefits that accrued to the community from using the taxpayers' funds in that particular way. It was essential to make explicit the arguments in favour of each programme, and to review the validity of each under the headings of social, economic, legislative, administrative, strategic, political, and any other relevant policy areas.

The CII recommended that the rigorous cost-effectiveness audit of programmes be extended to all programmes, both current and capital. The coverage should include every aspect of expenditure that eventually impacted on the size of the Public Sector Borrowing Requirement (PSBR). The relationships between the various programmes needed to be clearly traced and cross-referenced, as appropriate. As an example, there were obvious relationships between certain aspects of social welfare, the labour market and training. An attempt should be made in those areas to identify common target populations across different programmes.

The CII further believed that the analysis should be such as to enable a decision to be made on the complete or partial discontinuation of State involvement in a particular programme, or the extent to which a programme could be contracted out at an operational or delivery level. The latter point was of importance, because there were many areas where the State could influence the quantum and quality of delivery of a programme, without itself necessarily operationally delivering the programme. The State could influence programmes through the establishment of performance criteria, and through the on-going monitoring of performance. In at least some of those cases, it might be more cost-effective in terms of resource utilisation for the performance of a service to be undertaken on contract, awarded on a competitive basis involving public and private sector entities on an equal footing.

The CII believed that it was necessary to identify those people who benefited from a programme, and those who paid for the programme, because the same people from whom taxation was raised to fund the services consumed the vast majority of State services. The collection of taxation and the administration of the related services inevitably involved a real resource cost on the productive sectors of the economy, while the level of taxation necessary to support the programmes diminished the incentive for additional work effort throughout the economy. There is a *prima facie* case that subsidies and transfer payments should be reserved for genuine social, economic and strategic needs.

The CII recommended that Government look at the manner in which the services under each programme were delivered. At times, there seemed to have been no incentive to achieve value for money in the consumption of some services, because almost all of the services provided by the State were perceived to have been at no cost to the consumer. A cost-effectiveness audit of each programme by the Comptroller & Auditor General should include, necessarily, an examination of the manner in which the services under the programme were delivered to the consumers.

Performance criteria were advocated for each public expenditure programme. In some cases, it would not be possible to lay down financial criteria, but that need not result in the abandonment of an attempt to set criteria. In education and training, for example, criteria could include class sizes and pupil / teacher ratios. In other cases, such as social welfare, health, and public utilities, appropriate international comparisons could be relevant.

Publication of the annual *Comprehensive Public Expenditure Programmes* was discontinued after the 1986 volume in December 1986. Ray MacSharry TD, Minister for Finance, justified this in the Dáil in December 1987, by claiming that primary responsibility for ensuring that public expenditure programmes gave value for money and were managed efficiently lay with the relevant Government Departments, and that the Secretaries General of Departments, as accounting officers, were responsible for the efficiency and economy of administration in their Departments.[18] Other changes of a related nature made by the Government in 1987 were the abolition of the Department of the Public Service, which had been established in 1973, and the abandonment of the Dáil Committee on Public Expenditure. The functions of the Department of the Public Service were taken over by the

Department of Finance. The Minister announced that his Department (Finance) was reviewing the role of the Comptroller & Auditor General to see whether proposals could be prepared to extend his remit to include considerations of effectiveness and efficiency. This was done. The work of the Dáil Committee on Public Expenditure was subsumed into the Dáil Committee of Public Accounts.

AN ENVIRONMENT FOR ENTERPRISE

In the early 1980s, the public debate on competitiveness narrowly focussed on costs, especially wage costs. As stressed by me at a lecture to the Institute of Credit Management (ICM) in Dublin in 1984, the CII took the wider view that business competitiveness included all activities and constraints that combined to establish and sustain an economically viable enterprise.[19] Some factors were within enterprise and others were in the external envelope outside the enterprise. This was the view promulgated by the European Management Forum (EMF), 'an independent international organisation committed to improving the state of the world by engaging leaders in partnerships to shape global, regional and industry agendas'.

The 1981 *EMF Report* covered 21 developed industrial economies, including Ireland, and six developing countries.[20] The 21 developed economies were assessed and ranked according to 240 performance criteria. Of those, 180 criteria were based on international economic statistics and the remaining 60 related to surveys undertaken by the EMF in each of the 21 countries, based on subjective judgments made by industrialists in each country. The 240 criteria were divided into 10 *principal factors of competitiveness*:

◆ Dynamism of the economy.
◆ Industrial efficiency and costs of production.
◆ Dynamics of the market.
◆ Financial dynamism.
◆ Human resources.
◆ Role of the State.
◆ Infrastructure.
◆ Outward orientation of the economy.
◆ Forward orientation of the economy.
◆ Socio-political consensus and stability.

The top five positions, in descending order, were held by Japan, Switzerland, the USA, the Federal Republic of Germany, and Canada. Ireland was ranked 16th among the 21 developed economies. On the invitation of the EMF, I prepared a commentary on Ireland's performance, included as an integral part of each copy of the Report distributed in Ireland.

The number of criteria of competitiveness used by the EMF was increased to 245 in 1982, and to 284 in 1983. Ireland remained in 16th place, although, in the *business confidence survey*, Ireland performed relatively better in 12th place.[21] In 1982, the EMF appointed the CII as its liaison body in Ireland to promote and distribute its *Annual Report on Industrial Competitiveness* within the enterprise sectors, public and private. The EMF changed its name to the World Economic Forum (WEF) in 1987.

The CII emphasised cost competitiveness in its message to the new Government that took office on 10 March 1987, having a week earlier published its message to Government that 'the economic disease from which we suffer is loss of competitiveness; until the patient accepts this diagnosis, treatment cannot begin'.[22] The CII urged the new Government to work with industry to ensure that industrial input costs were brought into line with those of our international competitors. The CII view was:

> 'Economic recovery depends on many factors. It is fashionable to focus on high technology, marketing, design, and other similar essential issues, but we sometimes shy away from the more fundamental issues of industrial input costs and unit labour costs, because mention of these factors will ruffle feathers'.

The CII went on to say that any attempt to create a climate for investment and to generate economic growth in Ireland must solve the grave problem of the rapid deterioration of cost competitiveness, which resulted in loss of markets, enterprise closures, and job losses in the 1980s.

In order to focus the attention of the politicians and the workforce on the national need to be cost-competitive before Ireland could create more jobs and earn higher living standards, the CII catalogued eight headings under which cost penalties were imposed on industry. In each case, the CII explained the issues and gave relevant comparisons with Ireland's international competitor countries. The eight areas were:

- Interest rates.
- Unit wage costs.
- Energy.
- Transport.

- Telecommunications.
- Postal charges.
- Liability insurances
- Local authority rates on business premises.

In each case, action directly by Government could significantly improve the business cost environment.

Against that background, one of the important inputs to the negotiation of the PNR 1987 was the Working Party on the Cost Environment for Enterprise under the chairmanship of the Secretary General of the Department of Industry & Commerce.[23] The report of the Working Party listed eight conclusions, the most general being that the cost environment for Irish industry remained unfavourable in a number of important areas when compared to Ireland's main international trading partners. The CII undertook a survey among member enterprises in Summer 1987 to rank the importance of factors that impacted on the cost environment for enterprise. Industrialists identified and ranked factors in the following order:

- Personal taxation, with its knock-on effect on wage costs.
- Interest rates.
- Liability insurance costs.
- Energy.
- Telecommunications.
- Road transport.
- Air transport.
- Sea transport.
- Postal charges.

In retrospect, the social partnership programmes formed one of the most important background factors in the creation of an internationally-competitive cost environment for enterprise. This was recognised by Bertie Ahern TD, when he became Taoiseach in 1997. As he stated in Dáil Éireann, in answer to questions about his meetings with the social partners to begin the negotiations for *Partnership 2000 for Inclusion, Employment & Competitiveness 1997- 2000*:

> 'Also in my statement (*to the social partners*), I said Ireland's economic progress has been made against a background of wage moderation and industrial peace. I urged the maintenance of these policies to enhance our competitiveness.'[24]

HIGH PUBLIC UTILITY COSTS

Public utility costs dominated the list of factors that impacted unfavourably on the cost competitiveness of industry in 1987. The need to up-grade public infrastructure networks in areas such as energy, telecommunications and transport had been a recurring theme in the CII's pre-Budget submissions from 1981 onwards, together with the need to reduce public utility costs to levels comparable with Ireland's international competitor economies. In terms of Government-imposed public utility costs, for example, the following were the submissions made in 1985, prior to the 1986 Budget:[25]

♦ Energy: electricity prices. The CII noted that Irish electricity prices were about 20% higher than the European average for industrial users, although CII acknowledged that prices for domestic consumers were 5% lower. The CII noted that the levy on property imposed in lieu of rates by Government on the ESB was IR£22 million (€27.9 million) in 1985, equivalent to 14% of the total national revenue from local authority rates. The levy was disproportionate, because the ESB accounted for less than 3% of national economic output and less than 1% of employment. The CII recommended that the levy be reduced to a figure proportionate to rates charged throughout the rest of the economy and noted that the change would enable the gap between Irish and European industrial electricity prices to be halved.

♦ Road transport accounted for about 9% of industrial costs and this was at least 25% higher than in Ireland's main trading partners. The reasons were high excise duty on imported commercial vehicles, high insurance costs, exceptionally high road diesel costs and the poor quality of the national roads network. Taxation on auto diesel oil alone cost Irish industry IR£50 million (€63.5 million) *per annum* in excess of the average such taxation imposed in Ireland's European trading partners. CII recommended that taxation on auto diesel oil be reduced by 20% as a first step towards bringing Irish transport costs into line with the European average.

♦ The CII recognised that the cost of international telecommunications calls from Ireland was not increased in 1985. Despite this, the cost of international calls from Ireland to other European countries was 40% higher than calls in the reverse direction. Many enterprises had been forced to arrange that international business telephone calls would originate abroad to avoid high Irish charges. The CII recommended that the cost of international telephone calls be reduced to remove the disparity with other countries and to encourage the origination of more business telephone traffic in Ireland. The CII recommended that Government levies should not be imposed on Telecom Éireann because they would result either in uncompetitive pricing or in a transfer of borrowing within the public capital programme. The CII sought that Telecom Éireann be given the freedom to operate commercially within the public sector and to provide services at internationally-competitive prices.

The CII again sought reductions in the public utility costs of industrial electricity, international telecommunications, and postal charges in its 1987 pre-Budget submission, costs which were still well above the European average a year later, prior to the 1988 Budget.[26&27] The submission acknowledged that considerable progress had been made in reducing the gap between Irish and European average electricity costs since 1986, but much more was required, as recognised in the PNR:

> 'The State-sponsored bodies, which provide utilities and services, through greater efficiency and cost containment measures, must bring down the high cost environment which is now affecting the effectiveness of our economy and the growth of employment.'

EXCESSIVE PERSONAL TAXATION

The CII, in its 1988 pre-Budget submission, returned to the issue of implementation of the recommendations of the Commission on Taxation, including the introduction of a broadly based residential property tax, the proceeds from which would be applied primarily to reducing the PAYE tax burden.[28] This did not happen, although some progress was made in reducing personal taxation in the *Finance Act 1988*. In the following year, the submission sought a further widening of the 35% tax band, and a reduction in the top rate of 58%. In the event, tax bands were widened for 1989/1990, with a reduction in the 35% rate to 32% and in the top rate to 56%.[29]

The 1990 Budget submission went further and sought, within the framework of a continually falling EBR, that the burden of personal taxation should be further reduced gradually, with two income tax rates: 25% and 40%.[30] The CII further asserted that the higher rate of taxation not be reached by the taxpayer until a single person earned at least double the average industrial wage, with an increased threshold for a married couple.

The burden of high personal taxation was illustrated by reference to international comparisons.

In 1991 and 1992, the submissions highlighted the need to improve the tax treatment of lower-paid workers, particularly those with children, and to tackle the specific problem of poverty traps.[31&32] In the autumn of 1990, the CII commissioned a background study by PriceWaterhouseCoopers to identify and quantify 'disincentives to employment' relative to the operation of the personal taxation and social welfare codes. The CII discussed the report bilaterally with the relevant Ministers and Departments and recommended that such disincentives be eliminated during the period of the PESP, 1990-1993. The CII further sought to reduce taxation by recommending increases in the thresholds for income tax exemptions, enhanced tax reliefs at the lower income levels and increases in the Family Income Supplement (FIS). Additionally, because those tax allowances were under threat at the time, the CII supported the retention of mortgage interest relief and relief for health insurance. The submission expressed the view that one of the objectives of personal tax policy should be to encourage self-reliance to the greatest appropriate extent in both health and housing: the opposite approach would tend to encourage people to make greater use of public expenditure programmes, funded by the general taxpayer, who in many cases would be the poorer neighbour of the programme user.

Income taxation was reduced to two tax rates, 27% and 48%, in 1992/1993. Both rates were gradually reduced in subsequent years, and were set at 20% and 42% in the 'short' tax year 2001.[¶] The higher rate was reduced to 41% in the 2007 tax year.

BUSINESS TAX & INCENTIVES

In 1991, I expressed concern on behalf of the CII at the rapid increase in the yield from corporation tax that had a potentially counterproductive impact on international business location decisions, at a time when Ireland faced intense competition in the fight to attract and retain mobile international investment.[33]

The yield from corporation tax in Ireland in 1990 amounted to 2.1% of GNP, and was higher than Greece (1.7%), Germany (1.9%), and almost

---

¶   From 2001 onwards, the fiscal year, which previously ended on 5 April, was changed
     to the calendar year ended on 31 December. In the initial year of change, the resultant
     'short' tax year was from 6 April to 31 December 2001.

equal to Spain and Switzerland (both 2.2%). The yield as a percentage of total tax revenue at 5.7% was higher than Greece (4.4%), Denmark (4.5%), Germany (5.0%) and France (5.2%). On then current trends, the yield from corporation tax in Ireland in 1991 would move even closer to the yield in the richer OECD countries such as Austria, Finland, Germany and Switzerland. Additionally, the expected yield from corporation tax in the IFSC in Dublin would be significant and would far exceed the initial official estimates.

It was a matter of concern to note from the OECD Report that, side-by-side with the erosion of corporation tax incentives in Ireland, there were 21 zones with zero corporation tax spread throughout Belgium, France and Italy, which were then much richer EC Member States than Ireland. Some of those zones were large geographic areas with populations equal to a very significant proportion of the total Irish population. Not only was Ireland faced with competition from that large number of zero rate corporation tax zones, but a number of EC Member States gave direct cash grants to industry, which were significantly higher than those available in Ireland, both in absolute and in relative terms.[34]

The Netherlands and Belgium offered tax regimes for headquarters companies and holding and finance companies, with which Ireland could not then compete. The headquarters company concept was in place not only in the Netherlands but also in France and Belgium. The UK revenue authorities, on occasion, granted special concessions where headquarters operations had a significant employment content. Profits for those operations were determined on a *nominal* basis by reference to a percentage of direct costs incurred and tax was levied on that *nominal* basis. Many international corporations used the Netherlands as an 'intermediary' country because of the favourable tax treatment given to holding companies in receipt of foreign income. The tax concession was known as 'participation exemption', under which income from foreign shareholdings repatriated to the Netherlands was not liable to tax there. The holding company concept was often linked with headquarters and group finance functions.

The significant reduction in accelerated capital allowances in Ireland, and their abolition in April 1992, was an added disadvantage for Ireland, in stark contrast to the first year allowance of 50% then available in Germany, and to the investment tax credit system in Portugal and Spain.

One of the reasons why Ireland depended to a significant extent on corporation tax incentives was that Ireland did not have the capacity to pay huge up-front cash grants in order to attract mobile international investment here. It was essential that the OECD, in making any statement about corporation tax incentives in Ireland, should have looked at the position relating to cash grants given by richer EC Member States. State aid, per head of general population *per annum* on average during the period 1986-1988, amounted to 538 ECUs in Luxembourg, which headed the list in the EC according to statistics given by the European Commission. After Luxembourg, came Belgium (397 ECUs), Germany (391 ECUs), Italy (359 ECUs), and France (275 ECUs).

The EC average State aid per head of general population during the period 1986-1988 was 254 ECUs, with Ireland in 7th position at 198 ECUs. There was no suggestion by Irish industry that Ireland could, or should, pay higher cash grants; the recommendation of the CII had consistently been that the Irish Government should support the European Commission, and should persuade the European Commission to take an even firmer line in seeking the progressive reduction of State cash grants given to industry by the richer EC Member States.

Surprisingly, the Irish corporation tax regime came under attack from OECD in its 1991 Report.[35] This provoked a sharp response from the CII, whose view was that the OECD had made some dangerously naive and potentially damaging statements about the possibility of increasing the corporation tax yield in Ireland.[36] Because of the usual high quality of OECD Reports, and the authoritative standing of the organisation, there was a danger that its views might be accepted without question by the general public. In particular, the OECD suggested that the corporation tax system in Ireland offered scope for *improvement*, since it claimed that the cost-effectiveness of capital subsidies was to be questioned.

In the report, the OECD stated that profits were taxed 'relatively lightly' in Ireland. On the other hand, the OECD report acknowledged that the ratio of Ireland's corporate tax yield to GNP had increased from about half to about three-quarters of the OECD average between the mid-1970s and 1989. What the OECD report did not take into account was that there was a dramatic increase in the corporation tax yield in 1990; the increase was by more than 56% over the 1989 yield, from IR£303 million (€384.7 million) to IR£474 million (€601.9 million).

The CII stressed that the increase in the Irish corporation tax yield needed to be assessed in an international context. All other things being equal, the yield from corporation tax in Ireland as a percentage of GNP, and as a percentage of total tax revenue, should have been lower than the EC and OECD averages, due to the proportionately higher share of primary agriculture in Ireland in terms of employment and of economic output. Gross value-added contributed by agriculture in Ireland was more than three times the gross value-added contributed by agriculture in the then 12 Member States of the EC, on average. Agriculture was not structured on a corporate basis and so did not come within the scope of corporate taxation. Irish agriculture, in 1990, employed 15.4% of the workforce, in contrast to the EC average of 6.8%, and in contrast to the dramatically low figures for the UK (2.2%), Belgium (2.7%), Luxembourg (3.4%), Germany (4.3%), and the Netherlands (4.8%). Irish agricultural output contributed 9.7% of gross value-added of the economy, which was more than three times the EC average of 3.1%. The OECD 1991 Report failed to point out that the reverse was then the case, and that, in relative terms, companies in Ireland were more heavily subjected to corporation tax than in many other locations, including the average EC situation.

The OECD made no attempt in its report to analyse the reasons why Ireland initially granted corporate tax incentives, or to predict what was likely to happen to mobile international investment as a result of the significant reduction in corporate tax incentives over the previous years. Export Sales Relief (ESR) ceased after 5 April 1990, as did Shannon Relief. Companies that previously had availed of either of these reliefs were thereafter faced with the 10% Corporation Tax. It was obvious that the yield to the Exchequer from the replacement 10% Corporation Tax would depend on factors such as the extent to which the former ESR companies would continue to operate in Ireland after that relief had terminated. Both ESR and Shannon Relief were intended specifically to encourage the development of export companies.

Corporation Tax in Ireland needed to be lower than in many other industrial developed countries, in order that a sufficient amount of profit could be retained for business investment. An earlier OECD Report in 1990 stated that the rate of return on capital in the business sector in Ireland, at 9.6%, was significantly less than the average 13.5% for the EC and the European Free Trade Area (EFTA), and was still lower than the 16.2% average for all OECD countries.[37]

The CII view was that, if the average return was lower in Ireland than in most of our international competitor countries, then it was essential that Corporation Tax should be proportionately lower too, so that Irish businesses could retain adequate funds for investment to maintain and expand economic growth and employment.

US taxation was another issue that caused concern to the CII in the middle and late 1980s, when it was feared that new US legislation could diminish, or even negate, fiscal incentives given by the Irish Government to US multinationals. Such a move had a potentially negative impact on inward investment to Ireland from the USA. In May 1988, I was a member of a CII delegation that visited key members of the US Senate and the US House of Representatives in Washington DC.

CII Newsletters reported on developments relative to US taxation, including a comprehensive briefing on four important US tax and investment issues, contained in a *CII Newsletter* in October 1989:[38]

♦ Passive foreign investment companies (PFICs).

♦ Intercompany pricing.

♦ The *Tax Bill 1989*, with reference to Capital Gains Tax, interest payments, increased bureaucracy, and the tax treatment of expenditure on foreign R&D.

♦ The US *Omnibus Trade Act 1988*.

The CII mounted a vigorous campaign on US corporate taxation issues from 1988 to 1991 to protect Irish economic development interests. The campaign included direct dialogue with US politicians and tax authorities, and with the Irish Government, the Department of Finance, the Revenue Commissioners and the IDA. The CII participated in the submissions made by UNICE to the USA, to the European Commission and to national governments within the EC.

The representations to the US authorities were successful in delaying the implementation of the more restrictive elements of legislation. It was not until 2005 that US legislation impacted significantly and directly on repatriation to the USA of profits of US subsidiaries and branches, earned in Ireland!

BUSINESS LAWS THAT MAKE SENSE

In October 1984, I cautioned that proposed changes in company law relative to directors could adversely impact on enterprise.[39] Industry accepted that it was valid for the Government to legislate for directors who acted in a fraudulent manner. The Government already had sufficient power in that regard. The view of the CII was that diligence in the use of the existing powers should have been the focus of the debate, rather than dissipating energy by using a 'sledgehammer to crack a nut'.

In 1984, the CII believed that any changes in company law relating to insolvency should be guided by six basic principles:

- The need for equity and justice to all parties who were affected by insolvency, including the directors of the insolvent company.
- The need to ensure that change in the area of insolvency law would not hinder the many types of credit transactions that were an essential and integral part of Irish commercial life and without which the volume of trade would diminish to the detriment of the entire community.
- The need to ensure that legislative change would not be of an unduly punitive nature for business people whose actions, while they might have been commercially imprudent, were not fraudulent in a criminal sense.
- The need to ensure that each proposed legislative measure would be designed to help the continued existence of a potentially viable company in the interests of all parties, including employees, suppliers, and customers. In that context, a legal mechanism for the rescue or reconstruction of an ailing, but potentially viable, company would need to have regard to the personal situation of directors' liability before such a rescue mechanism could be used by a company.
- The need to ensure that legislative changes would not create any unnecessary additional administrative burdens for trading companies, in circumstances where enterprise in Ireland was already overburdened with administrative requirements and cost penalties, compared to businesses in many of Ireland's international trading partners.
- In a small country such as Ireland, which in 1984 had an extremely high level of unemployment, and living standards that were low relative to the EC average, the main focus of Government should be on creating a climate that would attract people to establish enterprises in Ireland. Consequently, Government should maintain a balance between the need to encourage enterprise, and the need to protect the legitimate interests of all parties on whom the operation of an enterprise would in any way impact.

Michael Noonan TD, Minister for Industry & Commerce, was responsible for the *Companies Bill 1987* that was presented in Seanad Éireann in January 1987, and published in February 1987. The *Explanatory & Financial Memorandum* stated as follows:

> 'The underlying aim is to create a climate of confidence for business activity in which genuine commercial endeavour will prosper, and the prospects for economic development in general will be enhanced.'

The CII welcomed the statement of underlying aim, and was in accord with the view that measures were needed, aimed specifically at curbing certain identified abuses, while at the same time introducing provisions that would inspire more confidence among all parties directly affected by the activities of companies, and encourage companies that got into difficulties to address those difficulties in a positive and constructive manner at a much earlier stage.

The CII supported the imposition of appropriate penalties on company directors and others who sought to trade in a fraudulent manner and accepted that the existence of those penalties would serve to protect *bona fide* business interests, as well as creditors and consumers.[40]

The *Companies Bill 1987* lapsed on dissolution of the Houses of the Oireachtas, the Dáil not having resumed after the Christmas recess and the Seanad having adjourned *sine die* on 21 January 1987.

The new Government that took office on 10 March 1987, in due course reintroduced the *Companies (No. 2) Bill 1987*. Albert Reynolds TD, Minister for Industry & Commerce, introduced an amendment that only the Courts could impose restrictions on company directors, and that such restrictions would not have automatic effect in insolvencies, as originally envisaged. The Minister added in his amendment, by way of safeguard, that restrictions would not be imposed where the Courts were satisfied that a director acted honestly and responsibly in the conduct of an insolvent company's business.

The CII responded to a number of major issues in the *Companies (No. 2) Bill 1987*, which included investigations; transactions involving directors; disclosure of interests in shares; insider dealing; winding up and related matters; disqualification and restrictions in relation to directors and other officers; receivers; companies under the protection of the Courts; and accounts and audit.

Desmond O'Malley TD, who became Minister for Industry & Commerce for his third time in July 1989, introduced 17 amendments that were contained in Sections 180 and 181 of the Act, a number of which related directly to points raised by the CII. The latter amendments included some relating to the *Companies (Amendment) Act 1990*,[41] which provided *inter alia* for the appointment of an examiner to report on a company under the protection of the Court for the period of examination.[42] The CII's amendments, accepted by the Minister, included some that related to the protection of employment, the protection of traders who provided goods and services during the course of the examination, and technical amendments related to the company under examination, creditors, banks, employees, and other interested parties. The *Companies (No. 2) Bill 1987* was finally enacted in December 1990, as the *Companies Act 1990*.

The cost of liability insurance was a specific issue of business costs influenced by legislation, which caused concern to the CII and its member enterprises from the early 1980s. The CII, from 1982 onwards, mounted a sustained campaign against the high level of liability insurance costs on industry. Employer's liability insurance in the mid-1980s cost between 2.5% and 3% of payroll in manufacturing industry but, in the case of some high risk manufacturing industries, and in the construction industry, the cost was sometimes as high as 10% of payroll. The premium level for manufacturing and construction was between three and 15 times higher than in comparable cases in the UK, depending on the sector of industry. Liability insurance premiums, in some cases, had become a factor in the assessment of Ireland as a location for multinational enterprise. At the same time, the liability insurers were incurring significant losses. In the five years, 1980 to 1984 inclusive, underwriting losses on non-life business in Ireland amounted to a cumulative IR£305 million (€387 million), before investment income was taken into account, and losses in 1985 and 1986 were averaging about IR£100 million (€127 million) *per annum*. The situation could not be allowed to continue; a developed industrial economy could not operate without insurance, and the liability underwriters could not continue indefinitely in a loss-making situation.

The CII welcomed the introduction of the *Courts Bill 1986* in February 1986, and the provision therein that certain civil actions in the High Court would be tried without a jury, but subsequently expressed concern at delay in enacting the legislation. In the event, the Bill was not enacted when the then Government went out of office early in 1987, but it was reintroduced by the next Government as one of the agreed measures in the PNR that was signed by the Government and the social partners in October 1987. The CII negotiated the inclusion of a paragraph on liability insurance costs in the PNR, as follows:

> 'Irish liability insurance rates place many Irish firms at a cost disadvantage, particularly in comparison with UK competitors. The Government will move quickly to facilitate a reduction in costs by proceeding with legislation to abolish juries in personal injuries cases, by introducing legislation to give effect to the main recommendations of the Commission of Inquiry on Safety, Health & Welfare at Work (the Barrington Report), and by promoting the introduction of safety audit arrangements by insurance companies. The scope for promoting the publication of a Book of Quantum of Damages, for introducing a pre-trial procedure system and reducing the level of legal representation in

the Superior Courts to help reduce legal costs, will also be examined. Insurance industry representatives have given assurances that reductions in liability insurance premia will follow the introduction of an improved framework.'

The provision, agreed by the Government and the social partners, contained all six issues on which industry had consistently sought progress since 1982.

A submission in 1985 to the Joint Oireachtas Committee on Legislation highlighted the desirability of a Freedom of Information Act, and a Data Protection Act.[43] There was a need for legislation in that area to allow Ireland to comply with the Council of Europe Convention on Data Protection. That was necessary *inter alia* so that the growing international trade by Irish companies in the information technology and data transfer industries could be protected and advanced by the introduction in Ireland of legislation that would not inhibit the flow of information across national boundaries. The Federal Republic of Germany, France, Norway, Spain and Sweden by 1985 had ratified the Convention, and the United Kingdom planned to do so in 1987, by which time the UK expected to have its own legislation in place.

The CII felt that a Data Protection Act should cover only personal data that related to an individual who could be clearly identified from the data and that data relating solely to commercial transactions should not be covered. Its submission sought a specific exemption in any new legislation for data that was held solely for payroll, accounting, and other administrative purposes strictly of an in-house business nature, and such exemption was needed for small firms in the generality of business and industry that did not hold sensitive personal information. The CII accepted that various principles applied to personal data that was held by industrial and commercial users.

In August 1989, the CII made a submission to the Department of Industry & Commerce on the review of the Fourth Council Directive on Company Law (78/660/EEC of 25 July 1978), which contained provisions and standards for the preparation of annual accounts of companies.[44] The submission sought that the EC should review the scope and character of the Fourth Directive, in comparison with the regulations that applied in other major world locations that attracted internationally-mobile investment, including the USA and Japan, together with smaller international financial and business centres such as the Isle of Man, Bermuda, Barbados, and Singapore. The CII's view was that international comparisons in relation to disclosure of accounting information were relevant, in view of the fact that a small number of multinational enterprises with plants in Ireland re-registered outside the EEC when the requirements of the Fourth Directive were introduced into Irish company law.

When the Fourth Directive was first discussed in Ireland, the CII referred to the need to protect commercially-valuable market and costing information. The CII repeated that point in a submission regarding the *Companies (Amendment) Bill 1985*.[45] The CII accepted as legitimate that companies should be required to disclose information on matters that directly impacted on employees, shareholders, suppliers, lenders and the general public, but it was not acceptable that a company be obliged to disclose strategic marketing information that was of interest primarily to commercial competitors. The CII sought that the focus of disclosure be on protecting the legitimate interests of all who were employed by, traded with, loaned to, or invested in a company.

Notwithstanding the comments relative to international business location decisions, and commercially-valuable information, the CII fully supported the need for companies to publish appropriate financial information on their affairs.

In the CII's view, the preferential position of the Revenue Commissioners for debts owing to them on the liquidation of a business was an issue relevant to the disclosure of information. Revenue preference was an issue in pre-Budget submissions to the Government and to successive Ministers for Finance over a number of years.[46] The concern was that the system, whereby the Revenue Commissioners enjoyed preference in the payment of debts in the event of bankruptcy and liquidation, worked to the detriment of unsecured trade creditors. It created unfair competition, because any delay in collecting taxes prior to bankruptcy or liquidation gave a competitive advantage to those who were allowed to retain money that should otherwise have been paid in full and on time to the Exchequer. Unsecured trade creditors were the main losers, when businesses failed, with large outstanding preferential debts due to the Revenue Commissioners. The CII believed that the Revenue Commissioners should be required to exercise the same discipline in collecting debts as other creditors. Any delay by the Revenue Commissioners in collecting taxes, in full and on time, placed unsecured trade creditors at an increased risk. Therefore, the CII sought that preferential status should apply to Revenue debts, and to debts due to other public authorities, only for a period of three months, with the possibility of an extension for a period of a further three months, provided that the Revenue Commissioners registered the outstanding debt with the Companies Registration Office (CRO), so that all who had a financial interest in the company would be aware of the preferential debt due to the Revenue Commissioners on inspection of the CRO file. The CII believed that the point deserved consideration within the EC in general. In that context, Denmark abolished the preferential debt status of the Exchequer in 1969, ranking the Danish Exchequer as an ordinary trade creditor.

SUMMARY

◊ Although control of public expenditure was one of the four main planks of the PNR, it was necessary for the campaign to balance the Government's current budget to continue long after 1987. That budget was ultimately balanced, in out-turn, in 1996 and on a planned basis in 1997. Control of public expenditure programmes was accompanied by a focus on value for money in all areas of public expenditure.

◊ The creation of an environment supportive of enterprise, job creation and economic growth required the reduction in business cost penalties that persisted throughout the 1980s, including in public utility areas such as electricity, postal services, telecommunications and transport.

◊ The CII campaigned against excessive personal taxation and sought an internationally-competitive corporation tax regime, together with corporate and business legislation based on equity and business ethics and on the protection of the *bona fide* interests of all stakeholders in business.

CHAPTER 7
THE ROAD TO TOMORROW

INVEST IN NATIONAL ROADS

Ireland's national road network is the predominant mode of inland transport. In the 1970s, roads carried 96% of passenger traffic in kilometres of travel, and 88% of freight traffic in metric tonnes per kilometre. The balance of inland transport was on rail, with internal air services making only a marginal contribution. Inland waterways were used solely for recreational purposes.

The national roads network, however, was in a poor condition in the 1970s as evidenced by a 1974 report from An Foras Forbartha (AFF), which surveyed the quality of the network, estimated traffic volumes to the early 1990s and the cost of up-grading the network to the average European level of operating efficiency.[1] AFF found that, relative to the norm in Europe, 18% of Irish national primary and secondary routes were either 'deficient' or 'seriously deficient'. By 1978, AFF estimated that 24% of the primary routes and 27% of the secondary routes had pavement in a 'poor' condition.

In 1978, the CII claimed that, even on the national primary routes, commercial vehicles averaged only 25 miles per hour compared with 40 miles per hour in other EEC Member States.[2] Total expenditure on both road improvements and road maintenance fell from 1.67% of GNP in 1962 to 1.27% in 1977. Furthermore, despite the growing need for improvements, only 31% of total expenditure in 1977 was on improvement works, in contrast to 51% in 1962, the balance being spent on maintenance. Consequently, the CII calculated the need for, and sought, a quadrupling of annual expenditure on roads over the following decade and recommended investment of private capital to provide toll roads and bridges, where appropriate, together with significant funding from the ERDF. Further, the CII called for the establishment of a National Roads Council (later, National Roads Authority) to co-ordinate the private and public inputs to an essential massive road construction programme.

On joining the CII in April 1979, one of my early responsibilities was to design and implement a major public affairs campaign aimed at achieving a higher political priority for investment in the network of national roads.[3]

My involvement began with inputs to the Roads Plan adopted by the Government in May 1979.[4] The CII subsequently discussed its response to the *Road Development Plan for the 1980s* with Sylvester Barrett TD, Minister for the Environment, and senior officials of his Department.[5] Points discussed included the need to establish a National Roads Council / Authority; the inadequacy of the 1979 Plan relative to industry's needs for national roads comparable with the European norm; the absence of multi-annual financing of the Plan; the need to monitor and annually update the Plan; the urgent need for local authorities to acquire land and to prepare detailed programmes; the need to study and to respond to the pattern of industrial traffic; the requirement to create public awareness of the economic and social benefits of an efficient national roads network; and the terms of the *Local Government (Toll Roads) Bill 1979*.

The establishment of the CII Roads Policy Committee followed the meeting with the Minister.[6] The terms of reference of this Committee were:

1. Promotion of a favourable public attitude to the development and use of roads as a significant national resource.

2. Formulation of the CII's policy towards the maintenance, development and expansion of Ireland's roads network, with particular reference to the National Primary Routes.

3. Representations to the Government, to the institutions of the European Community, to wider international agencies and to appropriate research institutions.

4. Promotion and encouragement of technological innovation in the areas of road construction and of road design.

5. Promotion of the optimisation of route selection policy in the context of regional, local, and national development, and in the context of European infrastructure policy.

The focus of the CII's discussions with the Minister and officials was on the *strategic national roads network*. The total roads network in Ireland measured 92,295 kilometres, of which the strategic national element was 7.6%, and comprised the national primary routes (2.8%), the national secondary routes (2.8%) and the access roads to ports and airports (2.0%). At the commencement of the *Road Development Plan for the 1980s*, the national primary routes, with 2.8% of the total roads network, carried 25% of all road traffic and 42% of all business road traffic.

The year 1980 was the first full year of implementation of the *Road Development Plan for the 1980s*. In order to stimulate public and political 'interest in the Plan, I undertook a widely-publicised lecture tour of selected cities and towns, addressing members of the CII and invited guests, including politicians, civil and public servants and other policy influencers.[7 & 8]

Irish Road Statistics, published by the CII Roads Policy Committee in 1980, gave a wealth of information about motor vehicle numbers, road traffic, the economics of road works, energy and transport, freight transport, household expenditure on transport, the road network, road expenditure, road administration, transport funding, and road accidents. The CII calculated that the total needs for the period 1980 to 1989, measured at constant 1980 prices, would amount to IR£2,468 million (€3,133.7 million) for road improvement works, compared with less than IR£1,000 million (<€1,270 million) provided in the *Road Development Plan for the 1980s*. In addition to improvements, the CII calculated that a special once-off road-strengthening programme was needed at a cost IR£600 million (€762 million). The Roads Policy Committee subsequently published an updated *Irish Road Statistics* in 1985.

The regrettable out-turn was that, in 1980, State investment in road improvement and maintenance amounted to only 65% of the projection for that year in the *Road Development Plan for the 1980s*. The PCP for 1981 only projected an investment of 80% of what had been promised in the Plan. In response, the CII Roads Policy Committee commissioned Irish Marketing Surveys to undertake a public opinion poll on *Attitudes to Irish Roads*, published in May 1981. Here is a summary of the findings:

♦ 90% of all persons interviewed considered that roads within and between the major towns and cities were inadequate to meet either present roads needs or foreseeable future needs.

♦ 60% of all interviewees believed that additional public money should be spent on new road construction and ranked expenditure on new road construction as the single highest priority for Government expenditure on the improvement of any transport mode.

♦ 30% agreed to the demolition of buildings, including private homes, to facilitate the construction of new roads and a further 34% agreed to demolition in certain circumstances only.

♦ 54% believed that the Government was not investing enough of the road users' direct payments to the Exchequer in new road construction and road maintenance.

♦ 42% believed that the condition of the Irish roads network was hindering industrial development.

Given this public acceptance of the importance of the roads network, the CII asked Government to accord to roads at least the priority given in the *Road Development Plan for the 1980s,* updated to meet the backlog caused by not keeping the Plan on target in 1980 and 1981. The CII subsequently supported the proposal by Ruairí Quinn TD, Minister of State at the Department of the Environment, made as early as July 1983, for the establishment of a Roads Finance Agency. Unfortunately, the Roads Finance Agency was not then established.[9]

In Autumn 1983, the CII Roads Policy Committee retained two leading journalists to prepare news media releases about the network of national roads. This ensured a high level of publicity in the national newspapers, on radio, and on television, together with comprehensive coverage in the local and regional newspapers and generated national and local political interest. The establishment of a Roads Authority was promised by Liam Kavanagh TD, Minister for Labour, but did not then materialise.[10]

Additionally, the CII organised a schools project in Autumn 1984, in co-operation with the Association of Geography Teachers of Ireland and the Department of Education, aimed at pupils between the ages of 15 and 18 years and inviting projects relating to the roads environment local to the school. As a follow-up, CII funded the preparation and distribution of classroom notes by the Association of Geography Teachers of Ireland. In addition, in 1985, the CII Roads Policy Committee inaugurated the award of an annual prize for the best roads-related project in the Geography Section of the Aer Lingus Young Scientists Exhibition and funded a project for young adults through Junior Chamber Ireland, on the theme of *Roads for a Better Future.*[11]

The New Ireland Forum, established by the Government to research relationships between the Republic of Ireland and Northern Ireland, published a number of sectoral studies, including one on transport.[12] The report supported the CII view by indicating that the standing charges on commercial vehicles were up to 30%, and operational costs were up to 25%, higher in the Republic of Ireland than in Northern Ireland and Great Britain. This resulted in such advantage for hauliers in Northern Ireland over their Southern competitors, that up to two-thirds of all cross-border trade was carried by commercial vehicles registered in Northern Ireland.

In 1983, the Government, under An Taoiseach, Dr Garret FitzGerald TD, appointed a National Planning Board to produce proposals for a National Plan for 1984 to 1987. The Board reported in April 1984, and stated *inter alia* that there were many road investments that were economically productive on any objective basis and that would even justify financing through foreign borrowing. The Board stated that there was a strong case for encouraging private investment to supplement public investment by enabling charges to be made for the use of roads, bridges, and bypasses. The Board pointed out that less than 1% of GNP had been spent annually on road building over the previous 10 years, despite the increase in the level of traffic congestion. The amounts allocated to road works in 1982, 1983, and 1984 had not been large enough to prevent the backlog in investment from increasing. The Board recommended streamlining legislation to reduce delays in planning, public hearings, and the making of compulsory purchase orders.

The Government published a National Plan, *Building on Reality 1985-1987*, in October 1984, which included emphasis on the development of the roads system. The Government acknowledged that, in the 1960s and 1970s, there had been serious underinvestment in road construction and maintenance, recognised the shortfall that had occurred in the *Road Development Plan for the 1980s* and gave a commitment to sustain planned expenditure in the years 1985 through 1987. This commitment was given in the revised plan, *Policy & Planning Framework for Roads*, in January 1985, and aimed at reducing the shortfall in investment under the previous Plan to 9% by the end of 1987 as against 17% at the end of 1984.

The European Parliament published a report on transport in Ireland in 1986,[13] which made a number of recommendations for initiatives at national level in Ireland and at EEC level. Among the proposals was one for the creation of a single Department of Transport, and increased investment in roads infrastructure on a planned multi-annual basis.

The CII organised conferences and seminars throughout the 1980s on the issue of road development, some of them in association with the Institution of Engineers of Ireland (IEI). Speakers were also provided for conferences organised by the public sector, including AFF.

In a comprehensive submission to the Minister for the Environment in October, 1987, the CII gave details of all national roads projects needed to bring the national roads network up to a European average level of operating efficiency and meet projected needs up to the year 2005.[14] The cost was calculated at IR£3,250 million (€4,127 million). In terms of benefit, the CII calculated that this could cut IR£300 million (€381 million) *per annum* off Irish freight transport costs, which then amounted to about IR£1,000 million (€1,270 million) *per annum*, and could have added to the overall competitiveness of the Irish business sector by about 3%. The level of annual freight transport outlay represented about 9% of the price of products on average, which required reduction to between 4% and 5% if

Irish business and industry was to compete on a par with the rest of the EEC. In addition to the 3% improvement in overall competitiveness that could accrue from an efficient roads infrastructure, a further 1.5% gain in competitiveness was potentially available from better traffic management, reduced customs delays at ports, and fuel taxes reduced to the EEC average. The CII emphasised that the road users paid a substantial price for an inferior level of service, and a greater proportion of net Exchequer direct receipts from road users needed to be invested in roads. In 1988, only 24% of the road users' taxes on vehicles, parts, and fuels was invested in road improvement and maintenance, 13% was invested in public transport, and the balance of 63% was used for general Government current expenditure.

AN INTERIM NATIONAL ROADS AUTHORITY

Roads were a major issue during the general election campaign of spring 1987. John Boland TD, on behalf of Fine Gael, and Ray Burke TD, on behalf of Fianna Fáil, undertook that their parties in Government would establish a National Roads Authority, and Ruairí Quinn TD, on behalf on the Labour Party, acknowledged the merit of the case made by CII. The Fianna Fáil Party, which subsequently formed the Government, published an election manifesto entitled *The Programme for National Recovery*. In the section dealing with *Roads*, it acknowledged that an efficient roads network was a vital component of national recovery and that road transport costs could be reduced by about 25%. The manifesto undertook to establish a National Roads Authority responsible for the development of an integrated network of national primary, national secondary, and access roads to ports and airports.

In May, 1988, the Government decided to establish a National Roads Authority (NRA) on an interim basis within the Department of the Environment, pending the introduction of legislation at an early date. Pádraig Flynn TD, Minister for the Environment, announced the interim NRA on 20 July 1988, with me as Executive Chairman. The Authority was mandated to commence operations immediately.

The Minister for the Environment, when launching the interim NRA in July 1988, stated that the investment needed to bring all roads up to an EC standard of operating efficiency would be IR£8.5 billion (€10.8 billion). Within this figure, the Minister estimated the investment needs on the

network of national roads to amount to IR£3.3 billion (€4.2 billion). This
sum was sub-divided into IR£2.2 billion (€2.8 billion) for the inter-urban
national roads, IR£0.3 billion (€0.4 billion) for the urban access roads to the
main ports and airports and IR£0.8 billion (€1.0 billion) for maintenance
and road pavement strengthening on the national roads network.
Meanwhile, in July 1988, the CII published a report on the public affairs
campaign and on the road developments undertaken during the decade
1979 to 1988.[15]

20 July 1988, on the establishment of the interim National Roads Authority:
(left to right) Paddy Dowd, County Manager, Cork County Council; Pádraig
Flynn TD, Minister for the Environment, and Con Power, Executive Chairman
of the interim Authority.

ROAD DEVELOPMENT, 1989–1993

The interim NRA was responsible for the national roads network element
of the *Operational Programme for Road Development 1989-1993*. The
Government, in the Operational Programme that formed part of the
National Development Plan 1989-1993, acknowledged the problem of
transport costs in the following terms:[16]

'It is estimated that transport costs for Irish exporters to Europe account for between 9% and 10% of export sales values and that these costs are approximately twice those incurred by Community countries trading with one another on the European mainland. This cost penalty applies to the great bulk of Ireland's international trade – not only exports but also imports of materials and capital goods.'

As Executive Chairman of the interim NRA, I spoke at the 1989 Annual Conference of the IEI and later to the Southern Section of the Chartered Institute of Transport in Ireland (CITI)[17] The preface to the latter talk was a quotation from the European Commission on Ireland's transport problems as a peripheral region within the EC:[18]

'Ireland's location on the western edge of the Community is a serious handicap to a country which is highly dependent on exports. If Ireland is to take full advantage of the potential benefits of the completion of the internal market, it is clear that measures are required to improve communications between Ireland and the rest of the Community.'

The *National Development Plan 1989-1993* was prepared by the Government, with the principal objective of addressing Ireland's problems as a less-developed peripheral region within the European Community.[19]

The Operational Programme for Road Development contained details of total expenditure of IR£755.2 million (€958.9 million) on the network of national roads over the period 1989 to 1993, only 23% of the total identified needs acknowledged by the Government in the National Development Plan. On a *pro rata* basis, that indicated a 22-year programme to bring the network of national roads to an EC level of operating efficiency, although the period probably could be considerably reduced as the annual investment was rising significantly over the period from IR£113 million (€143.5 million) in 1989 to almost IR£191 million (€242.5 million) in 1993.

The Government's objective was to complete that modest programme in full and on time, and to complete the balance of the programme to meet all acknowledged needs to bring the network of national roads up to a European average level of operating efficiency by the year 2000! In that context, by 1988 only 15% of the national primary roads, and 27% of the national secondary roads, met that standard. When completed, the proposed national roads network would consist of over 3,500 kilometres of two-lane carriageway, approximately 450 kilometres of dual carriageway, and 160 kilometres of motorway, plus 86 kilometres comprising a special Dublin circumferential motorway. That would make a total of 4,150 kilometres of up-graded roadway, and such a system would cost IR£3,250 million (€4,126.6 million) in 1987 prices.

On 20 September 1989, the European Commission allocated 3,672 million ECUs (1989 prices) (at the then exchange rates, about IR£2.86 billion (€3.63 billion)) for the period 1989 to 1993. Ireland, which then had 5.1% of the population of the less developed regions of the EC, was to receive 10.14% of the EC Structural Funds, amounting on a *pro rata* basis to twice the level of aid *per capita* received on average by all less developed regions. The higher *per capita* aid for Ireland was in recognition of three major national disadvantages: higher transport costs caused by being an island on the periphery of the EC; living standards about three-fifths the EC average; and the second highest unemployment rate within the Community.

The position for 1989 was that public finance for the network of national roads, Exchequer plus EC, would amount to IR£113 million (€143.5 million).

The allocation for 1990 in the Operational Programme was IR£134 million (€170 million), in 1989 prices. The PCP summary was published on 15 November 1989, and provided IR£184.5 million (€234.3 million) for all roads, a 12.5% increase over the 1989 total allocation of IR£164 million (€208 million). It contrasted with a 19% overall increase in the PCP, so that roads had not been awarded even the average PCP priority. Within the overall roads allocation, the allocation for the network of national roads at IR£116.5 million (€147.9 million) had been increased only in line with inflation, a reduction of 16% in real terms from the projection in the Operational Programme. In contrast, *other roads* had been allocated IR£68 million (€86 million) against IR£51 million (€65 million) in 1989, an increase of one-third. These figures reflected the political priorities and did not augur well for the network of national roads.

INTERGRATED TRANSPORT NETWORKS

The European Commission stated that aid from the European Structural Funds for roads and other transport infrastructures would be aimed primarily at overcoming the problems of peripherality. In that context, roads formed part of an integrated transport system, linked to the other transport modes in a rational, logical, and unified manner, with due weight given to investment in both public and private transport. Road development for Ireland was part of the wider issue of access transport as

Ireland, being an island, relied on sea and air transport for import and export trade and for the international movement of passengers.

Ireland's access transport problem was acknowledged by the European Commissioner for Regional Policy, Eneko Landaburu Illarramendi, who made public reference to it on a number of occasions. In particular, the Commissioner, addressing a national conference entitled *Around the Channel Tunnel,* in Britain in October 1989, stressed the need for the implementation of an efficient and fully-integrated European transport and communication system.

Commissioner Illarramendi stated that, without such an integrated transport and communication system, Europe's potential for increased internal trade could not be fully exploited, while the peripheral regions would remain at a distance from the EC central markets. It was self-evident that, without an appropriate policy, accompanying public investment and effective action, the peripheral less-developed regions of the EC, including Ireland, would become increasingly marginalised in the larger integrated European Internal Market. Operationally-efficient and cost-effective access transport was a precondition to the success of Irish merchandise trade and tourism.

The European Commission emphasised the need for a coherent transport policy between both parts of the island of Ireland, and with the rest of the EC. The objective of improving infrastructure, particularly the transport and communications infrastructure in the less developed regions of the EC was to enhance the capacity of those regions to create more jobs and earn higher living standards on a self-sustaining basis. The Commission stated that roads, rail, airport facilities, sea links, and the development of ports were all relevant to the peripherality programme, which accounted for 19.6% of the European Structural Funds allocation to Ireland. The programme was funded as to 65% by the EC, 23% by Government, and 12% by other public authorities.

The Commission agreed to provide road funds to aid the strategic Euro routes and related internal link roads, under the following headings:

♦ Completion of the *National Programme of (European) Community Interest Roads 1986-1990.*

♦ Supporting transport infrastructure for tourism.

♦ Supporting transport infrastructure for industry and services.

♦ Cross-border initiatives with Northern Ireland.

I will allow the book speak for itself, including the Introduction by your colleague, Ruairi Quinn TD, and the Foreword by Charlie McCreevy, both former Ministers for Finance. It has received eleven positive print reviews. I was particularly pleased with the two full pages devoted to it in one of the issues of the Journal of the Public Service Executive Union (PSEU).

I hope that you enjoy reading the book.

I look forward to your feedback and to discussing it with you in due course. I am convinced that there are lessons to be learned from the period 1979-1993 that are equally applicable to to-day's circumstances.

Kindest personal regards

Yours sincerely

Encl: book

Dr Con Power

BComm MEconSc MA PhD

FCCA FCMA FCIS

4 Hermitage Grove
Rathfarnham
Dublin 16

Telephone [Home] (01) 4946833
Mobile 087 2456917
E-mail: Con_Power@alumni.ucd.ie

4th November 2010

Ms Joan Burton TD
Labour Party Spokesperson on Finance
Dáil Éireann
Leinster House
Kildare Street
Dublin 2

Dear Joan

Despite the overall dominance of roads as the main transport mode for passengers and freight, roads were less dominant as a transport mode on the major inter-urban and inter-regional corridors, where rail had a 22% share of the overall passenger market (39% Cork / Dublin and 25% Tralee / Dublin) and a 25% share of all freight, measured in tonnes hauled distances of 150kms (90 miles) and over.

The ports handling the main volumes of freight were on the east and south coasts, as were the main passenger ports. The National Development Plan 1989-1993 proposed to concentrate commercial port expenditure primarily on the ports of Dublin, Rosslare, Waterford and Cork. Dublin, Cork and Shannon were designated the national airports.

My view, expressed throughout the decade prior to the establishment of the interim NRA in 1988, was that Ireland needed a Department of Transport with statutory authority for each of the four national transport networks: road, rail, sea, and air. The merit of the case was accepted by John Wilson TD, when Tánaiste and Minister for the Marine. The approach was similar to that taken in Denmark under the Danish *Roads Act 1972*, which established the Danish Road Directorate on a statutory basis as a Division within the Danish Ministry of Transport. Similar Directorates in the Danish Ministry of Transport had responsibility for each of the other transport modes. The Danish approach to roads administration was at three levels:

- National: 4,600 kms of main roads, including motorways. This road network was financed and administered directly by the statutory Road Directorate within the Ministry of Transport.
- Regional: 6,500 kms of regional roads that were administered by the 14 regional authorities.
- Local: 55,500 kms of local roads that were administered by the 275 local authorities.

Appropriate operational relationships existed between each of the various levels of public administration to ensure value for money in the use of scarce resources. A fundamental point of difference between Denmark and Ireland was that, in Denmark, each level of public administration – local, regional, and national – had its own dedicated sources of finance and taxation was levied at each of the three levels. In 1989, through the good offices of the Danish Ambassador to Ireland, I arranged for the Director General of the Danish Road Directorate to visit Ireland and meet with the Minister for the Environment, Pádraig Flynn TD, and senior staff of the Department.

I argued the case for a Department of Transport in April 1990.[20] I found that the greatest objection came from the Department of the Environment. That was probably understandable because of the dominance of roads as a transport mode in Ireland and the fact that the local authorities, under the aegis of the Department of the Environment, were the roads authorities within their administrative areas. After I spoke at the University College Dublin (UCD) conference in April 1990, in my capacity as Chairman of the interim NRA, Minister Pádraig Flynn TD told me that for so long as he remained Minister for the Environment, no part of his Department would move to a Department of Transport! That was also the view given to me by senior officials of the Department during my time as Chairman from July 1988, to December 1993! It was not until 2002 that the transport sectors of the then Department of the Marine & Natural Resources were combined with the Roads Division of the then Department of the Environment & Local Government to form a new Department of Transport. The NRA, established under the *Roads Act 1993*, with effect from 1 January 1994, remains an independent statutory body under the aegis of the Department of Transport. Significant progress has been made in terms of administrative structures, and of operational delivery.

I still believe that the Government should revisit my fundamental proposition of 1990 for a Department of Transport with four integrated divisions, where each division would be the National Authority for road, rail, sea, and air transport, respectively and each would be underpinned by its own consolidated Act for that particular transport mode. I believe that the governance of each public infrastructure network should be a reserved central core function of the State, administered by a Division of a Government Department. Operational aspects of the provision, maintenance and operation of each network would be a matter for public and private entities within the framework set and regulated by the National Authority. Any public entity involved in operational activities would not be an 'Authority' in the sense of policy co-ordination and deployment of scarce national resources. Policy and public finance clearly and correctly would rest with the relevant Minister, subject to the concurrence of the Minister for Finance, and subject to the ultimate sanction of Government and of the Houses of the Oireachtas in the Annual Budget and in applicable legislation and regulations.

THE DUBLIN RING ROAD

The Dublin Ring Road was an important element in the National Development Plan 1989-1993. The proposed motorway ran from the Airport Road to the Bray Road, via a new tolled Liffey crossing to the west of the City.

A major problem still to be solved was access to Dublin Port. When the Minister for the Environment, Pádraig Flynn TD launched the NRA on 20 July 1988, he announced the establishment of a separate Working Party to assess and report on that issue. Much remains to be done in 2009, 21 years thereafter!

THE DUBLIN LIGHT ELECTRIC TRAMWAY

The traffic and roads situation in Dublin gave rise to much debate, including regarding its environmental impact. The Government made a decision in 1987 that required CIÉ to prepare public transport investment plans for the Dublin area involving only bus-based options, or diesel rail services on existing lines. One solution that had not then been given sufficient attention was the possibility of using a light electric tramway system. Such a system could have been put in place to service Dundrum by using *inter alia* the old Harcourt Street railway line, and eventually the line could be extended to other parts of south and southwest Dublin. The use of a tramway system could deliver not only a public transport solution, but could have a beneficial impact on the environment, with no exhaust emission and little noise pollution. The proposal could significantly reduce both peak hour congestion in Dublin city centre and the demand for long-term car park facilities in the city centre. Electric tramway systems then were being recognised increasingly as a significant solution for inner city mass transit in major European cities, whereas the creation of extensive busways to solve those inner city problems had been clearly demonstrated elsewhere to be an out-of-date and ineffective solution.

The case existed, therefore, for the Government to modify the 1987 decision in the light of new possibilities for private investment in electric tramway systems and also because of the compelling environmental and cost arguments. In terms of cost, there had been a major economic change since 1987 due to a significant drop in the real cost of electricity. There was evidence that the cost of rolling stock for electric tramway systems was becoming much more competitive. Therefore, it appeared that environmental and economic considerations were in harmony at the beginning of the 1990s and both indicated that serious consideration should be given to the light rail alternative in the context of endeavouring to solve Dublin's traffic problems. The CII had not taken a view on the issue by 1990; it was one of the options being examined by the CII Transport Council. My personal view in favour of a Dublin light electric tramway, given at a Fine Gael seminar in July 1990, received significant news media coverage.[21]

Four years later, in April 1994, the Dublin Transportation Initiative (DTI) produced a report with a wide range of transport recommendations for the Greater Dublin Area, including a three-line Light Rail Transit (LRT) system linking Ballymun, Cabinteely and Tallaght to the city centre at a cost of about IR£300 million (€381 million). In May 1998, the Government decided to proceed with an LRT system comprising a surface line from Tallaght to Connolly Station (Red Line) and a line from Sandyford Industrial Estate to Ballymun and Dublin Airport using the disused Harcourt Street and Broadstone railway routes. The Government also decided that a section of the LRT system would run underground in the city centre between St Stephen's Green and Broadstone. The system is known as the LUAS. In due course, Public Private Partnership (PPP) contracts were awarded for the operation of the LUAS transport system, for the maintenance of the light rail vehicles and for the provision of the automated fare collection system. The LUAS Green Line from Sandyford Industrial Estate to St Stephen's Green went into public service on 30 June 2004, and the Red Line from 26 September 2004.

ACCESS TO DUBLIN PORT

Access to Dublin Port was another transport issue that had given rise to much debate and serious questioning on environmental grounds. It seemed that two concepts had been merged into one – the need for access to Dublin Port and the separate, but related, need for an eastern by-pass of the city to cater for interaction between the north and south of Dublin. It was obvious that both of those problems would have to be solved, with due weight given to environmental considerations and to economic aspects of access to Dublin Port. It was essential that protection be given to jobs and living standards by ensuring that Ireland had an effective central sea corridor through Dublin to Britain. This required ease of access to Dublin Port and efficient sea services to connect with Holyhead and Liverpool, together with an efficient roads network out of those British ports, important to Irish traffic.

I suggested, in my address to a Fine Gael seminar in July 1990, that the question of access to Dublin Port should be separated from the question of an eastern by-pass and that a solution to the traffic problems of the port and the city could be found more effectively by treating them separately.

SUMMARY

◊ Ireland's national road network is the predominant mode of inland transport for passengers and freight. The poor condition of the national primary and secondary roads, including access to the principal ports and airports, imposed a significant cost burden on business and industry from the 1970s onwards and provoked a major campaign to achieve improvements.

◊ The campaign was a major factor leading to a significant increase in public investment in roads, including assistance from the EU, and to the establishment of the interim NRA in 1988, under my chairmanship.

◊ The European Commission placed an emphasis on the preparation of integrated transport programmes, including roads, rail, sea, and air, and on the transport programmes to overcome Ireland's problems of geographic peripherality.

◊ Other issues addressed by me during the period included a proposal for a Dublin Light Tramway system in 1990, issues relating to the Dublin Ring Road, and access to Dublin Port.

CHAPTER 8
KEEP IT CLEAN

MANAGEMENT OF INDUSTRIAL WASTE

Management of industrial waste was another major national infrastructure area that posed serious problems for Irish industry in the 1970s and 1980s and that, regretfully, continues to cause problems into the 21st century. Ireland industrialised rapidly since 1960, and was classified as a developed industrial economy by the United Nations (UN) in the 1980s. The industrialisation process was achieved by leap-frogging many of the stages experienced by other industrialised countries over the previous two centuries, avoiding most of the problems that others experienced and solved. Since 1960, the IDA had placed emphasis on attracting high technology, science-based industries with minimal adverse impact on the environment. The Institute for Industrial Research & Standards (IIRS) and AFF jointly assessed environmental aspects of all IDA-proposed industrial projects. The result of vigorous assessments was that there had been few industrial incidents of environmental damage or nuisance. In addition, the IDA ensured that modern pollution control equipment was installed in existing enterprises when those enterprises applied for grants for modernisation and re-equipment. In general terms, manufacturing industry, while it was a major discharger of effluent, was not a major cause of environmental pollution. That point was borne out in a national survey of air and water pollution in Ireland, commissioned by the IDA and under-taken by the IIRS, a summary of which was published in 1976 as a contribution to public knowledge of the subject.[1] The report gave the IDA some pointers to the areas where it was necessary to install modern pollution control equipment and procedures and to ways in which future industrial progress could be achieved at little or no risk to the natural environment.

I initiated the establishment of the CII Environment Policy Committee in November 1980, to advise the National Executive on all aspects of environmental protection. My initiative in this regard was informed partly by pioneering work in the area of environmental science, including water quality, done by colleagues in Sligo RTC (now the Institute of Technology,

Sligo) during my years as Principal of the College (1972-1979). Within the CII, one of the reasons for the establishment of the Environment Policy Committee was the concern of many industrialists at the absence of an adequate national waste disposal infrastructure, and at the absence of an informed political and public debate on the issue. Thirty-one local authorities operated tip-heads, but only 16 accepted industrial waste. In many cases, where facilities were available, the sponsoring local authorities described them as 'small', and only four tip-heads in the entire country had facilities for waste oil reception. Very few legal tip-heads were operated by the private sector, so that industrial waste disposal facilities were few in number and the distance travelled to a tip-head could be considerable. The absence of an adequate national network of tip-heads added to the cost of industrial waste disposal, due mainly to high transport costs.

A NATIONAL STRATEGY FOR WASTE DISPOSAL

Peter Barry TD, Minister for the Environment, announced a national strategy for waste disposal on 18 May 1981, with the following elements:

- A central depot and possible treatment facilities for industrial and other waste for which alternative acceptable means of disposal were not then available.
- Development of a network of co-disposal tips around the country at which industrial and other wastes could be accommodated satisfactorily; provision of financial support for local authorities for the upgrading of existing tips and for the acquisition and development of new ones for co-disposal use.
- Consideration of sea disposal services and, where appropriate, of local authority sewerage treatment plants for liquid wastes suitable for disposal by such means.
- Extension and improvement of tips to meet local needs for disposal of trade and domestic wastes to acceptable standards.
- Strengthening the powers of local authorities to control waste and to prosecute offenders; the undertaking of a new planning activity by the local authorities to promote proper waste disposal; and the implementation of the strategy as it affected their respective administrative areas.

The CII rejected the Minister's argument that legislation should be strengthened or enforced immediately and sought postponement of legislative change, pending the provision of the essential national infrastructure services essential to permit compliance.

On behalf of the CII Environment Policy Committee, I undertook an industrial waste management survey in summer 1981, to obtain feedback from industry on environmental issues covered by the national strategy for waste disposal of May 1981, and to identify issues for representations to Government and public authorities.

The major problem areas identified by enterprises were:

♦ The escalating cost of waste management, including disposal and storage.

♦ The inadequacy of approved dumping sites for various types of industrial waste, including solid waste.

♦ The absence of any facilities for the disposal of toxic waste.

♦ The enforcement of legislation and regulations in the absence of an adequate national network of public and private waste management facilities.

♦ The scarcity of recycling facilities, in particular for materials other than oil.

♦ The slow pace of development of a private sector waste management industry.

♦ The inadequacy of public awareness of environmental protection, and of the relationship between industrial development, job creation, and the environment.

♦ The absence of information about certain types of industrial waste produced in Ireland, with the consequential lack of information on how those wastes should be managed.

♦ The absence of appropriately-located and technologically-advanced public incineration facilities.

♦ The absence of facilities for the safe disposal of confidential documents.

The CII view, discussed with the Department of the Environment on an on-going basis, was that the other problems identified could be solved by the private sector, once the Government ensured the provision of a national network of public infrastructure facilities and once the general public was educated as to the social and economic importance to the community of industrial waste management.

A positive finding was that 85% of enterprises surveyed were recycling oil and a further 6% undertook the recycling of oil as a direct result of the survey, bringing the total to over 90% before the end of 1981. Recoverable solvents were recycled by about 75% of the enterprises, and solid industrial waste was recycled by almost 50%. The proportion of waste recycled was lowest for aqueous effluents, which were suitable for discharge to waters under the *Local Government (Water Pollution) Act 1977*, where the figure was slightly above 10%. In addition, more than 30% of the enterprises were considering the installation of recycling plants, the installation of incineration equipment or other methods of improving industrial waste management. The CII response to the national waste disposal strategy announced by the Minister for the Environment in May 1981, reflected the feedback from the survey.[2]

WASTE CONTRACTORS

Two serious structural deficiencies faced Irish industry relative to waste management. The first was an acute scarcity of public and private sector infrastructure facilities for waste disposal. The second was that waste management service providers generally had a poor image, were disorganised, and there was no mechanism for dialogue on key issues either with them or on their behalf. I held exploratory discussions with waste contractors and with officials in various public authorities in the autumn of 1981 with a view to assessing what could be done to improve the structure and organisation of the private sector waste management industry. There was unanimity among the waste contractors and the public officials that the provision of waste management services should be organised on a more formal and structured basis, in the interests of manufacturing industry, of the waste contractors and of the conservation and enhancement of the natural environment.

The outcome was that, on my initiative, the Irish Waste Contractors' Federation (the successor organisation within IBEC is the Irish Waste Management Association) was established within the CII to represent the interests of waste contractors, recycling contractors, manufacturers of equipment and suppliers of environmental protection services. The inaugural meeting of the Federation was held in Confederation House in February 1982.[3] One of the first actions of the Irish Waste Contractors' Federation was to agree a Code of Conduct for members.

ENVIRONMENTAL COSTS

The OECD first promulgated the 'polluter pays' principle in 1972,[4] and it was adopted in the EEC First Environmental Action Programme in 1973. Article 25 of the *Single European Act 1986* provides that action relative to the environment will be based on the principle 'that environmental damage should, as a priority, be rectified at source and that the polluter should pay.'

The polluter pays principle provoked much debate in Ireland, within the OECD and within the EEC in the 1970s and thereafter. Notwithstanding the varying interpretations of the principle, the reality was that some industries, because of the nature of their products and processes, necessarily invested heavily in pollution control installations and, for certain high technology industries, that investment could have been as much as 25% to 30% of the total investment in plant. That was a high proportion of overheads for a business to carry, as such investment did not directly generate revenue. Industry accepted that the maintenance and improvement of environmental quality was a benefit to the entire community, but the benefit needed to be related to the costs borne directly by the general community, in the form of higher production costs. Pollution control was a cost of production and entered directly into price. In the final analysis, it was the consumer who paid.

WATER RESOURCES

The availability of water resources was important not only for social and environmental reasons, but it also influenced industrial location decisions. The Water Pollution Advisory Council, which operated under the aegis of the Department of the Environment, was a statutory body appointed under the *Local Government (Water Pollution) Act 1977* to advise the Minister for the Environment on all aspects of water pollution. The Council was representative of industry, fishery, agricultural, scientific, conservation, professional, local authority, and other relevant interests, as well as of Government Departments and State-sponsored bodies. The CII was represented both on the Council and on its Executive Committee.

In summer 1982, the Water Pollution Advisory Council published an advisory booklet for industry.[5] The CII welcomed the publication, endorsed the guidelines recommended by the Council for the prevention of water pollution arising from industrial activity and widely promulgated the guidelines among member enterprises.[6]

The CII was vigilant to ensure that unnecessary costs were not placed on industry. To protect the interests of member enterprises, the CII made a submission to the Minister for the Environment in April 1982, on the question of any proposal under consideration by the Minister to authorise local authorities to introduce effluent discharge charging schemes.[7] Local authorities had power under the *Local Government (Water Pollution) Act 1977* to make charges for effluent discharge, provided that the Minister introduced regulations to that effect. No regulations were made up to autumn 1982, although the CII understood from the Department that the Minister had made a decision in principle to authorise such charges. Over and above any question of the introduction of charges for the discharge of effluent, a local authority could be authorised to charge for all or part of the costs incurred in monitoring a discharge of effluent. Regulations authorising a local authority to require certain payments relating to an application for a licence to discharge effluent, including the cost of investigations carried out concerning the application, had been made in 1978.[8]

In its submission to the Minister for the Environment, the CII emphasised that industrial development in some cases was hampered in the early 1980s because of the absence of adequate infrastructure facilities for the acceptance of essential effluent discharges from industry. The CII emphasised the inequity of charging industry alone for services that were supplied to all sectors of the community and emphasised that, in considering any proposals for additional charges on industry, account should be taken of the economic difficulties faced by industry and of the adverse impact on employment of introducing additional charges. Environmental limitations and the costs of meeting environmental controls needed to be fully justified against the need to protect jobs.

TOXIC & HAZARDOUS WASTE

EEC Regulations on toxic and dangerous or hazardous waste came into operation on 1 January 1983. The Regulations covered substances and materials, including arsenic, cadmium, cyanides, lead, mercury, chlorinated solvents, organic solvents, chemical laboratory materials, pharmaceutical compounds, soluble copper compounds, and acids, and affected many CII member enterprises, particularly in the chemical and allied industries.[9]

The 1982 Regulations established a mandatory permit system. Under that system, persons who treated, stored or deposited toxic and dangerous waste on their own behalf or on behalf of others required a permit. Thus, an entity that performed any function of treatment, storage, or disposal of toxic and dangerous waste needed to obtain the necessary permit from the relevant local authority. The CII advised member enterprises that, by law, the primary responsibility for proper disposal rested with the producer, and urged enterprises to familiarise themselves with their obligations, contact the appropriate local authority, and obtain the necessary permit.

Peter Barry TD, Minister for the Environment, as part of the national strategy to provide the necessary waste management infrastructure, announced a proposal to establish a National Centre for Hazardous Waste at Baldonnel, Co. Dublin, early in 1982. The plan was to use the facility, if provided, for the assembly of toxic and dangerous waste for export, and it was possible that treatment facilities would be available later. The CII welcomed the proposal when it was made, and subsequently actively pressed for the provision of the facility at an early date. In its 1982 and 1983 pre-Budget submissions to Government, the CII listed a number of areas where the private sector could be involved in the provision of public infrastructure and of public services, including waste disposal and treatment facilities.[10] The proposed National Centre for Hazardous Waste at Baldonnel did not proceed, due mainly to a strong local campaign against the proposal that succeeded in winning wider public and political support.

A further part of the strategy, outlined by Minister Peter Barry TD, was a request to the local authorities to provide a network of sites in their respective administrative areas where non-hazardous industrial waste could be deposited in conjunction with household waste. The CII welcomed that part of the strategy, but a decade later was still awaiting a progress report on what action, if any, had been taken by each of the local authorities.

JOINT STUDY WITH AN TAISCE

Responsibility for the Environment Policy Committee, established on my initiative in autumn 1981, was transferred to Dr Aidan O'Boyle, on his return to the CII in Dublin from the Irish Business Bureau in Brussels in 1986. In 1988, under his leadership, the CII Environment Policy Committee published a joint study with An Taisce entitled *Study on Industry & the Environment*. The introduction to the study, by the Minister for the Environment, Pádraig Flynn TD, welcomed the agreed statement of the principles for harmonising industrial development and environmental protection, made between representative bodies for industry and the environment.

The joint recommendations by the CII and An Taisce in 1988 showed that it was possible for industrialists and environmentalists to reach a consensus on issues of mutual interest. Sixteen recommendations were made, aimed at achieving more effective environmental planning. The CII noted that, for many enterprises, the new environmental obligations had not come as a surprise or as an imposition. Multinationals, in particular, accepted that the host country was obliged to set environmental standards for manufacturing companies; planning control was, therefore, invariably seen by industry as normal and necessary. Most modern industries themselves needed a good physical environment. Clean water and air were needed for processes, safe disposal sites were needed for waste, and the living conditions for the workforce, including management, needed to be environmentally acceptable and attractive.

The June 1990 meeting of the European Council at the Dublin Summit noted that, while completion of the European Single Market would provide a major impetus to economic development, a corresponding acceleration of effort was needed to ensure that the development was environmentally sound. The European Council warned on the need to counter, in particular, the environmental risks inherent in greater production and increased demand for transport, energy and infrastructure and emphasised that environmental considerations required effective integration into all relevant policy areas.

SUMMARY

◊ In 1981, the CII Environmental Policy Committee was established on my initiative to focus industry's concern for, and involvement in, environmental protection and enhancement.

◊ Industry welcomed the announcement by the Minister for the Environment of a national strategy for waste disposal in May 1981, but sought the provision of essential infrastructure services before strengthening enforcement legislation.

◊ A CII industry survey in May 1981 identified 10 problem areas relating to waste management, many of which could be solved by the private sector, subject to the provision by Government of the necessary public infrastructure facilities and to the education of the general public as to the social and economic importance to the community of industrial waste management.

◊ In 1982, the Irish Waste Contractors' Federation was established on my initiative, and one of its first actions was to agree a Code of Conduct for members.

◊ Industry pursued issues including the interpretation and enforcement of the 'polluter pays' principle; water pollution control; management of toxic and dangerous waste; and environmental costs to industry.

◊ In 1988, CII and An Taisce jointly agreed 16 recommendations aimed at achieving more effective environmental planning.

CHAPTER 9
SHARE IS FAIR

LOCAL TAXATION

The CII's views on participation and co-operation in the workplace were reflected also in its approach to subsidiarity in Government and to local democracy. The CII made common cause with the local authorities on issues such as enterprise development, housing, roads, the environment and local government finances.

It is not possible to focus adequately on the restructuring of local government without addressing the question of finance, with the related issue of local taxation. The CII participated in the preparation of the NESC Report *The Financing of Local Authorities* in 1985, and publicly supported its recommendations, including the introduction of a broadly-based property tax.[1] The introduction of such a tax, together with a corresponding *pro rata* reduction in personal taxation, could have brought a greater degree of equity into the tax system. The CII suggested that the property tax could be levied on the imputed income from the ownership of property, with liability consequently arising only if the taxpayer's total income, including the imputed income from property, exceeded tax-free allowances. The CII suggested that the introduction of such a tax did not necessarily require a separate tax collection mechanism. In Switzerland, for example, the individual taxpayer received a single annual tax assessment, and the tax payable was divided on a statutory basis between the three levels of government: the commune; the canton; and the Federal Government. The Swiss system had the added advantage that it automatically took into account the taxpayer's ability to pay, with net tax payable only if the taxpayer's income, including the imputed income from property, exceeded the taxpayer's tax credits and allowances. The introduction of the tax would be accompanied by the immediate abolition of the residential property tax.[1]

---

[1]   A Fine Gael / Labour Party Government introduced the Residential Property Tax (RPT) in the Finance Act 1983. It was a self-assessed tax of 1.5% on the excess of the market value of all residential properties owned by a person over an exemption limit and was

While the Council of the NESC favoured the principle of a property tax, there was some disagreement among interest groups as to the precise coverage of tax. The agreement of the ICTU was subject to the principle of the tax being applicable, as recommended by the consultants who prepared the report, to all property, including farmland. The IFA, however, vigorously expressed the view that farmland constituted the basis of production in agriculture and, therefore, should not be subjected to a property tax.

The *Fourth Report of the Commission on Taxation: Special Taxation* was published in May 1985. The Report covered local taxation, *inter alia*. In July 1985, in a submission to the Minister for Finance, Alan Dukes TD, the CII urged the Government to address immediately the question of funding local authorities.[2] It was essential that the question of funding local authorities be addressed in the context of the overall burden of taxation at national and local levels, both direct and indirect. Subject to the overall issues being resolved by Government, if there were to be a system of direct funding for the services of local authorities, then the CII urged the Government to adopt a broadly-based approach related to a just and equitable apportionment of the aggregate cost of the provision of local services, with no exemptions as to types of property to which services were provided. The CII envisaged that the base for funding local services would include all land, domestic dwellings, farms, factories, commercial premises, industrial premises, and every other type of property, the possession and occupation of which placed demands on the services of the local authorities. The CII believed that the objective should be to ensure that all who used the services of local authorities should make an equitable contribution towards the funding of those services. The CII stressed that its support for the main thrust of the recommendation was given on the strict understanding that there would be no increase in the overall national tax burden at all levels of public administration.

THE CASE FOR LOCAL DEMOCRACY

In a talk to the General Council of County Councils in 1986, I advocated three fundamental principles: first, the merits of the Swiss model of government, both in terms of a comprehensive range of societal

---

payable subject to the household income exceeding an income exemption limit, set in the annual Finance Act. The Fianna Fáil / Progressive Democrats Government abolished the RPT in the *Finance Act 1997*.

governance issues and of the Swiss three-tier system of public finances;[3] second, a wider role for the local authorities in constructing 'affordable' homes for those on local authority waiting lists, including construction on dormant land banks then held by many local authorities, and joint venture house construction with the private sector; and third, the introduction in Ireland of a scheme of shared equity home ownership, under which a purchaser could move in stages towards full ownership over a number of years. Five years later, a shared equity / ownership scheme was introduced.[1] My 1986 suggestions on housing received contemporaneous favourable media attention, as did the suggestion about a wider economic development role for the local authorities.[4]

In the period 1985 to 1989, the CII published a series of nine articles in support of the policy for autonomous local government. There followed in September 1990 a submission to the Advisory Expert Committee on Local Government Reorganisation & Reform, appointed by Pádraig Flynn TD, Minister for the Environment.[5] The submission dealt with issues such as the principle of subsidiarity, local government structures, local taxation, regional authorities, and key questions relating to reform.

In general, the CII favoured devolution to the greatest possible extent to that level of government closest to the delivery of a service. This was the operating principle of the relationship between the European Commission and Member State governments, and it was the norm for the relationship between Government and regional and local authorities in many European countries.

The economic difficulties experienced by Ireland in the 1980s should have served as a stimulus for Government to undertake a fundamental reappraisal of the role of local authorities and of their financing. The CII offered to play its part with Government and with the local authorities to try to work out the best ways in which essential services could be provided in a cost-effective manner and how those services could be financed. The public authorities at national and local levels did not take up that offer.

One practical reason why the business community was concerned with the financing of local authorities was because the business community alone, in both the private and the State commercial sectors, paid local authority rates. The assessment of rates on domestic dwellings ceased after

---

[1]   Pádraig Flynn TD, Minister for the Environment, introduced shared equity ownership (Shared Ownership Scheme) in the *Plan for Social Housing 1991*. A number of schemes were initiated subsequently to facilitate the building of affordable homes on sites owned by local authorities.

1977. Such rates were subsequently paid by grants from the Exchequer to the local authorities. The Supreme Court in 1984 declared that the basis used for the calculation of the rateable valuation of agricultural land was unconstitutional.

The issue of payment of rates by the business community alone led to a campaign by the CII against the terms of the *Valuation Bill* published in March 1985. The history of that campaign, and of its outcome, was published in a number of *CII Newsletters*, both before and after the enactment of the *Valuation Act 1986*.[6]

IN PRAISE OF BUCHANAN

Balanced regional development was another aspect of subsidiarity and local democracy advocated by the CII. By way of background, the first comprehensive attempt to produce a regional development policy in Ireland was in October 1966, when the UN, at the request of the Government, commissioned a report on *Regional Development in Ireland*.[7] This, the *Buchanan Report*, researched the prospects in agriculture, other natural resource-based industries, tourism, transport, public utilities and manufacturing industry. The report examined economic development at four levels: the National Capital; the National Framework; Regional; and Local. Having assessed alternatives, the Report recommended:

♦ Dublin as the national capital.
♦ Two designated national growth centres in Cork and Limerick / Shannon, intended for significant development to counterbalance what was recognised by Buchanan as the proportionately-excessive growth of Dublin relative to the rest of the State.
♦ Six regional growth centres in Athlone, Dundalk, Drogheda, Galway, Sligo and Waterford.
♦ Three local growth centres in Castlebar, Letterkenny and Tralee.

Following the Buchanan Report, Regional Development Organisations (RDOs) were established during 1968-1969. Additionally, under the *Industrial Development Act 1969*, the IDA formally was given a regional remit, leading to the publication of the *IDA Regional Industrial Plans 1973-1977*.

The conclusions of the Buchanan Report remain relevant. Despite various spatial planning initiatives and programmes to decentralise elements of the public service, there is still a need to develop viable counterpoles to Dublin not only for economic development reasons, but also for pressing social reasons, such as the availability and price of serviced land for housing, traffic congestion, and drive times to work. Buchanan observed:

'Cork, the second city of the Republic, with its port, airport, industry, commerce and social facilities is well placed to become one of the proposed two new major centres, and so also is Limerick, third city in population and range of facilities, with the thriving industrial estate and international airport nearby at Shannon. We propose that the development of both should be pressed vigorously, for example, by the provision of industrial estates with advance factories and a high standard of services and by the provision of additional housing and social facilities. There is also a strong case for the construction of a motorway link to Dublin. In this way, we believe, that they can become points of major growth, offering economic and social opportunities which could not otherwise be created outside Dublin.'

Post-Buchanan, a variation on the theme of growth-centre development was followed in practice, although no Government formally adopted or implemented the Buchanan Report. The IDA strategy for the decentralisation of manufacturing industry conformed to a regional development template. Shannon Development and Udarás na Gaeltachta worked towards the achievement of a more balanced geographic spread of industry, each within its own quite narrowly-designated geographic area.

Although the Government announced in 1972 that it intended to adopt an overall regional policy for the following 20 years, little of major substance happened between 1972 and 1985, with the exception of proposals by the short-lived Department of Economic Planning & Development, 1977-1980, which included a policy decision to decentralise some sections of the Civil Service. The approach to regional planning by Government and the IDA had been largely one of endeavouring to increase manufacturing employment in the regions. The virtual neglect of a policy for the strategically-structured decentralisation of high quality services employment, with the possible exception of the development of internationally-traded services at Shannon Airport, has been a major weakness.

The CII's view on the need for balanced regional development was formulated following publication of an Eastern Regional Development Organisation (ERDO) report of 1985.[8] The ERDO study highlighted the problems posed by urbanisation and particularly by over-concentration of population and economic activity in the East Region, which contained 23% of the population of the State at the Census of 1926. This grew to about 33% by 1961, and the East Region in the mid 1980s contained almost 40% of the national population.

The CII's view was that the ERDO study was excellent and served as a warning to Government as to what would happen unless the Government adopted an explicit policy for regional development and ensured implementation of that policy. This view was given in my keynote address at a conference in Limerick in November 1986, the proceedings of which were later published.[9] The conference was organised by the Mid-West RDO to mark the decision by Government to abolish the RDOs. Senator Michael Smith, a participant at the conference, who subsequently held Ministries for Energy, Environment, Education, and Defence, as well as a number of posts as Minister of State, supported my views on the pressing need for balanced regional development.

In CII's view, Ireland's search for a more successful economic development model in the mid-1980s needed to focus on comparisons with small successful countries. These included Austria, Denmark, Finland, Sweden and Switzerland, most of which combined economic success with a high degree of decentralisation of Government. Denmark, for example, which in 1985 earned the highest national output per head of population in the EEC, followed a pattern of administrative decentralisation throughout the 1970s, beginning with the establishment of boundary changes and new local authorities in April 1970. By 1986, Denmark, in addition to central Government, had 273 local authorities, and 14 regional authorities for a population of about 5.2 million. Each level of government had its own autonomous system of financing.

In my view, the main reason for the absence of a more robust approach to balanced regional development in Ireland is the dominant position of central Government, the absence of structured regional authorities and the narrow remit of the local authorities. I believe that the system of national taxation and the absence of any meaningful system of broadly-based taxing powers for other public authorities is the root cause of the problem.

In the late 1980s, the focus of the European Commission was on the preparation of integrated programmes that drew together plans for support from each of the EEC Structural Funds: the ERDF, the ESF, and the European Agricultural Guarantee & Guidance Fund (FEOGA).[10] The Taoiseach, Charles J Haughey TD, in an address to the CII in 1988, stated that a Steering Committee had been established to agree terms of reference for a study, and to supervise the preparation and implementation of a programme for the Dublin region.[11] Business interests were included on the Steering Committee. The Taoiseach stated that there would be studies and programmes for the Cork region, the Mid-West region, and the West region, and that it was intended, in time, to take a similar approach in all regions. He added that the national roads network and the natural gas grid were being structured to enhance the potential for regional development.

THE MID-WEST REGION

In relation to the Mid-West region, my public intervention on the future of Shannon Airport in 1991 was reported widely in the national and local media.[12] The intervention came in a talk at the University of Limerick, intended by me in response to a high profile campaign by the Dublin Chamber of Commerce and others to have direct US flights into Dublin *in lieu* of the continued designation of Shannon Airport as the transatlantic gateway to Ireland. I expressed the view that the political and public debate about the 'status' of Shannon Airport placed too narrow a focus on perceived conflicts of interest between Dublin and Shannon, relative to transatlantic air traffic. In my view, the debate failed to recognise the success of Shannon Development in terms of balanced regional development or to give sufficient weight to the pivotal role of Shannon Airport in the Mid-West and as a gateway for tourism along the entire Western Coast. I perceived a new and enhanced role for Shannon in a national context in the Single European Market, and the inevitable shift of the economic centre of gravity in Europe to the centre and the east following changes in the former socialist republics. Shannon could play a national role of *strategic centrality* as a hub between North America and Continental Europe. I sought to change the focus of debate to one of enhancing the role of Shannon in a regional, national and European Community context.

SUMMARY

◊ In 1985, the NESC recommended the introduction of a broadly-based property tax to finance the local authorities, but there was disagreement between the social partners on the coverage of the tax. In the same year, the Commission on Taxation recommended the introduction of such a tax, subject to no increase in the overall burden of taxation on the community.

◊ In many papers between 1985 and 1989, I advocated greater autonomy for local government, similar to the structure of government in Switzerland and some other small successful economies.

◊ CII advocated a greater role for local authorities in constructing affordable homes, mainly for persons on public waiting lists and in the operation of shared equity / ownership schemes.

◊ Throughout the 1980s, I advocated balanced regional development along the lines of the *Buchanan Report*, 1968.

◊ In 1991, I publicly advocated an enhanced role for Shannon Airport in a regional and national context, including as a hub between North America and Continental Europe.

CHAPTER 10
THE MONEY ILLUSION

INFLATION EXPLAINED

Industry was concerned at the high level of Irish cost and price inflation in the early 1980s and at the consequences for business competitiveness on domestic and export markets. To help promote an understanding of the nature and impact of inflation, the CII commissioned a book on the subject that was distributed widely, including to post-primary schools.[1] Subsequently, on my initiative, the CII commissioned a brief animated film, with commentary, on the subject of inflation.[2] The background was that rising prices, growing unemployment and falling living standards were problems of everyday life in Ireland in the early 1980s. Despite the urgency of finding a solution to the problems, technical jargon and a constant stream of economic statistics induced bewilderment and a sense of helplessness in the general community. The objective of the film was to relate the working of the national economy to everyday life and to show that the solution to pressing national economic problems lay mainly in Irish hands. Scenes from working life and the lives of consumers were interspersed with animated graphics to illustrate basic economic principles. The film portrayed the national economy as no more or no less than the aggregate of the aspirations, attitudes and efforts of individuals. Human behaviour, rather than technical jargon, was both the material and the message of the film. After looking at the helplessness and gloom that surrounded the subject in contemporary political and media debate, the film revealed the positive message that lay just beneath the surface. Ireland had the resources necessary to overcome the economic difficulties of the early 1980s, and could generate more jobs and higher living standards, provided the community worked in partnership towards that objective.

The film was shown to a broad spectrum of Irish society, and was aired on RTÉ 1 television during the week before the 1984 Budget.

The following graph puts Ireland's inflation in a historic context and displays the annual percentage increase in the CPI in each year from 1961 to 2007.

Graph 10.1: Annual Inflation 1961-2007

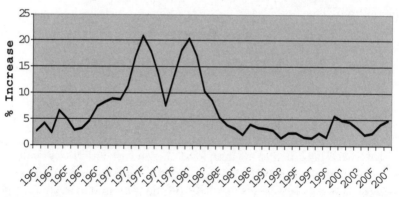

Source: *Budget & Economic Statistics*, Department of Finance, various years.

The graph shows inflation rising sharply in the years immediately following Ireland's entry to the EEC, from the already high level of 8.7% in 1972 to 20.9% in 1975. It then fell over the next three years to 7.6% in 1978, rose sharply to reach 20.4% in 1981 and fell continuously over the next seven years to 2.1% in 1988. Inflation increased again to 4% in 1989 and fell thereafter to reach the lowest level for the entire period, 1.5%, in 1993 (repeated in 1997 and almost equalled at 1.6% in 1996 and 1999). Inflation rose sharply to 5.6% in the year 2000, the highest level since 1985. It then fell steadily in each year to 2004, after which it began to rise again.

FUELLING THE FLAMES

Chapter 3 records that the seeds of the disastrous spiral of Government current borrowing were sown in the 1972 Budget.[3] The Minister for Finance was conscious that he was taking the risk of '... fuelling the fire of inflation rather than the engine of growth'. The Minister added that '... there should be a widespread acceptance of the need to redouble our efforts to check price and cost inflation'. In reference to the boost that the current Budget deficit gave to the economy, the Minister warned against allowing '... the additional purchasing power to be eroded through continuing inflation'. Instead, the Minister urged that the national aim be '... a worthwhile reduction in the rate of increase in costs and prices'. He pointed out that, in 1972, for the first time since 1959, prices would not be increased because of changes in taxation, and he urged that this contribution by Government to price stability be matched by 'a positive response' from employers and trade unions through the next National Pay Agreement. The Minister linked a low inflation regime to increasing employment and growth, and he gave the warning that:

> 'Without the co-operation of employers and employees, these objectives will be frustrated and the external deficit, which in any event is likely to increase substantially, could well be pushed to such a level that corrective measures would be unavoidable.'

In the event, Irish inflation in the years 1971-1977, at an annual average of 14%, was the highest among our trading partners in the EEC. While there was a welcome drop in 1978, the upward spiral began again in 1979.

The CII *Annual Reports* for each year from 1979 to 1987, inclusive, made significant reference to inflation and related issues. The *Annual Reports* for the years 1980 to 1983 show the extent to which high inflation was crippling manufacturing industry. Michael McStay, in his 1980 CII *President's Report*, focused on inflation as the top priority issue against the background that 1980 saw a reversal of the fortunes of Irish industry. Manufacturing output declined by 2% compared with the previous year, and manufacturing employment fell by about 5,000. McStay acknowledged the adverse impact of international recession on industrial output. He pointed out, however, that significant blame lay with the high rate of cost inflation since Ireland joined the EMS in early 1979. In his 1981 *Annual Report*, he noted the falling inflation rates in many of Ireland's international competitor countries, while Irish inflation was running at around 20% *per annum*. The excess of imports over exports rose from 23% in 1977 to 36% in 1981, and the deficit on the international balance of payments amounted to 13% of GNP. McStay called for the adoption of consistent incomes, fiscal and monetary policies so that competitiveness could be improved, inflation reduced, the value of the Irish currency protected and employment expanded.

Dr TP Hardiman, in the 1982 CII *President's Report*, welcomed the fall in inflation by about 3% from the 1981 out-turn of 20.4%. He pointed out, however, that inflation at just over 17% in 1982 was significantly in excess of the rate of price increases in nearly all of Ireland's trading partners. Irish manufacturers were severely damaged by the excessive level of inflation. As an example, Hardiman mentioned that the output price index of manufacturing industry rose by only 2.5% in the second six months of 1982 which, when compared to the rate of increase in costs, disclosed the very severe price / cost gap faced by many Irish manufacturers. Imported inflation contributed only 4% to the 1982 Irish inflation rate of 17.1%; indeed, in the final few months of 1982, import prices had stopped rising.

The picture was brighter when Hardiman came to present his 1983 *President's Report*. The rate of inflation was down to 10.5% and was expected to fall still further in 1984. Ireland's international balance of payments had improved remarkably, and he expressed the hope that 1983 marked the end of a period of deep economic recession, both in Ireland and internationally. Unemployment, however, was still rising, albeit at a slower rate. His conclusion is interesting in the context that it took a further four years before the economic turning point was finally reached:

> 'We can report progress in some areas in 1983, but we are a long way from achieving our desired objective of creating in Ireland the kind of internationally-competitive economy which will promote the rapid growth of industry and which will achieve the solution of our social and economic problems.'

The 1985 *Annual Report* records that Ireland's inflation gap with the EEC average was closed during that year. By the end of 1985, the interest rate differential between Ireland and the EEC average was reduced to about 1%, Ireland's balance of international trade moved into surplus, retail sales showed modest growth, and the rise in unemployment appeared to be slowing down. Nevertheless, Liam Connellan, the CII Director General, recorded in his *Annual Report* for that year that many problems remained.

Connellan's *Annual Report* for 1986 noted the continued fall in inflation as a key feature of the year. Average inflation throughout 1986 fell from 5.4% in 1985 to 3.8%, on a downward slope that started the year with a rate of 4.6% and ended with 3.2%. The Irish rate of inflation was, however, still 1% higher than the EEC average due to more rapidly falling inflation in some other Member States. Side-by-side with the fall in inflation, there was a continued improvement in Ireland's current account balance of payments deficit from 3.5% of GNP in 1985 to an estimated 1.2% in 1986.

Terry Larkin, the CII President, recorded in his 1987 *Annual Report* that the year '... brought a marked and welcome return of confidence to our economy'. He noted the reduction in inflation as one of the significant features. Liam Connellan, in his 1988 *Annual Report*, noted that the business climate remained favourable that year, with inflation falling to 2.1%, its lowest level in almost three decades.

Dr Dermot Whelan, the CII President, in his 1989 *Annual Report* expressed some concern at the rapid increase in consumer spending, particularly in the purchases of motorcars, and expressed the view of industry that, if sustained, it could lead to a resumption of inflationary pressures. Inflation did not, however, rank as a major issue in the CII *Annual Reports* in the remaining years of CII as a separate organisation up to 1993.

GOVERNMENT & INFLATION

Throughout the years of high inflation, the CII consistently called on Government to recognise the problem and its consequences, and to take corrective action. In the early years, the CII warnings about the social and economic damage of high inflation went unheeded; in some instances, the CII was criticised by politicians and by some interest groups for raising the issue.

The CII's pre-Budget submission for 1982 expressed serious concern at the level of Government current borrowing and made a number of recommendations for the control of Government spending programmes.[4] In the context of fuelling inflation, the CII made special reference to the need to freeze the total public sector pay bill that had grown at a phenomenal rate, particularly in the previous three years. The following table illustrated the extent of the problem.

Table 10.1: Pay Increases & the CPI, 1979-1981

Year	Public Sector Pay Bill %	Weekly Earnings in Manufacturing Industry %	Consumer Price Index %
1979	25	15	13
1980	34	18	18
1981	22	15	20

The situation continued to deteriorate and the CII's pre-Budget submission 1983 listed inflation and competitiveness as the first of three issues under the heading *The Government's Financial Crisis*.[5] The other headings were profitability and investment and the current account international balance of payments, the latter then seen by the CII to have reached an unsustainably high level.

The CII's view was that:

'The rapid growth in public expenditure for current purposes and capital projects which do not yield an adequate return, has been financed by foreign borrowing, and has increased inflation by stimulating domestic demand beyond the capacity of the productive sectors to support it. This has led to a cost and price spiral, which has made Ireland the highest inflation country in the EEC.'

The following table provides the statistical evidence:

Table 10.2: EEC Annual Inflation %, 1971-1981

Country	1971-77	1978	1979	1980	1981
Belgium	8.3	4.5	4.5	6.6	7.6
Denmark	9.5	10.1	9.6	12.4	11.7
France	9.0	9.3	10.7	13.6	13.4
Germany	5.6	2.7	4.1	5.5	5.9
Ireland	14.0	7.6	13.2	18.2	20.4
Italy	13.1	12.2	14.8	21.2	19.5
Netherlands	8.3	4.2	4.3	6.5	6.7
UK	13.9	8.3	13.4	18.0	11.9

The CII observed that, when currency realignments were taken into account, Ireland's comparative situation was even worse, with an increase in costs and prices of 30% since 1979, relative to trading partners in the EMS. The financing of high levels of consumption through borrowing created a climate that fuelled increases in domestic costs. Wage costs, in particular, stimulated by high public sector pay settlements, and unrealistic expectations financed by recourse to personal borrowing, continued to grow at exceptionally high rates in comparison with those of major trading partners. The CII pointed out that further inflationary aspects of the financial crisis arose from the need to levy higher indirect taxes, which had boosted consumer price inflation by about 10% in the previous two years and, in turn, had increased the pressure on wage demands. In addition, costs levied on the productive sectors by way of increased oil, electricity, postal and other charges, as well as through various taxation increases, significantly reduced the funds that should have been retained in enterprises as working capital to maintain and expand production.

The CII concluded that, as a direct result of higher inflation and higher wage costs than those of international trading partners, there was a substantial loss of competitiveness of Irish goods on both domestic and export markets. This militated against the creation of long-term sustainable employment for the increasing labour force.

The CII's pre-Budget submission for 1984 urged Government action to reduce inflation, on the grounds that very high rates of inflation relative to Ireland's main trading partners over the previous five years had led to a substantial erosion in the international competitiveness of Irish goods and services, to loss of home and export markets, and to job losses.[6]

The situation improved during the following year and the CII in its pre-Budget submission for 1986 noted:[7]

> 'The inflation gap with the EEC average, which was 2.5% in 1984, was closed in 1985. The elimination of the inflation gap with the rest of Europe is now beginning to have a favourable impact on the output of many of the traditional sectors of Irish industry, which had been in continuous decline since 1980.'

The CII, in its pre-Budget submission for 1989, noted among the steps taken by the Government to improve the environment for enterprise, that inflation, then at an annual rate of about 2%, was significantly below the EC average and that interest rates were in line with ECU rates.[8] The CII welcomed the growth in manufacturing output, together with the consequential increase in employment, shown in the Central Statistics Office (CSO) *Labour Force Survey* of mid-April 1988. The out-turn for 1988 was that employment rose by 1% and exports increased by 8.7% in volume, in contrast to a 3.9% increase in imports, so that there was a surplus on both the balance of trade and the balance of payments.

The reappearance of inflationary pressures during 1989 was a matter of concern against the background of Ireland's past inflation rates being consistently higher than the EC average.[9] The trend prompted the CII to return to the issue of inflation with the publication of the following table (**Table 10.3**).[10]

The CII noted that Ireland's inflation rate in the 12 months to mid-August 1989 was 4.5%, more than double that for the previous 12 months. The Irish rate contrasted with rates in the Netherlands of 1.1%, Germany 3%, Belgium 3% and France 3.5%. Even high inflation countries such as Denmark dropped from 4.8% to 4.5%, while the UK dropped from 8.3% to 7.3%.

Table 10.3: Annual Inflation %: Ireland & the EMS, 1979-1988

Year	Ireland	EMS Narrow Band
1979	13.2	7.3
1980	18.2	9.9
1981	20.4	10.6
1982	17.1	9.7
1983	10.4	7.1
1984	8.6	5.7
1985	5.4	4.2
1986	3.9	1.7
1987	3.2	1.6
1988	2.1	1.9

Source: Derived from the *OECD Economic Outlook, No. 45,* June 1989.

When making its 1991 pre-Budget submission, the CII acknowledged the significant progress made under the PNR in terms of strong economic growth, including low inflation relative to the EC average and to the main trading partners.[11] The CII recommended that a major focus of public policy be to maintain inflation at a very low level and acknowledged that a continuation of the policies being pursued under the PNR would have led to Irish inflation below 3% in 1991 but that the international situation had changed dramatically because of the Gulf crisis of autumn 1990, with adverse knock-on effects on energy availability and energy pricing. In the latter context, the CII urged Government to stabilise its total Exchequer receipts from the taxation of petroleum products rather than fuel further increases in prices through the *pro rata* taxation of the higher-priced petroleum imports. The CII's view was that international developments reinforced the need for even greater domestic discipline relative to business cost inputs and public expenditure. International developments brought sharply into focus the need for greater emphasis on reductions in indirect taxes as a contribution to counterbalancing international inflationary trends. It was vital, in an international trade context, to maintain Ireland's relative advantage of low inflation. The CII pointed out that there was scope to do this within the framework of the movement towards indirect tax harmonisation within the European Community.

In its 1992 pre-Budget submission, the CII urged Government to continue to take all necessary steps within its control to ensure the continuation of low inflation in Ireland.[12] The CII acknowledged the progress made over the previous number of years, which resulted in achieving and maintaining one of the lowest inflation regimes in the EC. The CII urged that indirect taxation be kept as low as possible consistent with EC regulations and that Government-controlled business input costs be kept at or below those of international competitor countries.

INTEREST RATES

The CII expressed serious concern at the interest rate increase of 2% announced by the Associated Banks in March 1982.[13] That brought the commercial bank interest rate to 19% and, in the absence of remedial action, it would have imposed on manufacturing industry an additional cost of IR£22 million (€28 million), equal to the working capital required by manufacturing to maintain about 3,500 people in employment. The Irish three months interbank rate was almost 20%, in contrast to some major competitor countries, such as The Netherlands 9.4%, Federal Republic of Germany 10.0%, UK 13.7%, Belgium 13.8%, and France 15.0%.

The CII contended that, in order to be competitive on domestic and international markets, Irish enterprises needed access to funds at rates available in the main competitor markets. Two established mechanisms enabled the sector to achieve that objective. These were the Exchange Rate Guarantee Scheme and Tax-Based Lending under Section 84 of the *Corporation Tax Act 1976*. The Exchange Rate Guarantee Scheme is revisited later in this Chapter. The other mechanism, Section 84 lending, enabled the benefits of the capital allowances to be set directly against bank profits, and the resultant tax saving to the banks was passed on to the manufacturing sector as low cost finance. CII believed that there was scope to further extend that scheme to the benefit of the productive sectors of the economy. CII believed that action by Government was vital, as the IDA had indicated early in 1982 that about 350 manufacturing enterprises were at risk and needed help to reduce costs and sustain output in what were exceptionally difficult trading circumstances.

The situation continued to deteriorate and the CII's 1984 pre-Budget submission contended that, based on the total credit outstanding in February, 1983, Irish manufacturing industry had to pay an additional IR£50 million (€63.5 million) in interest charges in the previous year in contrast to what would have been paid on average in the main competitor countries.[14] The interest rate disadvantage suffered by Irish business was 4% at the beginning of September, 1983, when the CII submission for 1984 was drafted. Over and above core interest rates set by international conditions, rates in Ireland were raised as a direct consequence of high Irish inflation rates. The CII urged the Government not to directly add to inflationary pressures through additional Budgetary and other fiscal impositions.

The NESC published an in-depth financial study that included the financing of indigenous Irish manufacturing industry in 1984.[15] The CII gave extracts from this study in a *Newsletter* of December 1984, including the conclusions and recommendations relating to the financial institutions; the Stock Exchange; the personal investor; the regulation of financial institutions; and the State as a source of finance.

The CII prefaced the extracts from the NESC Report with an assessment of Irish interest rates.[16] Three points of significance were:

♦ 'The recent increase in interest rates will have a serious impact on manufacturing industry. The increase will bear particularly heavily on firms supplying the home market.'

♦ 'The main reason for the increase in Irish interest rates when international rates are falling is the extent of public sector borrowing. The blunt fact must be faced that the public sector overhead is so high that it is now stifling the expansion of industry. Public sector borrowing is crowding out the private sector, whether corporate or individual, and, in the process, is forcing the contraction, and sometimes the closure, of manufacturing firms.'

♦ 'Irish interest rates are much higher than in our main competing countries. The three month interbank rate in Ireland is now over five percentage points higher than in Britain and the US, and nine percentage points higher than in Germany.'

In its pre-Budget submission for 1986, the CII welcomed the progress achieved during the previous year in a number of areas that impacted on the climate for industrial development. In particular, because of the reduction in the inflation gap with the EEC average, the disparity between Irish and European interest rates, which was 3% in 1984, was reduced to 1% at the end of 1985.

Despite the improvement in inflation, Irish interest rates remained high and this obliged the CII, in January 1987, to take a strong stand on the impact that high interest rates were having on unemployment.[17] The CII pointed out that, although Irish inflation was in line with the EC average, Irish interest rates were much higher than in competitor countries in Europe. CII estimated that the exceptionally high interest rates represented a cost penalty of about IR£80 million (€101.6 million) *per annum* on Irish enterprises, equivalent to the sum required to pay the annual wages of 8,000 employees.

After the 1987 General Election, a week before the new Government took office on 10 March, the CII called on Government to work with industry to ensure that industrial input costs were brought into line with those of international competitors in an effort to help to solve the grave problem of rapid deterioration of cost competitiveness, which resulted in loss of markets, enterprise closures, and job losses in the 1980s.[18] The CII listed eight cost areas directly influenced by Government, and placed interest rates in first place. The CII message to Government about interest rates was:

> 'Irish interest rates are astronomically high in real terms. The small Irish business is currently paying about 17% for borrowed money; this is somewhat double the EEC average, more than three times the rate of return on a public infrastructure project as required by the Department of Finance, and around five times the rate of inflation.'

In June 1987, the CII again emphasised the urgency of achieving a significant cut in interest rates.[19] The CII calculated that additional cost burdens in terms of interest rates, some telecommunications charges, postal charges, transport, some energy charges, and liability insurance premiums imposed a cost penalty of more than IR£200 million (€254 million) *per annum* on manufacturing industry. Interest rates alone accounted for about 20% of the total cost penalty under the six headings. The CII view was that the reduction in Exchequer borrowing by about 2.3% of GNP in the March 1987 Budget, the Government policy to maintain a stable exchange rate within the EMS, and the return of business confidence, set the preconditions for a return to growth in productive investment. The excessively high level of interest rates was the single most serious constraint on making investment decisions, without which there could be no growth in economic output, employment and living standards.

The CII's 1988 pre-Budget submission recorded that the reduction in Exchequer spending during 1987 had a significant influence in reducing interest rates from 14% to 9%.[20] The CII concluded that the continued application of strict financial discipline would ensure that the gap between Irish interest rates and the ECU rate, then between 1.5% and 2%, could be eliminated.

In its 1991 pre-Budget submission, the CII sought that Government intensify policy initiatives to achieve a further convergence of Irish real interest rates towards the most favourable interest rate levels in the narrow-band EMS countries.[21] The CII sought the abolition of the arbitrary and discriminatory Bank Levy, which was contrary to EC competition policy rules, together with the removal of regulatory anomalies that placed Irish banks at a competitive disadvantage relative to other European banks. The CII referenced an acknowledgement by Albert Reynolds TD, Minister for Finance, of the disproportionately heavy burden of interest rate increases on small business enterprises and personal borrowers, in his address to the International Monetary Fund (IMF) and the World Bank in 1990.[22]

In its 1992 pre-Budget submission, the CII complained that, notwithstanding Ireland's position as one of the lowest inflation economies of the EC for a number of years, Irish interest rates were consistently higher than in some of the other narrow-band economies of the Exchange Rate Mechanism (ERM) of the EMS.[23] The CII recommended that everything possible be done by Government to ensure that the risk premium element of interest rates in Ireland be reduced to a minimum. The CII urged that an objective of Government's budgetary strategy be to ensure that real interest rates in Ireland were significantly reduced in a manner consistent with the policies of the ERM of the EMS.

BORROW ABROAD!

Currency exchange rates were extremely important for a small open economy where exports and imports, combined, significantly exceeded GDP in value. In 1979, Government stated its objective of maintaining the value of the Irish currency against its EMS partners. The CII responded in October 1979, by asking Government to recognise that the cost to industry of covering the exchange risk inherent in foreign borrowings would bring the cost of interest plus exchange risk cover back to the high cost of borrowing in Ireland.[24] It sought that Government underwrite the exchange risk for industry, and pointed out that the cost to the Exchequer would be zero, if the Irish currency maintained its value against EMS currencies, in accordance with Government policy. The Minister of State at the Department of Finance, Pearse Wyse TD, speaking in Dáil Éireann on behalf of the Tánaiste and Minister for Finance, George Colley TD, in December 1979, stated:[25]

> 'I have recently authorised the Industrial Credit Company Ltd to negotiate foreign borrowings in EMS currencies so that it can continue to meet the high level of demand by industry for investment funds ... No exchange risk will arise for the ultimate borrower; the risk will be borne by the Exchequer in return for regular payments to it by the company.'

The President of the CII, Edmund Williams, in the *Annual Report 1979*, made reference to the international pressures and problems of adjustment to the EMS that resulted in a significant increase in interest rates for industry in 1979. He said that these high interest rates, together with the slow down in international trade, resulted in a large number of enterprises cutting back on working capital to seek to survive. Williams added that relatively few projects remained economically viable when the cost of funds exceeded 20% *per annum*, as it had done for most of the previous year. He went on to say that the Central Bank of Ireland had indicated its desire that industry should seek additional funds abroad. The CII President observed that while this was valid for economically-viable projects, when the cost of foreign exchange risk cover was added, industry was still faced with high borrowing costs. For this reason, the CII Director General, Liam Connellan, throughout 1979 and the first half of 1980, continued to urge the Government to underwrite an exchange rate guarantee scheme for manufacturing industry for the duration of the transition period while Ireland was adapting to the fiscal discipline imposed by membership of the EMS.

The issue was debated at length in Dáil Éireann in April 1980, following the announcement by the four Associated Banks of significant increases in their lending and deposit interest rates.[26] The Minister for Finance, Michael O'Kennedy TD, made reference to loans for investment by small and medium-sized enterprises available at attractive rates of interest from the EIB through the Industrial Credit Corporation (ICC), with the Exchequer carrying the exchange risk, and a similar scheme for agri-business available through the Agricultural Credit Corporation (ACC). The Minister added that he had authorised the ICC to borrow additional funds in foreign currencies on the capital markets for on-lending to industry, without exchange risk to the final borrower. He said that a similar scheme had been authorised for the ACC in 1979.

The Minister for Industry, Commerce & Tourism, Desmond O'Malley TD, during the course of that debate said:

> 'In this regard, one source of regret to me is that our smaller and more sensitive firms do not choose to avail themselves more of the lower interest rates prevailing in certain other EEC states. I understand that there has been some move in our bigger firms in recent months to borrow in these attractive markets. I hope that this development will increase and intensify in the months ahead.'

The Government responded by introducing an Exchange Rate Guarantee Scheme of limited scope in autumn 1980, which allowed eligible manufacturing enterprises to borrow Deutsche Marks at an interest rate of about 14% *per annum*, without a currency exchange risk. The scheme was restricted to small and medium-sized enterprises, with a fixed asset limit of IR£2.5 million (€3.2 million). The CII sought to have the scheme extended to all manufacturing enterprises that were exposed to international competition and to their working capital requirements, but that did not happen.

EXCHANGE RATES

In relation to exchange rates, Edmund Williams, the then CII President, in his 1979 *Annual Report*, noted that, in March 1979, Ireland joined the EMS and the Irish Pound moved from its one-to-one parity with Sterling, which had obtained for over 150 years.[*] He stressed that industry supported the decision to join the EMS, as it offered the prospects of lower inflation, lower interest rates, better control of development policies and a deeper commitment to the EC. Williams noted that, during 1979, the EMS was a zone of monetary stability in a world where major currencies fluctuated violently. The Irish Pound held its value within the EMS and industry supported the policy of the Central Bank of Ireland to maintain the value of Ireland's external reserves with the objective of maintaining the exchange rate within the EMS.

In the CII's 1980 *Annual Report*, Liam Connellan, Director General, reported that the CII pressed Government for a policy stance that would maintain the exchange rate of the Irish Pound, and consequently requested that there be no net increase in indirect taxation.

Liam Connellan, in the 1981 CII *Annual Report*, complained that failure to implement the disciplines that should have accompanied Ireland's entry to the EMS in 1979 were still evident in 1981. Increased domestic costs,

---

[*] Ireland broke parity with Sterling in March 1979, because Sterling rose in value on the international foreign exchange markets to a rate above that of the currencies participating in the EMS exchange rate mechanism, including Ireland. The break in parity with Sterling meant that Ireland was faced with the task of managing its own currency on the foreign exchange markets for the first time in the history of the State. Parity with Sterling began in 1826, although for more than 100 years prior to that the Irish Pound had an independence of its own on the foreign exchange markets of the time. The rate of exchange of the Irish Pound against Sterling for the 100 years or more prior to 1826 was 13 Irish Pounds to 12 Pounds Sterling, varying in response to the balance of payments between Ireland and England.

including wage cost increases at over twice the average in other EMS countries, coupled with the relative stability of currency, resulted directly in a loss of competitiveness on many export markets.

There were 12 currency realignments within the EMS, which lasted from its establishment in 1979 until the end of 1993. Ireland was involved in only three of the 12 realignments, those of March 1983, July 1985, and August 1986. This was the lowest number of involvements of any of the participating currencies, which currencies were, with the number of involvements of each in the 12 realignments, the Belgian and Luxembourg Francs (5), Danish Krone (6), Deutsche Mark (7), Dutch Guilder (6), French Franc (5), Italian Lira (6), and the Irish Pound (3).

In a talk to the CII South East Region in Waterford in July 1982, I expressed concern that the merits or otherwise of exchange rate movements were being discussed in isolation from, and without equal weight being given to, fundamental domestic economic issues.[27] After the EMS realignment in March 1983,[¶] the first that involved the Irish Pound, the CII, in a press release that I prepared, commented on the 3.5% devaluation of the Irish Pound.[28] It pointed out that devaluation had the immediate effect of increasing the price of imports, which represented a heavy burden for manufacturing industry because about 60% of Ireland's total import bill was for materials for further production. On the other hand, there was the potential to regain some lost export markets, but that was contingent on keeping all other costs under strict control and on intensifying marketing efforts. The CII stressed that, in order to be successful, currency devaluation had to be accompanied by action under fiscal policy, monetary policy and incomes policy. It stressed also the need for partnership between all sectors of the community to ensure that price increases were kept to a minimum for the foreseeable future.

The second EMS realignment in which Ireland was involved was on 22 July 1985. The realignment arose to facilitate an 8% devaluation of the Italian Lira against all other EMS currencies. The 8% was achieved through a downward realignment of the Lira by 6% and an upward revaluation of all other participating currencies by 2%, including the Irish Pound.

There was an EMS realignment on 7 April 1986, when the Government opted to maintain the existing central parity of the Irish Pound. The

---

¶ The Finance Ministers and the Central Bank Governors of the EMS participating EC Member States agreed on 21 March 1983 to adjust bilateral central currency rates as follows, with all currencies being adjusted: Deutsche Mark + 5.5%; Dutch Guilder + 3.5%; Danish Krone + 2.5%; Belgian and Luxembourg Francs + 1.5%; French Franc – 2.5%; Italian Lira – 2.5%; and Irish Pound – 3.5%.

realignment involved all EMS currencies except the Italian Lira and the Irish Pound. At the time, the CII's view, which I gave at a talk in Mullingar, County Westmeath, was that, because of the openness of the Irish economy in trade terms within the EMS, and on a broader basis within the EEC and the world economy, it was impossible for Ireland to operate an exchange rate policy in isolation from the aggregate of social and economic policies.[29] The CII called on Government to take all appropriate action within its power to reduce interest rates, and the costs to enterprises of energy, transport, telecommunications, and all other input costs influenced by the action of public authorities, and to dramatically reduce Government expenditure. It pointed out that cost structures needed to be corrected, not least because Irish exporters faced a wide variety of foreign exchange risks due to the composition of export markets. Irish exports were valued at IR£9,744 million (€12,372 million) in 1985 and the profile of exports in currency terms can be judged from the following Table.

Table 10.4: Currency Zone Destinations of Irish Exports, 1985

Destination	% Irish Exports
United Kingdom	33
EMS Countries	34
Other EEC Countries	2
USA	10
Rest of the World	21
Total	100

The last EMS realignment in which Ireland participated was on 4 August 1986. This comprised solely an 8% reduction in the value of the Irish Pound within the EMS. During 1986, because of the weakening of Sterling, competitive cost pressures were a major focus of the CII's activities. This led to the establishment of a Joint Working Party on Industrial Costs between the CII and Government Departments, which reported to the Government in July 1986. Undoubtedly, cost-competitiveness pressures were a significant factor in the Government's decision to seek a unilateral devaluation of the Irish pound within the EMS in August 1986.

Currency stability thereafter prompted Dr Dermot Whelan to make the following statement in his 1988 CII *President's Report*:

> 'The Irish economy is now operating as a full and active member of the European Monetary System and its currency is ranked among the three

strongest within the EMS. It has one of the lower rates of inflation and interest rates within the European Community and Irish industry wants this position to continue … our currency should retain its current relationship with the Deutsche Mark if there were a realignment of currencies within the EMS in the coming year. This will ensure that inflation remains low and that Ireland remains an attractive place for investment.'

The only revaluation within the EMS after that of August 1986, was in January 1990, when the Italian Lira alone was devalued by 3.7%. The Irish Pound retained its relationship with the Deutsche Mark.

THE LINKAGE BETWEEN POLICY AREAS

There is a direct link between inflation, interest rates, exchange rates, international competitiveness, jobs and living standards. The CII consistently emphasised the linkage, with special reference to inflation, inflation-imposing public expenditure and currency exchange rates. In early 1987 at a talk to the College of Business in the NIHE, Limerick (now the University of Limerick), I emphasised that, while Irish exchange rate policy was rooted in membership of the EMS, it was clear that Ireland had not followed the disciplines implicit in EMS membership.[30] As a result, the money economy had decoupled from the real economy of goods and traded services, with a resultant strain on many enterprises. Loss of markets, enterprise closures, job losses, and low living standards followed. I argued that the economic problems of the 1980s had their roots in a loss of competitiveness. Notwithstanding the complexity of definition, it was a truism that cost competitiveness was one of the most important issues in the short-term. Cost-competitiveness for Ireland was a factor of domestic costs and of the relationship between the home currency and the currencies of our trading partners. In other words, cost competitiveness was a factor of domestic costs and of the exchange rate. A quotation from *The Economist* in 1986 gave a very simple and pragmatic massage to illustrate the relationship between the money economy and the real economy:[31]

'Of all the ways for poor countries to become less poor, one stands out: make sure exchange rates reflect internal-*versus*-international costs, so that exporters are not squeezed while (*others make*) a fortune importing shoes and ships and sealing wax at what, in local currency, are dirt-cheap prices.'

I further emphasised that industry's approach to issues such as the exchange rate debate was pragmatic and based on the requirement for a long-term stable cost / price competitiveness relationship. The ideal from an industrial viewpoint was a combination of, at minimum, three conditions:

♦ A strong and stable currency based on industrial cost parity.

♦ Inflation no higher than international competitors.

♦ Industrial cost inputs, including interest rates, at internationally-competitive levels.

Some elements of that policy linkage were alluded to, for example, in the CII's pre-Budget submission for 1990:

> 'Low inflation last year helped international competitiveness to a considerable extent, as a result of which exports in 1988 increased by 8.7% in volume, while imports increased by only 3.9% and there was a surplus both on the balance of international trade and on the current balance of international payments. As a consequence, employment rose by 1% in 1988.'

SUMMARY

◊ The high level of Irish cost / price inflation in the 1970s and early 1980s and the adverse consequences for the economy in terms of lost domestic and export sales led the CII to mount a public awareness campaign about the nature of inflation.

◊ The campaign contributed to the achievement in 1988 of an inflation rate of 2.1%, the lowest for almost three decades. The campaign placed special emphasis on Government-generated inflation, fuelled by excessive public borrowing and poor control of some public expenditure programmes.

◊ High interest rates imposed an additional cost on business and industry and led the Government to introduce an Exchange Rate Guarantee Scheme, in the early 1980s, to facilitate low-interest foreign borrowings by certain manufacturing enterprises.

◊ Industry representatives supported the decision of the Government to join the EMS in March 1979, subsequently resulting in a break in parity with Sterling.

◊ The CII consistently emphasised the direct policy links between inflation, interest rates, exchange rates, international competitiveness, employment and living standards.

CHAPTER 11
BACK TO BASICS

The educational and instructional activities of the CII, in helping to generate a public awareness of the principal economic, social and political constraints to Ireland's economic development, played a vital part in the creation of the conditions leading to the Celtic Tiger economy. Although frequently mundane in character, and certainly lacking in drama, the work justified the resources invested in it, as subsequent events have proven. Much of this work was in direct collaboration with the education system, mainly at post-primary and higher education levels.

CURRICULUM DEVELOPMENT

From 1979 onwards, I sought to strengthen the links between industry and the post-primary schools to ensure that the education system was continuously informed of, and responsive to, the rapidly-changing needs of enterprise.[1] Against that background, I prepared a detailed response in which the CII welcomed the 1980 *White Paper on Educational Development*, in particular the undertaking given by Government that the education system 'will undergo a continuous process of adaptation and development'.[2] Particularly welcome was the *White Paper's* recognition of the accelerating pace of change in society and its recognition of the role of the education system in helping to prepare young people to meet that change.

The CII expressed concern at the quality of the statistical base for population projections and noted the need for an early up-date. It welcomed the Government's commitment to an accelerated programme for the provision of specialist teachers, particularly in areas such as woodwork and metalwork, and recommended a similar programme for the provision of specialist teachers in the technological sector at the higher education level.

In relation to the Irish language, the CII was impressed by the detail of analysis and proposals, welcomed the emphasis on spoken language, suggested that the proposals applied equally to other languages essential to international marketing and recommended that well-researched methodologies for teaching Irish be used as a model for all language teaching at both primary and post-primary levels.

At the primary school level, the CII welcomed the *White Paper*'s recognition that the school was an integral part of the community, and the proposal for school publications to aid the teaching of Environmental Studies and to reflect the economic interests of local areas. The CII recommended that, additionally, emphasis be placed on the fundamentals of wealth creation so that young children could learn how jobs are created and sustained and living standards earned. It welcomed the proposal for special support for the handicapped and the educationally-disadvantaged.

In line with the *White Paper*'s recognition of the place of the school in the community, the CII sought a review of the constitution of Boards of Management of national schools, to include a consideration of the extent to which it was desirable to include an appropriate mix of people from the various socio-economic groups, sectors of the economy, and employer / employee backgrounds.

The CII welcomed the proposed establishment of a Curriculum Council at post-primary level and recommended the inclusion on each Syllabus Committee of persons from sectors of the economy outside of education, including from enterprises and from consumer / user groups. Further, the CII welcomed the proposal to introduce career-oriented courses at the senior cycle, and recommended that they be structured as alternatives within the formal Leaving Certificate validation system, rather than being isolated outside that system. In practical terms, the CII pledged curriculum support for a number of schools / industry initiatives.

The CII expressed concern that the only firm proposal in the *White Paper* for the treatment of the Arts in education was the establishment of a committee to examine the extent to which artistic and creative activities were catered for in the post-primary schools. The CII welcomed the statement that 'competition in the marketplace puts a premium on the element of design in commercial products', but regretted that the statement was not further elaborated on, and that there were no proposals to follow through on the practical implications of acceptance of the place of the design element in the promotion and marketing of products. The CII recommended that a greater emphasis be placed on the role of visual education, as an aid to the promotion of industrial development, and on the relationship between product design, economic development, job creation and job retention.

The CII also welcomed the continuing development of the post-primary sector and the innovative steps taken to introduce new types of post-primary education. It recommended that the Department of Education review the rationale behind the different types of post-primary school, in consultation with the management organisations, teachers' unions and other interested parties, with a view to eliminating any confusion caused by the proliferation of different types of schools.

In relation to teachers' in-service courses, the CII welcomed the emphasis on oral competence in Irish and in modern continental languages and recommended that a similar approach be taken to emphasise communications in the teaching of the English language. The CII argued that the Committee on In-Service Training of Teachers should have regard to the in-service needs of guidance counsellors and that the committee should include persons from economic and social sectors outside of education to ensure that cognisance would be taken of developments in industry, agriculture, commerce, services and the professions.

On the subject of school transport, the CII advocated a review of the restrictive contract conditions to ensure provision of the best appropriate quality service in a cost-effective manner. One consequence of the restrictive clauses in school transport contracts was the use, on occasion, of old and poorly-maintained buses, due to the inherently uneconomic nature of 'stand-alone' school bus contracts, resulting in many buses being used only for limited periods of the day and of the year.

The CII recognised the importance of 'continuing education' in view of the rapid pace of change in society, which made the idea of a job for life an out-dated concept. The CII observed at the beginning of the 1980s that up to two-thirds of industrial jobs would have changed in form and / or content to a greater or a lesser extent by the year 2000. The result would be people returning to the education system periodically to up-date their technical knowledge and skills, and to acquire further education of an economic, social, cultural, or linguistic nature. The CII recommended that, within the wider societal remit of adult education, emphasis be placed on courses linked to career progression and change, and that people from the enterprise sector ought to be included in membership of the Adult Education Sub-Committee of each Vocational Education Committee and on similar committees in the higher education sector.

In relation to sport, recreation, and youth activities, the CII welcomed the suggestion that the institution of a national awards scheme for young people would be examined in the context of youth services. The CII sought further elaboration of the Government's thinking, in which 'on the industrial side, where State funds are used in the setting up of an industry, it is proposed to endeavour to provide for adequate recreational needs of workers'. In response, the Department of Education invited views from the CII on how to meet the recreational needs of employees, which resulted in my appointment to the Department's Steering Committee on Recreation Management, which functioned from April 1983 to August 1985.[3]

The CII's view of the overall philosophical framework for education was given in the conclusion to the CII's response to the *White Paper*, notably that the education system needed to address the preparation of each pupil in at least three major areas:

♦ As an **individual**, to be given every opportunity to develop his or her own potential in the broadest sense, and not solely in terms of being equipped with a balanced range of social, economic, societal, and cultural accomplishments.

♦ As a **member of a group**, with an interdependent role in harmony with each other member of the group. The young person needed to learn how to work with other people, and to communicate with other people both formally in the classroom, and in the informal setting of the various cultural, social, and sporting clubs and societies that played a vital role in the development of a balanced environment in the school. The preparation of the individual in that respect was towards equipping the young person with all of the skills necessary to live as a citizen in a democratic society, which was by definition a participative community where the individual citizen had both a right and a duty to participate within the capacity of each.

♦ As a **worker** required, within the capacity of each individual, to contribute either directly or indirectly to the production of those goods and services that determined the living standards of every member of the community.

The CII submitted that education did not exist as a self-contained system; that educational planning needed to go hand-in-hand with planning all other social, economic, cultural, and political developments in society. In particular, but not limited to an economic view, the CII believed that, as one element, the inter-linking of educational planning with planning for economic development should aim at ensuring that the educational qualifications of young people would give them the best opportunity to make a significant contribution to their own development and to the overall development of their community.

INVESTMENT IN EDUCATION

The CII consistently supported investment in education in many pre-Budget submissions to the Government, throughout the 1980s and into the early 1990s, and in other submissions to Government of a social and economic nature.

In the depths of national economic crisis in summer 1986, the CII made a number of proposals to reduce public expenditure and to create conditions that would enhance the environment for economic activity and viable long-term job creation in the productive sectors.[4] Education was the sole area of current public expenditure that the CII exempted from the proposed financial cuts. The CII recommended that the total expenditure on the Exchequer Education Vote should be maintained in inflation-corrected terms, because investment in education increased the capacity of the national economy to create more jobs and earn higher living standards.

In its 1991 pre-Budget submission, the CII sought that public policy should concentrate on increasing the proportion of 16, 17, 18 and 19-year olds who remained in school at the post-primary level, and should significantly increase the participation rate at the higher education level.[5] The percentage of young people, then in full-time education in each age group, was 16 (87.5%), 17 (73.2%), 18 (44.5%) and 19 years (26.9%). An increase in the participation rate for 17-year olds to 87.5%, the same percentage as 16-year olds, and an increase in the average participation rate of 18 and 19-year olds to 55%, would mean an additional 35,000 pupils *per annum* in education. The CII believed that a significant improvement in the full-time education participation rates in this way would not only enhance the capacity of the national economy to create additional viable long-term jobs and to achieve higher living standards, but it would also improve the general quality of life of the population. Increasing the participation rate at senior cycle post-primary level was one of the most effective ways in which to solve the problem of poverty, through enhancing skills and job prospects.

One of the beneficial results from increasing the participation rate in education could be a reduction of not less than 14,000 (40% of 35,000) in unemployment *per annum* because, for every 10 who stayed on longer in school, four jobs, which would otherwise have been held by them, could be available for others.

The CII did not consider that these measures would result in any increase in State expenditure, because the cost of unemployment assistance and related benefits to a single person, prior to the 1991 Budget, was about

IR£3,175 (€4,031) *per annum,* rising to IR£8,866 (€11,257) *per annum* for a married couple with four children. The cost of a second-level education place in 1990 was about IR£1,525 (€1,936) *per annum,* and IR£2,001 (€2,541) *per annum* per place for Vocational Preparation & Training (VPT) courses, so that, even when allowance was made for jobs filled by those not on the Live Register and for reduced migration, there was a potential gain to the Exchequer as a result of this measure.

GUIDANCE COUNSELLING

The CII was anxious to ensure that guidance counsellors in post-primary schools were familiar with the work environment in enterprises. In furtherance of that objective, I initiated the CII Annual Careers in Industry Conference, in association with the Institute of Guidance Counsellors (IGC). The first conference was held in UCD in October 1979.

September 1986: (left to right) Con Power, CII Director of Economic Policy; Enda Kenny TD, Minister of State for Education; Albert O'Ceallaigh, Chief Executive, Curriculum & Examinations Board; and Arthur Dunne, President, Institute of Guidance Counsellors at the Eighth Annual CII Careers in Industry Conference.

The CII Manpower Policy Committee, from 1979 onwards, included in its membership *inter alia* one representative each from the Psychological & Guidance Counselling Inspectorate of the Department of Education, the IGC, the NMS, AnCO, the National Council for Educational Awards (NCEA), and the Chartered Institute of Personnel & Development (CIPD). Prior to the publication of the *White Paper,* I initiated projects to assist guidance counsellors in familiarising themselves with work in industry. Those projects, described in the CII response to the *White Paper*, included:

♦ Publication in October, 1979 of a booklet, *Your Future in Industry*, with the objective of assisting pupils, parents, and teachers to obtain a better understanding of careers in industry. Copies of the booklet were distributed to each registered post-primary school in the country, and the assistance of guidance counsellors was enlisted to obtain a feedback on the value of the booklet. A second, and much expanded, edition was published at the end of 1980.

♦ Talks on careers in industry to pupils, parents, and teachers in over 100 post-primary schools during the school year 1979/80. The talks were continued at an accelerated pace during the year 1980/81. By 1981/82, the CII arranged about 300 careers talks *per annum* in schools.

♦ Preparation and distribution of a *Resource Directory* that was sent to each registered post-primary school, giving details of some of the ways in which the CII and its participating member enterprises could directly help to strengthen the links between industry and the individual schools.

♦ As part of the programme for distributing information to the schools, copies of the published proceedings of the 1980 CII Annual Economic Conference, *Industry Report 1980*, were distributed to each registered post-primary school to be deposited in the school libraries, and to be used by teachers of subjects such as economics, business organisation, geography and civics.

♦ In summer 1979, the CII commissioned an audio-visual slide / tape presentation for use as an aid to industrialists when giving talks in the schools.[6]

♦ At the request of the Dublin Branch of the IGC, the CII organised a scheme of work experience in industry for guidance counsellors in summer 1980. A similar arrangement was made for the Waterford Branch of the IGC in summer 1981. The CII welcomed the proposal in the *White Paper* that provision would be made to secure exposure to industrial employment environments as part of the training of the guidance counsellors, and the CII recommended that provision be made for the periodic up-dating of that experience.

The CII recommended that training be given to guidance counsellors in the use of audio-visual aids, and expressed concern that the recommendations of the Educational Media Review Committee, which reported in December 1975, had not been fully implemented by the Department of Education.

LINKS WITH POST-PRIMARY SCHOOLS

The CII's on-going educational links with post-primary schools were mainly at national level with the Minister for Education and the Department, the Government, the EC Commission, the National Council for Curriculum & Assessment (NCCA), and teachers' subject associations, rather than with individual schools. In the latter case, following some demonstration projects, the CII encouraged member enterprises to link directly with local schools, including through local Chambers of Commerce, Junior Chamber Branches, Rotary Clubs and similar organisations.

In addition to the formal links at institutional and organisation level, the CII continually advocated the development of the education system, for example, in the negotiations for the National Understandings (1980 and 1981), the PNR (1987-1990) and the PESP (1990-1993). Booklets and films / videos were produced from time-to-time on topics including economics, environmental issues and careers in industry, and these were distributed to the post-primary schools.

I initiated and organised the CII Awareness of Irish Industry Awards scheme for the post-primary schools, in co-operation with the Irish Goods Council, in each of the five school years from 1981 / 1982 to 1985 / 1986. Plaques were awarded annually to post-primary schools that made a significant contribution to improving the relationship between industry and the school. Enda Kenny TD, Leader of Fine Gael, then Minister of State at the Department of Education, presented the 1985 / 1986 plaques at the 8th Annual CII Careers in Industry Conference held in Dublin on 19 September 1986. During the school year 1986 / 1987, the scheme received major sponsorship from the Irish Life Assurance Company, and was re-launched by Irish Life as a stand-alone scheme with that enhanced level of sponsorship.

CURRICULUM & SYLLABUS INPUTS

Subsequent to the CII response to the *White Paper on Educational Development*, the Department of Education arranged that, when reviewing a syllabus, each Syllabus Committee consulted the CII. Between 1981 and the end of 1983, the CII made submissions to the Syllabus Committees for accountancy, art & design, chemistry, commerce, English, mathematics and physics, together with a number of broader overall curriculum submissions. In January 1984, the Minister for Education designated the CII as an organisation with which the Curriculum & Examinations Board was required to consult. The NCCA, launched in December 1987 to advise the Minister on all matters relating to curriculum and assessment in first and second-level education, made a similar arrangement with the CII.

THE CII EDUCATION COLLEGE

The CII promoted curriculum development in the post-primary schools through funding projects by teachers' subject associations. On my initiative, the *CII Education College* was established in December 1984. It is now the *IBEC Centre for Educational Research & Development.*[7] The objective of the College was to assist teachers' subject associations financially to undertake curriculum research and development work, which would directly influence the curriculum in the post-primary schools in a practical and directly beneficial way.

The initial collaboration was with the Irish Science Teachers Association (ISTA), beginning in April 1981, prior to the incorporation of the CII Education College. The project involved development work on the chemistry and physics syllabuses for the Leaving Certificate. Subsequently, the CII Education College, in the years up to 1993, funded projects undertaken by the undermentioned teachers' subject associations and by other formal groups of teachers:

- Art Teachers' Association.
- Association of Geography Teachers of Ireland.
- Association of Teachers of Spanish.
- Applications Oriented Mathematics Project (North Tipperary VEC).
- Business Studies Teachers' Association of Ireland (BSTAI).
- Cork-Brittany School Exchange Programme.
- German Teachers' Association.
- History Teachers' Association of Ireland (Dublin Branch).
- International Skill Olympics (Irish Apprenticeship Participation).
- Irish Agricultural Science Teachers' Association.
- Irish Science Teachers' Association.
- Italian Teachers' Association.
- Marino Curriculum Support Services.

- Mathematics Teachers' Association.
- *Unter den Linden* Project for the teaching of the German language to primary school pupils.

Some projects were once-off, while others, such as those with BSTAI and ISTA, involved multi-annual funding. The collaboration with ISTA included curriculum development work for the Junior Certificate and the Leaving Certificate, publication of a series of illustrated wall posters of famous Irish scientists, publication of booklets on Leaving Certificate Chemistry, the making of videos on Leaving Certificate Physics experiments, and the production of a polymer experimental kit.[8]

The CII arranged work experience for business studies teachers, in addition to the schemes mentioned earlier for guidance counsellors. In summer 1987, in co-operation with BSTAI, the CII placed 42 business studies teachers in enterprises for between two and four weeks. The programme was repeated in summer 1988, with 30 business studies teachers. In 1991, the CII adopted a team approach involving the principal, a business studies teacher and a guidance counsellor from each of 12 schools in the Dublin area. They were linked with six companies, two each in the food, high technology and services sectors. Collaboration was with three teachers' organisations: the European Secondary Heads Association (ESHA), representing the principals; the BSTAI, representing the business studies teachers; and the IGC, representing the guidance counsellors.

As mentioned earlier, the CII, in association with the IGC, organised an annual conference for guidance counsellors, beginning in 1979. The CII, in association with the BSTAI organised an annual conference for business studies teachers from 1985 onwards. *Ad hoc* conferences were held in other subject areas.

THIRD LEVEL EDUCATION:
THE 1980 WHITE PAPER

The CII welcomed the proposal in the 1980 *White Paper* that the Government would examine the funding for third-level education, 'with a view to ensuring priority of allocation of resources for identified areas of national development'. By way of background, in August 1978, a CII survey among member enterprises identified a number of key skills areas, at craft, technician, and technologist levels, where enterprises were unable to recruit staff because of the inadequate supply of skilled workers. In response, in autumn 1978, the Minister for Labour established the Manpower Consultative Committee (MCC), under his chairmanship. The MCC provided a forum for the assessment of national development priorities by employer and industry organisations, trade unions, Government Departments and State agencies. Projects were undertaken to increase the supply of skilled persons, initially in engineering and applied science disciplines, including a recruitment campaign abroad, special relocation grants administered by the NMS, short-term conversion courses for persons with certain technological skills to equip them with skills in short supply, and additional technological courses offered in the universities and in other higher education courses.

The CII noted that the qualifications to be awarded in the National College of Art & Design (NCAD) would be those of the NCEA and recommended that the design needs of industry be emphasised within this qualification awards structure.

The CII welcomed the proposals for distance learning programmes as a support for training within the workplace, as well as within the community generally.

HIGHER EDUCATION & INDUSTRY

In 1981, the CII commissioned and published a report by a working party drawn from the universities and led by Professor Vincent J. McBrierty, Physics Department, University of Dublin, Trinity College.[9] The report, *Strategy for Industrial Innovation: The Role of the Third Level Institutions*, was a discussion document for widespread dissemination and a contribution to the development of CII policy on the subject. It examined the process of innovation, the nature and role of Irish industry, the national research institutes and State agencies, the nature and role of the third level education sector, employment implications of industrial growth in Ireland, and mechanisms for promoting innovation in Irish industry.

The report developed three major themes:

♦ The need for Government funding and facilitation of research and innovation.

♦ The need for academics and industrialists to breach institutional and attitudinal barriers to co-operation, and for industry to increase significantly its investment in research and development (R&D).

♦ The need for a continuing supply of well-trained and motivated employees to carry out applied R&D.

It went on to examine 14 factors that underpinned success in achieving efficient technology transfer and made recommendations relative to each:

- The post-primary curriculum, including gender equality in access to each subject.
- The post-primary funding mechanism.
- The teaching of critical numerate and technical subjects in post-primary schools.
- Mobility of post-primary and third level academic staff.
- Training assignments within industry for undergraduates and post-graduates in engineering and applied science to reflect sensitivity to industrial needs.
- Recognition of the enterprise role of graduates in disciplines other than engineering and science.
- Provision of retraining programmes in good time to benefit those affected by redundancy.
- Facilitation of academics and industrialists to contribute to the process of technology transfer.
- The need for a long-term Government commitment to adequate funding for research at a steadily increasing level.
- Encouragement of multinational industry to establish strong Irish roots through participation in local R&D programmes, including the allocation of a small percentage of the IDA budget to R&D activities in the third level institutes, selected on the basis of industrial relevance.
- Provision of facilities to enhance the transfer of technology, including industrial science parks and applications laboratories alongside academic institutions and the co-ordination of the inter-disciplinary effort of a number of departments within a university to serve designated sectors of industry.
- The infrastructure for technology transfer to serve national rather than parochial needs, with management committees of applications laboratories drawn from the best experience available at national level.
- Initiation in Ireland of a scheme similar to the Teaching Company Scheme, introduced in the UK at the beginning of the 1980s.
- Encouragement to groups of small and medium-sized enterprises to establish joint research R&D initiatives in conjunction with third-level institutions.

The CII held a conference in follow-up to the report in April 1981.[10] It dealt with four main topics:

♦ Strategy for industrial innovation.

♦ The link with third-level institutions.

♦ Manpower development for technological innovation.

♦ Technological innovation in practice.

The CII emphasised the relationship between design, production, and marketing. Technological innovation required development to the point where it benefited the ultimate consumer. As an example, Xerox copying was the brilliant idea of Chester Carlson in the 1930s, but it did not cause an office revolution until Joseph C. Wilson of the Haloid Corporation turned the technological idea into a marketable reality in the 1960s. In the quest for what the consumer would purchase, the artist, the architect, and the product designer have a vital role to play, as have behavioural scientists, market analysts, marketing specialists, including geographers and linguists, engineers and applied scientists, cost accountants and business administrators and other creative persons from any academic background.

In Ireland, in the early 1980s, the demand for innovation was not great among the majority of industrialists, but the demand for innovation, when articulated, usually presented a welcome challenge for academics. There was a public policy need to stimulate the demand for innovation, with a particular focus on the marketplace, nationally and internationally, consistent with the fulfilment by third-level institutions of their unique role in society.

Speaking at a seminar on industry and higher education in 1983, my view was that far too high a proportion of highly-skilled people in Ireland were involved in activities which, although important, did not directly add to the economic living standards of the community through the production of goods or the performance of traded services.[11] There was a need to swing the balance so that slightly more highly-skilled people would work in productive enterprises, in the narrow economic sense, subject to Ireland not creating a new imbalance in personnel deployment. The universities and higher education colleges could contribute by:

♦ Helping to create widespread economic awareness.

♦ Relating the content of appropriate courses more directly to economic activities.

♦ Arranging relevant work familiarisation and experience for students.

♦ Permitting academic staff to engage in consultancy and in applied R&D projects, compatible with their academic mission.

♦ Permitting academic staff to become directly involved in enterprises through, for example, non-executive directorships, compatible with their academic mission.

♦ Where appropriate, allowing enterprises to use the specialised facilities of the universities and higher education colleges.

THE RTCS & NIHES

The CII supported the work of the RTCs throughout the country and the National Institutes for Higher Education (NIHEs) in Limerick and Dublin. It recognised at an early stage that the RTCs were developing rapidly and to a high level of academic excellence that required appropriate management structures.[12] In relation to the NIHEs, the CII made a detailed submission to the Minister for Education on the *National Institute for Higher Education, Limerick, Bill 1980*. In the submission, it sought changes aimed at enhancing the role and the operating structures of the NIHE. Of significance in a later context was the request by the CII for clarity to ensure that the NIHE had the capacity to evolve into an independent award-making body as a university or technological university.

In 1987, the CII responded to an invitation to make a submission on the question of technological education and a Technological University.[13] The CII did so in the belief that the NIHEs in Limerick and Dublin brought a new dynamism to the higher education sector, and provided a much greater direct industrial focus for higher education on a broader institutional basis than had previously been the case.

With the change in Government in March 1987, action was suspended on the establishment of a National Technological University. The CII focused on the achievement of individual university status for the NIHEs in Limerick and in Dublin. Mrs Mary O'Rourke TD, Minister for Education, announced in October 1987, that the Government would establish the NIHEs in Limerick and Dublin as universities, and appointed Governing Bodies to each NIHE on that basis. I was appointed to the Governing Body of the NIHE Dublin and, in February 1988, on the Minister's invitation, I prepared a briefing note on the upcoming university designation for the NIHEs. The main points were that university status having been earned, a change in title was needed nationally and internationally; the required changes could be readily achieved in legislative terms; the functions of the new universities were straightforward; the administrative and academic structures relative to accreditation would mirror the *NCEA Act*; and academic and governance titles should be those used as the norm in universities. In my briefing note to the Minister in February 1988, I recommended that the titles of the universities be the Dublin City University, and the University of Limerick. Legislation establishing the two universities was enacted in 1989. They were the first universities to be established by the State since its foundation in 1922.

COMPETITION PUTS A PREMIUM ON DESIGN

In the 1980s, the CII placed an emphasis on industrial design education in the context of the *IDA Industrial Plan 1978-1982*, which included, as key target sectors, the production of goods with a distinctive Irish quality, not only of craft goods, but also high technology engineering products of good design, quality, finish, and presentation.[14]

The *White Paper on Educational Development* 1980, stated that 'competition in the marketplace puts a premium on the element of design in commercial products'. The CII welcomed the statement and concurred with its implications, believing that all higher education courses in art and design should include a module on product marketing techniques. In that context, in October 1982, the CII made a submission to the NCEA on art and design education at the higher education level. The NCAD was, at that stage, designated as a recognised higher education institution under the *NCEA Act*, and many of the other higher education colleges designated under that Act, including most of the RTCs, offered courses in art and design.

The CII believed that art and design modules should be included in all marketing and graphics courses, because of the need to use modern marketing visual aids. It also believed it essential that, in those courses, some emphasis be placed on the production of good technical trade literature, good promotional trade literature, and on the production of audio and audio-visual aids to marketing. The CII recommended a work familiarisation module in manufacturing industry for students in their final year of art teacher training. The objective would be to demonstrate to the student how the element of aesthetics combined with other disciplines to produce the finished product and thus help to correct the imbalance between fine art and industrial design. The background was that art teachers in the post-primary schools seemed to concentrate almost exclusively on the aesthetic aspects of art, even seeing their subject as divorced from the day-to-day activities of business and industry. The situation seemed to differ from that in the Scandinavian countries, where the approach to the aesthetic was through the functional.

In a 1984 article, I examined international comparisons, and discussed issues such as the dynamics of the market, meeting the needs of the consumer, marketing, innovation, and visual education.[15] My conclusion was a conviction of the pivotal role of visual education, and of the relationship between product design, production, marketing, and the improvement in living standards of the entire community. The article urged that art and applied science be given the opportunity to work together as equal partners for the benefit of society. In 1988, I examined issues such as art and science in the context of those key growth areas in the PNR 1987-1990 that related to industries requiring a high craft and design input and I assessed the role of art and design, including industrial design, in an overall industrial development strategy.[16]

MARKETING & EUROPEAN LANGUAGES

Reference to the CII and higher education would be incomplete without mention of a major initiative related to marketing and modern European languages. The European Orientation Programme (now the Export Orientation Programme) (EOP) was the initiative of Paddy Jordan, who had been the Director of the Irish Business Bureau in Brussels, and was subsequently the Director of the CII's Food, Drink & Tobacco Federation. The EOP was established with the dual objectives of building up a corps of young business executives capable of relating effectively to their Continental European counterparts and of developing the skills and expertise urgently needed to strengthen the international marketing capacity of Irish industry in all sectors. Each trainee was sponsored by an Irish exporting enterprise, with which the trainee spent the first three months learning the basics of the business. The second three months period was spent in a language laboratory in a relevant European country. The final six months were spent working in a commercial environment in an enterprise related to the business of the sponsoring Irish enterprise. The EOP was managed by the CII and, in the initial years, was jointly funded by the YEA, Córas Tráchtála and the Bank of Ireland. The first programme trained 30 participants, while the second was formally launched by Ruairí Quinn TD, Minister for Labour in June 1985.[17]

GRADUATES FOR BUSINESS & INDUSTRY

The CII, in its 1986 pre-Budget submission, emphasised the need to increase significantly the recruitment of science and technology graduates by industry.[18] This was against the background of an OECD 1985 Report that Irish industry had proportionately only one-third the number of science and technology graduates compared to other industrialised countries.[19] In 1984, Irish industry recruited 700 new science and technology third-level award holders, an increase of 30% on the previous year. However, a further 700 award holders emigrated or were unemployed. A 1985 study conducted by Córas Tráchtála indicated that each new export marketing executive generated sufficient orders to underpin between seven and 10 additional jobs in Ireland. The CII considered that a similar multiplier could apply to additional science and technology graduates engaged in industrial product and process development. A Government *White Paper* in 1984 pointed to the urgent need to increase investment in brainpower, particularly related to marketing and technology.[20]

Since 1983, two schemes had operated for the placement of young marketing and technology award holders in small manufacturing firms. These were 'Marketplace', operated by the Irish Goods Council, which provided a maximum grant of IR£3,600 (€4,571) towards the first year's salary of a new marketing graduate employed by a small manufacturing firm, and the 'Young Scientists & Technologists Employment Programme' funded by the YEA, which provided a similar grant to small firms recruiting young people with science and engineering qualifications. Those schemes proved successful.

In its 1986 pre-Budget submission, the CII recommended that the Marketplace and Young Scientists & Technologists Employment Programmes be extended to all of the older established industries, and that a target be set to recruit an additional 500 marketing and technology graduates to these firms in 1986. The cost was about IR£2 million (€2.5 million), and could have been more than recovered as a result of the increased contribution to innovation made by those young people.

More fundamentally, the CII pointed out that there were 20,000 applicants for 14,000 places in third-level institutions in 1985. The great majority of the available places in all third-level institutions were filled. In view of the low proportion of technical and business graduates in the population, and the relatively low proportion of the 18 to 20 years age cohort in third-level education in Ireland, compared with countries such as the United States, Japan, France and Denmark, a further investment in third-level education would have contributed significantly to future economic development. The CII calculated that the average, non-capital, annual cost of a third-level place was IR£3,000 (€3,809), somewhat lower than the average cost of unemployment benefit, so that a redeployment of funds could have been achieved at no net cost to the Exchequer. More young people would have remained in third-level education, and there would have been more jobs available for the unemployed. The CII recommended that an immediate study be conducted into how student intake could be increased by one-third or about 4,000 places, in the autumn of 1986. Implementation of that proposal would have ensured that, by 1989, Ireland would have had an annual supply of new science, technology and business studies graduates more in line with the requirements of an advanced industrial economy.

TRAINING WITHIN THE WORKPLACE

In 1980, the CII expressed support for the apprenticeship system.[21] At that stage, about 65,000 students left post-primary school each year, the majority after completing all or part of the Leaving Certificate course. About 10,000 continued in full-time further and higher education, and the remaining 55,000 entered the labour market; of the latter, about 4,000 became apprentices in the various designated trades. Of those 4,000, about 45% spent their first 40 weeks in training centres run by AnCO; 10% spent a similar period in training centres within industry, such as in CIÉ and Bórd na Móna; and 3% participated in training schemes run by the VECs, including in the RTCs. The CII urged a wider role for training within industry, in partnership with the VECs and training centres, to deepen the apprentices' awareness of the actual industrial environment, rather than of a simulated environment, and to facilitate the apprentices' gradual participation in the productive process. The CII called for an independent, external, inspection system to ensure that the training programme was fully implemented, together with certification of standards by an independent agency, in a system similar to Germany, France, the Netherlands, Switzerland and Italy. The CII suggested that the cost of providing apprenticeship training within industry could be lower than the cost of providing similar training in an external training centre, school, or college, as factory space and specialised equipment could be used partly for training and partly for productive purposes.

In the early 1980s, the External Training Division of AnCO, with the support of the CII, actively campaigned to arrange training places within industry both for apprentices and for general trainees.[22] The CII / ESRI *Monthly Industrial Survey*, December 1981, showed capacity utilisation in Irish industry at 58%, thus indicating that there was significant scope for the accommodation of training places within industry. At the beginning of 1982, there were 3,500 enterprises in the manufacturing sector covered by the AnCO Levy / Grant Scheme. Many of those enterprises not only had spare plant capacity, but they employed training instructors and training managers.

In 1987, the CII published a discussion document on a broadly-based structured system of training in business and industry, as an input to the manpower policy issues to be examined by the proposed National Employment & Training Authority.[23] The strategy was to extend the concept of 'apprenticeship', based on a system of fixed-term training contracts, along the lines followed in countries such as Austria, Germany, and Switzerland. The proposal envisaged the possibility of an initial increase in the numbers involved, from the 1987 intake of 3,000 craft apprentices *per annum*, to 10,000 trainees across the whole spectrum of industry and business. The ambition was to build to an annual aggregate of 30,000 indentured places covering all years of apprenticeship, within a period of three to five years.

The proposal envisaged a broader approach to the widespread use of training contracts as necessary, not only in Ireland's national interest, but also in the context of harmonisation of education and training within the EEC, and the reciprocal recognition of certificates within and between Member States of the EEC. The move towards rationalisation and harmonisation was already taking place in the area of higher education and the principles and practice involved were expected to extend in time to cover all levels of certification.[24]

In 1990, the CII welcomed a major new training scheme in Shannon, announced by Mr Bertie Ahern TD, Minister for Labour. The CII had suggested such a scheme in 1980.[25] The Shannon scheme provided an intensive two-year training programme, in Ireland and abroad, for about 700 young people, recruited by Shannon Aerospace over a period of four years. On successful completion of the programme, the trainee would qualify as an aircraft maintenance technician for Shannon Aerospace, a joint venture between Guinness Peat Aviation, Lufthansa, and Swissair. Recruitment for three main specialist programmes started at the beginning of 1990, with FÁS assistance.

HEALTH & SAFETY

The Minister for Labour, Tom Nolan TD, in April 1981, brought into operation the provisions of the *Safety in Industry Act 1980*, to secure greater co-operation between employers and employees in promoting a safe and healthy working environment.[26] The Minister of State at the Department of Labour, Seán Calleary TD, in 1981, appointed a Commission on Safety, Health & Welfare at Work (the Barrington Commission) to review the system for preventing accidents and diseases at work; the CII made a comprehensive submission to the Commission.[27] The issues covered in the submission included economic literacy, safety literacy, employee motivation, management action, the codes of taxation and of social welfare, employer's liability insurance, short-term sickness claims, the medical referee system of the Department of Social Welfare, and Employee Assistance Programmes (EAPs).

In the late 1970s and early 1980s, a focus on absenteeism levels in Irish industry drew attention to the problem of alcoholism in the workplace and to wider issues of health and safety. The CII recognised that it had a role in endeavouring to promote a climate of awareness in industry and within the general community that would support the efforts of management to combat absenteeism. In that context, in 1985, I collaborated with Dr Michael ffrench-O'Carroll, Director, Alcoholism & Drug Abuse Prevention Centre, Southern Health Board, Cork, in his efforts to establish in Dublin a pilot programme to help combat absenteeism in industry through the prevention of alcohol and drug abuse.[28]

The Minister for Industry, Trade, Commerce & Tourism, John Bruton TD, announced details of a Government action programme to help combat absenteeism in industry, in September 1985. The Minister outlined the work of a Ministerial Task Force that, on his initiative, was established by the Government to examine the problem of absenteeism. The Task Force invited submissions from key interests, including the CII, FUE, ICTU, IMI, and IPC. On receipt of the submissions, the Minister noted the unanimity in all submissions from those interest groups that absenteeism control was primarily a management responsibility, best tackled at the level of the individual enterprise.

In May 1988, the CII referenced Ireland's high 'sickness absence', and emphasised that Irish business and industry had a significant interest in promoting healthy living.[29] The concern of business and industry was not only the control of issues such as alcoholism and substance abuse, but also the positive issue of enhancing the living and working environment.

In March 1988, an ESRI publication quoted, in summary, a 1985 OECD Report that the duration of illness per worker was considerably higher in Ireland than in other OECD countries. In 1981, for example, 34 days per worker were lost in Ireland because of sickness absence, in contrast to Sweden 23, United Kingdom 20, Italy 17, France 14, Luxembourg 12, Netherlands 9, USA 5, and Finland 4.[30] The OECD Report quoted by the ESRI observed that the number of days lost per worker *per annum* through sickness in Ireland increased from 19.5 in 1960, to 25.6 in 1970 and 33.8 in 1978.

By 1988, it was obvious that, with the constraints on public expenditure in Ireland, there was an urgent need to reduce public expenditure on sickness benefits by lowering the sickness absence rate. Irrespective of the constraints in public expenditure, absenteeism was a factor reducing the capacity of the nation to earn more jobs and higher living standards. The ESRI Report observed that 'very few studies have been carried out in Ireland of the factors which influence the national sickness absence rate' and drew attention to the urgency with which the problem needed to be addressed and solved.

The view of the CII was that a solution to absenteeism was only part of the equation. The other part, and perhaps the more important part, was the need for a positive focus on human resource development, through what were known in the USA as 'employee wellness programmes'. Towards the end of 1986, the Minister for Health, Barry Desmond TD, issued a discussion document, *Health: The Wider Dimensions*. The CII enthusiastically supported proposals therein on preventive medicine and health promotion.[31] His successor as Minister for Health, Dr Rory O'Hanlon TD, stated, in 1988, that Ireland intended to follow policies to improve lifestyles, promote good health and put greater emphasis on preventive medicine, in line with the view expressed in the World Health Organisation's policy document, *Health for All*. The CII identified closely with that policy.[32]

In 1989, health and safety legislation was enacted, extending occupational safety and health protection to all persons in the workplace, employees, employers and self-employed.[33] The legislation embodied a preventive approach and provided for the participation of employers and trade unions to develop better safety and health measures, at national level and at the level of the individual enterprise. The new legislation had its roots in the Report of the Commission of Inquiry on Safety, Health & Welfare at Work, July 1983, the 'Barrington Report', which stated that:

> 'We doubt if safety and health can be advanced by an excessive reliance on detailed and increasingly complex regulations imposed on workplaces from the outside'.

The members of the Barrington Commission placed the emphasis on reform within the workplace, and said that this should be based on clearer ideas about the responsibilities of employers, employees, and the self-employed. The Barrington Commission spoke about its proposals being a negotiated consensus, and expressed the belief that the significant changes proposed could not be introduced at the workplace level, without at the same time the recommended adjustments taking place at the national level.

It was the view of the CII that one of the important national framework issues that needed to be addressed in Ireland, and which impacted on the workplace, was the question of community health and, within this, there was a need to place a greater emphasis on health promotion and on preventive medicine. That needed a change in attitude and a move away from health issues being seen primarily as a problem in terms of sickness, absence, and low productivity. The new focus required was one of seeing health issues as a development factor, in terms of good health, high employee motivation, full attendance and high productivity.

In summary, the enactment of the *Safety, Health & Welfare at Work Act 1989* was accompanied by a renewed focus on the working environment. Health programmes in the past had mainly been based on the disease model, but it was accepted in the 1980s that there were valid social and economic arguments in favour of the redeployment of some resources to the area of health promotion, including in the workplace.

The CII believed that there was a need for professionals in the workplace who would have knowledge of the organisation of work, human resource management, labour law, counselling, intervention strategies, and healthcare issues. Those persons needed to be able to deliver the main elements of the prevention and intervention components of a comprehensive care programme, with appropriate direction from, and access to, medical and other professionals. Towards that end, a number of new developments were taking place in Ireland in the late 1980s: the then Institute of Personnel Management in Ireland and Stanhope Consultancy Services were offering a Certificate Course in the area of employee assistance programmes, while the Association of Labour Management Administrators & Consultants on Absenteeism (ALMACA), offered a Certification Examination for Employee Assistance Professionals. General management needed sufficient training to identify employees with personal problems, but the CII called for the diagnosis and intervention process to be handled by trained professionals.

SUMMARY

◊ From 1979 onwards, the CII sought to strengthen the links between business and industry and the post-primary schools to help ensure that the education system was continuously informed of, and responsive to, the rapidly changing needs of economic development.

◊ Towards that end, I undertook initiatives related to curriculum development, and syllabus support. These included the establishment of an Education Trust, called the *CII Education College*, that funded syllabus-related projects by teachers' subject associations, and the organisation of careers talks in schools.

◊ I collaborated with many teachers' associations, particularly the IGC, BSTAI, and ISTA, of the last of which I was elected President for the years 1988-1990.

◊ The CII worked closely with academic staff in the universities and other higher education colleges and produced reports and organised conferences on issues such as industrial innovation. Other higher education initiatives included modern language training through the EOP, the promotion of programmes to increase recruitment of graduates by business and industry and the placing of an emphasis on industrial design.

◊ Industry submissions advocated increased emphasis on training within the workplace and on health and safety issues, including employee assistance programmes.

CHAPTER 12
A NEW DAWN

PROMOTION OF ECONOMIC AWARENESS

From the late 1970s, the CII was conscious of the need to promote community economic awareness as a foundation for enlightened public policy formation. **Chapter 11**, *Back to Basics*, described how the CII recognised and fostered the role of post-primary schools, as a uniquely useful medium of communicating with critically important cohorts of the population, either as persons approaching adulthood, or as adults and parents:[1]

> 'In October 1979, the Confederation embarked on an extensive campaign to explain the vital role of industry to teachers, parents and post-primary pupils, through talks in schools by industrialists, plant visits, and conferences.

> The climax to the campaign was reached in a massive public relations exercise in autumn 1981 with the launching of the film, *The Voice of Industry*, viewed by over 600 non-cinema audiences – clubs and societies, trade unionists, teachers and opinion-makers at large – within six months of its release.'

The CII view was that community understanding of the economy was an essential prerequisite to the generation of public and political willingness to take the steps necessary to achieve economic progress, create more jobs and earn higher living standards.

The societal importance of economic literacy was stressed by the CII in publications[2 to 22], and in public lectures.[23 to 32] My belief was that one reason for past incorrect national economic decisions was a societal misunderstanding of the role of the State. The popular misconception seemed to have been that Government *per se* was an independent agent of economic growth and was a provider of *free* services to an almost unlimited extent. Perhaps this misperception could be traced back to the view in Ireland that Government was a 'foreign imposition', separate from the general community, coupled with the fact that Ireland came late to industrialisation. The reality is that Government *per se* has only one ultimate economic power: the right to tax some citizens, and, directly or indirectly, make real resource transfers to others. Government can, and does, help to create the environment for enterprise in the public and private sectors.

Two definitions are important:

Economic growth
'Economic growth can only come about through an increase in the production of goods and the performance of traded services by enterprises – public and private – at costs which are internationally competitive.' (Joint Programme for Government of Fine Gael & Labour, December, 1982)

Competitiveness
'The immediate and future ability of, and opportunities for, entrepreneurs to design, produce and market goods and traded services within their respective environments whose price and non-price qualities form a more attractive package than those of competitors abroad or in domestic markets.' (European Management Forum)

In 1979, the CII referenced a number of studies published in the 1970s that indicated a conflict between the expectations of young people and job opportunities then on offer.[33][¶] Those expectations were formed by social attitudes and by the traditional relationship between schools, colleges, and universities and the labour market. The influence of parents was important, and their attitude was conditioned by their knowledge of the labour market and of general economy. In many cases, that knowledge had not kept pace with rapidly changing technological developments and with the establishment of many new high technology and high value-added service industries.

The use of the film, *The Voice of Industry*, commissioned by the CII in 1981, on my initiative, was particularly effective in creating widespread public awareness of economic issues.[34] The film gave a vivid portrait of the nation at work, and presented the views of industrialists, employees, academics and community leaders. Not only was it shown to over 600 non-cinema audiences during the first six months after release, it achieved over 1,100 screenings during its two years' effective life. Discussions with the audience that followed each screening gave valuable feedback to the CII of the economic mood of the general community.

[¶]   The studies referenced by the CII had been undertaken by AnCO, the Irish Foundation for Human Development, the European Centre for the Development of Vocational Training, Gaeltarra Éireann, and a number of other organisations.

October 1981, at the first viewing of *The Voice of Industry*: (left to
right) Liam Connellan, CII Director General; Con Power, CII
Director of Economic Policy; and film producer, Louis Marcus.

I also was responsible for a second CII public awareness film, *Inflation*,
launched in November 1983.[35] This is described in **Chapter 10**, *The Money
Illusion*. In addition to extensive non-cinema screenings, the film was
broadcast on RTÉ 1 television during the week before Alan Dukes TD,
Minister for Finance, introduced the Budget 1984![36]

CII maintained a well-resourced Press & Publications Office, with a
high profile in the print media, local and national radio and television. The
CII *Annual Report 1980*, for example, records that industrialists filled the
key interview spot in the RTÉ radio series, *Face the Future*, from October
1980 to May 1981 and, in the following year, industry spokespersons were
on 29 such programmes.

In summer 1980, the CII, jointly with ICTU, made a submission to the
RTÉ Authority on the subject of economic awareness programmes on
television and radio. The CII *Annual Report 1981*, records that 'close liaison
was maintained with RTÉ, and, as a result, the CII made a significant input
to the research for the television series, *A Future in Mind*'. The relationship
with RTÉ was of fundamental importance in helping to ensure that

industry's views on economic development issues were disseminated to the widest possible audience.

Five years later, the CII *Annual Report 1986* states:

> '*Radio Series on Careers*: The Confederation has been keen to encourage a comprehensive radio series on careers in Irish industry. A Sub-Committee of the Manpower Policy Committee has been considering various features and characteristics that could be included in such a radio series. Proposals have been put to RTÉ, and it is hoped to have a response from RTÉ Radio 1 in the first half of 1987.'

In addition to central policy and sectoral publications for member enterprises, the CII annually published a number of booklets for post-primary schools and for the general distribution. Some examples are listed in the CII *Annual Report 1981*.[37] The CII continued to distribute publications of an economic awareness nature to post-primary schools, until that project was superseded by the work of the CII Education College, incorporated in December 1984.

The CII distributed its regular publications to public authorities and to each member of Dáil Éireann and Seanad Éireann. The regular publications included the weekly *CII Newsletter*, the *CII Monthly Economic Trends*, and the *CII / ESRI Monthly Industrial Survey*.

Senior staff met on an on-going basis with the Taoiseach, Ministers, Opposition Leaders, Opposition spokespersons and groups of national politicians to brief them on issues of importance to business and industry. Staff occasionally spoke as invited lecturers at political conferences. One-to-one briefings were given at the request of senior politicians on issues contained in CII's regular publications, on submissions that were made by the CII or on topical economic issues. The CII made formal submissions to Government on issues that impacted on business and industry and most of these were published in the weekly *CII Newsletter*.

In 1987, on my initiative, the CII organised a programme to link individual TDs and Senators, on a one-to-one basis, with enterprises for the purposes of obtaining short structured business briefings and to give senior business management the opportunity to learn about the functioning of the political process. The idea of linking individual politicians with business, in a formal programme organised by a trade association, began in Sweden in 1980 and subsequently spread to other Scandinavian countries and to the UK. The CII programme was organised in consultation with the Leaders of the then four main political parties – Fianna Fáil, Fine Gael, Labour, and the Progressive Democrats and took place in autumn 1987. By early December 1987, 47 politicians had volunteered to participate in the programme, of whom 41 were TDs and six were Senators.

NATIONAL ECONOMIC STRENGTHS & WEAKNESSES

The CII accepted and promoted the fundamental economic reality that, in the long run, a nation must establish its industrial development strategy on the firm foundation of promoting those economic areas with comparative advantages over its international competitors on home and export markets. The message for Ireland, as for every other developed and developing country, was to identify niches of national comparative economic advantage and to promote those with thoroughness and consistency.

The complexity of the task of auditing Ireland's strengths and weaknesses was demonstrated in the annual *EMF World Competitiveness Report 1986*, published prior to the PNR in 1987. The EMF Report assessed the competitiveness of 31 countries under each of no less than 340 criteria.[38]

The CII list of Ireland's economic strengths was given in my talk in November, 1987:[39]

♦ Stable Government within the European Community.

♦ Well-developed financial, commercial, and industrial framework.

♦ Sophisticated fiscal and other incentive packages for the promotion of industrial and commercial development.

♦ An open, internationally trading economy.

♦ A well-educated young population with high technology, applied science, and other business skills.

♦ A clean living and working environment that was ideal for many types of tourism.

♦ An indigenous supply of natural gas, with the prospect of developing oil and renewable energy resources.

♦ Mineral resources, not yet fully explored.

♦ Agricultural land, technically among the best in the world for many agricultural and horticultural purposes.

♦ Significant potential for forestry.

♦ Marine and inland fisheries potential.

♦ A modern telecommunications network, nationally and internationally, with the potential to underpin data processing and related services.

♦ International renown in areas of literature, culture, and sport.

♦ The success of having attracted more than 900 multinational manufacturing plants to Ireland up to 1987, ranked first by the EMF Foundation in 1986 and in a number of previous years for the extent to which inward foreign investment was nationally welcomed.

Against those 14 strengths, the CII identified only four primary weaknesses, against each of which it vigorously campaigned:

♦ The low level of economic literacy in the general community.

♦ The inordinately high level of Exchequer expenditure, mainly through transfer payments, with gross current Exchequer spending plus the PCP amounting to 68.2% of GNP (60.4% of GDP) in 1987.

♦ The massive burden of National Debt, which was projected to reach at least 151% of GNP by the end of 1987, and which consumed a sum in debt servicing equal to almost the entire proceeds of PAYE tax, thus considerably reducing the ability of Government to bring order to public finances.

♦ Poor public infrastructure networks, particularly the transport infrastructure, including the network of national roads.

In retrospect, it is interesting to compare the CII's list of national economic strengths and weaknesses given in November, 1987, with the results of a survey of the poorer regions of the EC carried out in May 1990.[1] The study listed the five most positive factors for Ireland:

♦ A very modern telecommunications network.

♦ General availability of labour.

♦ Availability and quality of the education and training facilities.

♦ Favourable social climate.

♦ Availability of skilled people.

Four out of the five positive factors related to people and to intellectual skills, and the fifth related to telecommunications technology, in which a geographically peripheral region did not necessarily suffer from infrastructural cost disadvantages. The five factors provided a template

---

[1] The study was undertaken by the *Institut für Wirtschaftsforschung* of Munich on behalf of the European Commission.

against which to assess the business areas in which Ireland had comparative economic advantages.

MOVE UP THE KNOWLEDGE CHAIN FOR JOBS

The major thrust of the PNR 1987 was on economic development, with a special focus on job creation. Many of the solutions proposed and implemented under the PNR and its successor, the PESP 1990-1993, both at macroeconomic and sectoral levels, had been advocated by the CII throughout the previous decade and the CII provided the input data for a range of proposals adopted in the PNR.

The main development areas identified in the PNR were:

♦ Manufacturing industry, including toolmaking, automotive components, mechanical engineering, electronics, multinational enterprises, clothing, craft products and DIY products.

♦ State enterprises export services, including through the State agency Development Co-operation Organisation (DevCO), with the focus on technical assistance and training for developing countries by such as Aer Lingus, the ESB, Bórd na Móna, and FÁS.

♦ The IFSC in Dublin.

♦ Knowledge-based industries, including computer services, health services, education services, and architectural and engineering services.

♦ Natural resources, including the food industry (beef, pig processing, and sheep meat), horticulture, forestry, and the marine (both sea fishing and inland fisheries).

♦ Tourism.

In September 1986, the CII's assessment of growth industries with employment potential was given at a conference for the IGC.[40] The list is interesting in the light of the sectoral proposals subsequently contained in the PNR.[¶] Some months prior to the publication of the PNR, the CII

¶   The growth sectors proposed by me at the CII *8th Annual Careers in Industry Conference* were: (1) high technology engineering and science-based industries, including small indigenous enterprises with materials, components, and services linkages to major enterprises, including multinationals and State enterprises; (2) processed consumer food products, including meat, fish, vegetables, snacks, and prepared meals; (3) goods with a distinctive quality Irish image, including craft goods; (4) internationally-traded

published its own national development policy, which concluded that, given a competitive environment for enterprise, supplemented by internationally-competitive business development incentives, Ireland could achieve a sustained industrial growth rate of 7% *per annum*, resulting in the creation of an estimated 100,000 additional jobs during the decade of the 1990s.[41]

The acceleration of centralisation of heavy production facilities, in the geographically and demographically more favoured locations in Central and Eastern Europe, meant Ireland was necessarily obliged to focus on industries that did not rely on heavy plant, and that, consequently, did not suffer from infrastructural cost disadvantages. Suitable activities included high technology industries, knowledge-based industries, internationally-traded professional services, internationally-traded financial services, and education and training services. The CII's view was that knowledge, in the widest sense, was the key to Ireland's economic progress and it worked with senior academic staff in the universities and technological colleges to help to promote a climate favourable to such developments.

Liberalisation of international trade in services, then the subject of negotiations within the EC in the context of the completion of the European Single Market by 1992[42] and within the General Agreement on Tariffs & Trade (GATT),[43] would present both a challenge and an opportunity for a small, open, trading economy, such as Ireland. In the CII's view, the industrial development strategy of a small, island nation needed to include a major emphasis on the development of traded services. These services depended primarily on the skills of people and on information technology. There was a need to ensure that the legislative and administrative environment in Ireland was supportive of the development of internationally-traded services, and that the foreign language expertise of people matched the information technology skills that provided instantaneous global communications. Legislation,

---

professional and financial services and knowledge-based industries, together with education and training services, including training in high technology skills and English language training for overseas students; (5) areas of import substitution, including agricultural and horticultural products, clothing, and furniture; (6) infrastructure provision, including the network of national roads, the completion of the natural gas grid, other elements of the transport infrastructure, and essential economic and social infrastructure; (7) natural resource development, including forestry, mining, gas and hydrocarbon exploration, agriculture, horticulture, and mariculture; and (8) the products and services of the tourist industry, with particular emphasis on high-added-value market niches, and business tourism, including fishing, boating, equitation pursuits, cultural events, and the ranges of activities related to Ireland's rich cultural, sporting, and natural resources.

regulation, administration, personnel skills, and communications technology were available equally to a small island nation as to a larger nation and, in Ireland's case, they could be brought together to provide a significant input to economic wealth generation and job creation.

IRELAND'S SERVICE INDUSTRY DEVELOPMENT STRATEGY

While international developments within the EC and GATT served to put in sharper focus Ireland's industrial development strategy, the promotion of internationally-traded services using Ireland as a base was not a new concept. The *Finance (Miscellaneous Provisions) Act 1958* exempted certain traded services operations carried on within the Shannon Free Zone from taxation for a period of 25 years. The *Corporation Tax Act 1976* continued the exemption until the year 1990 for businesses established prior to 1 January 1981. The *Finance Act 1981* extended the 10% manufacturing tax rate to those service companies until December 2000.

Ireland gave its first formal recognition to the national economic importance of developing internationally-traded services, when the services of architects and engineers were designated within the mandate of Córas Tráchtála in 1969. The move was followed by the addition of the services of quantity surveyors in 1971. However, it was a further 12 years before a wide range of other internationally-traded service areas were included within the mandate of Córas Tráchtála under the *Export Promotion (Amendment) Act 1983*. These additional services ranged from agricultural development and processing services to training, technical consultancy, and public administration.

High added value in manufacturing was emphasised in the *IDA Industrial Plan 1978-1982*, with the statement that:

> '... the central industrial strategy in the IDA Plan is to shift our industry into products with higher added value based on good quality and design aimed at specialist market niches using well planned professional marketing'.

Prior to that, in 1974, the IDA had extended its activities to include assistance of non-manufacturing or service enterprises able to secure business outside Ireland, while creating jobs in Ireland. The primary focus from the earliest stage was on engineering, architectural, and financial services, together with computer software. The IDA was empowered, in

1981, to give employment grants to international service projects that contributed to regional and national development. Examples included data processing, software development, technical and consulting services, commercial laboratories, administrative headquarters, healthcare services, research and development centres, recording services, training services, publishing houses, and international financial services. The IDA had been intensively marketing the concept of Ireland as a centre for international services and had been stressing factors such as the abundant source of well-educated labour, political and economic stability, and a strategic location within the EEC. The IDA stressed the generous incentive package that Ireland had developed for service industries. The key elements of that package were employment grants, training grants, a favourable corporate tax environment, capital grants, business parks, and low cost finance. The IDA was, at that stage, developing a business park at Sandyford and intended to develop another on land south of Dublin Airport.

ADVANCES IN INFORMATION TECHNOLOGY

The application of information technology and the tremendous growth in trade in financial and other information technology services had given rise to new systems linking the users and the providers of information. These were known in the industry as 'value-added communication networks', and operated at three levels:

♦ Some multinational organisations maintained their own private international communications networks for internal corporate communications purposes.

♦ Some international networks operated on an industry basis, and provided access for participant organisations within the industry. The industries covered by such networks ranged from banking to oil exploration. These networks were not new. One of the early industry networks was the *Societé Internationale de Telecommunications Aeronautiques* (SITA), which had been established in 1947 and, in 1986, had 240 airlines in membership. Another relatively early industry organisation was the Society for Worldwide Interbank Financial Telecommunications (SWIFT), established in 1973 and with a membership of more than 1,000 banks in nearly 50 countries by 1986.

♦ There were publicly available networks that allowed private individuals with the appropriate communications technology to send

messages *via* the normal telephone lines, and to obtain instantaneous
access to information stored in a wide range of databases. The majority
using those public networks worked in research institutions and
libraries, professional practices, and major commercial enterprises.

Thus, by the late 1980s, based on developments over the previous 40 years,
it was possible to foresee the early establishment of major international
communications networks that would provide an international
marketplace for trade in information. The technical capacity existed for
financial markets to operate on a worldwide basis and, within the EEC,
there were many legislative proposals that would impact favourably on
such a development.

An EEC telecommunications report of 1986 reviewed the priority areas
for action, with special reference to co-operation on the development of
EEC telecommunication services and networks; joint infrastructure
projects; the creation of an EEC market in telecommunications terminals
and equipment; provision of a programme to develop the necessary
technology for increasing the use of wideband networks; improvement of
access to advanced networks and services for less-favoured regions; and
co-ordination of negotiating positions in wider international bodies.[44]
Arising out of this, the EEC Council of Industry Ministers adopted a
resolution on the intergovernmental use of videoconference and
videophone techniques.

The European Commission, in 1991, stated that the electronics and
information technology industries within the EC represented a very
important sector of business with a turnover of 175 billion ECUs, and a
market that was rapidly growing at nearly 5% of GDP *per annum*, with
significant progress in fields such as computer software and services, and
industrial automation.[45] The Commission proposed five types of action
within the EC to help firms through the adjustment process, without
taking artificial measures to support the enterprises: demand for products
and services; technology, including the launching of a second generation
of research and technological development (R&TD); training, particularly
in multi-disciplinary skills, and the provision of networks of excellence,
composed of both academic and industrial teams geographically
distributed throughout the EEC; external relations, including the seeking
of a satisfactory conclusion for those industries in the multilateral
negotiations of the Uruguay Round of the GATT negotiations; and the
creation of a healthy business environment, including improvement of the
financing systems, faster standardisation and integration of standards into

products, and closer involvement of the development of electronics and information technology in the introduction of structural policy.

The Commission pointed out that the impact of information technology on employment was considerable. Between 60% and 65% of the working population in the EEC was directly or indirectly affected by these technologies and their applications. The Commission also noted that there were about 13,000 computer services and engineering companies in the EEC whose strengths lay particularly in the integration of customised software and systems.

In 1991, about 5,000 people were employed in software development in Ireland, almost a five-fold increase on the 1985 figure of 1,100. Software products contributed significantly to export earnings, and accounted for about IR£600 million (€762 million) in exports in 1990. The European Commission pointed out that, within the EC as a whole, there were not enough engineers and researchers in the labour market with up-to-date training in the production, adaptation and use of information technologies. The Commission added that, due to a lack of qualified staff, such as systems engineers and staff trained in computer-aided management, user industries and small businesses were unable to benefit from the competitive openings in the information technology field. The Commission stated that Japan trained 80,000 engineers a year compared with 41,000 in Germany and France combined, which between them have a similar population to Japan.

The structure of Ireland's manufacturing industry continued to change in the 1980s, side-by-side with the increasing emphasis on internationally-traded services. New technology industries, such as electrical, electronics, chemicals and pharmaceuticals, increased output by an average of 15% *per annum* over the 15 years prior to 1990, well anticipating the Celtic Tiger.[46] During the same period, the food, drink and tobacco sector increased output by an average of only 3% *per annum*. The traditional low added-value, labour-intensive industries, in aggregate, suffered a decline in output by about 2% *per annum*, but reported a significant increase in output in 1989. By 1990, Ireland was unusual within the EC in that half its total manufacturing output was from the fast-growing new technologies sectors, auguring well for a continuation of faster growth in industrial output than the rest of the EC, thus putting in place the conditions necessary for the growth to come. New technology enabled industry to improve its competitiveness, expand exports and output, and achieve a relatively good employment performance. R&D was one of the key elements in promoting the process of change.

In that context, the CII welcomed the announcement by the EC Council of Research Ministers of the Third Framework Programme.[47] The six elements of the Programme were information and communications technologies; industrial and materials technologies; the environment, life sciences and technologies; energy; and human capital and mobility. The CII sought to ensure that the Third Framework Programme responded more clearly to the needs of indigenous enterprises in sectors where Ireland had a comparative advantage, such as agribusiness, agriculture, forestry and fishing, including through the development of centres of excellence in the higher education sector. The CII encouraged the higher education sector to act as both catalyst and coordinator for coalitions of SMEs engaged in R&D, in view of the very small size of Irish SMEs. Across the EC in aggregate, according to the EC Commission, SMEs participated to a considerable extent in EC R&D programmes, and were involved in more than half the European projects that dealt with industrial-based R&D. In 1989, about 66% of the budget for the European BRITE / EURAM programmes went to industry, of which 30% was allocated to SMEs.[¶]

INTERNATIONAL FINANCIAL SERVICES

In the GATT Uruguay talks that opened in 1987, the EC emphasised the need to improve the functioning of the international monetary and financial system, in parallel with efforts to improve international trade. Ireland was ahead of that move by including international financial services in the *Export Promotion (Amendment) Act 1983*. The financial services industry had grown rapidly over the previous two decades, and was still growing in 1987. In addition, there was significant internationalisation of the financial services business in Ireland since the start of the 1970s, not least as a spin-off from the establishment of more than 850 multinational manufacturing plants here, primarily under the IDA programme. Many multinational financial services institutions followed their manufacturing clients to Ireland, as well as generating international business for Irish financial services providers.

[¶]   The BRITE (Business-Related Initiative for Technology-based Enterprises) programme is a two-year schedule of one-to-one mentoring, business networking and business skills training, funded by the ESF and the National Development Plan. The European Academy of Management (EURAM) is a professional society for scholars in the field of management.

Chapter IV of the 1985 European Commission's *White Paper, Completing the Internal Market,* was divided into three sections that dealt with financial services, transport, and new technologies and services.[48]

The section that dealt with financial services was further sub-divided into banks and insurance. The programme for the completion of the European Internal Market by the end of 1992 included 43 legislative proposals to create a common market in services; of those, 23 related directly to financial services – banking, insurance, and transactions in securities. Almost one-third of the package of more than 300 legislative enactments required to complete the European Internal Market related directly to finance, including the legislative and fiscal environment within which financial transactions took place.

The 1985 *White Paper* detailed issues relating to the accounts of banks; accounts of foreign branches of banks; freedom of establishment and freedom to supply mortgage credit services; re-organisation and winding up of credit institutions; harmonisation of the concept of 'own funds'; establishment of a guarantee system of deposit within the Community; and control of large exposures by credit institutions. Developments at EEC level on liberalisation of trade in financial services were proceeding rapidly on some fronts.

A major breakthrough came on 28 October 1985, when the Council of Finance Ministers approved a Directive governing 'undertakings for collective investment in transferable securities' (UCITS), whose rules applied to unit trusts and other mutual funds. Member States had until October 1989 to incorporate the Directive into national laws. Without these EC provisions of 1985 and, thereafter, the establishment of an international finance centre in Dublin would hardly have been possible.

THE IRISH FINANCIAL SERVICES INDUSTRY

In the early to mid-1980s, the financial services industry in Ireland numbered about 2,000 institutions. They employed between them almost 45,000 people or 4.1% of the total at work in the economy, an increase of more than 150% over the preceding two decades, and the sector was still growing. The Irish figure was proportionately the third highest in the then EEC 9, after the UK at 19.7% and Luxembourg at 5.5%. The percentages for other EEC countries were Italy 1.8%, France 2.6%, Denmark 3.6%, Belgium 3.7%, Netherlands 3.8%, and the Federal Republic of Germany 2.8%. In

1985, despite a fall in overall employment in the Irish economy, employment in the overall services sector increased by 3,000 persons.

One essential part of the framework necessary for Irish financial services to participate fully in international business was the enactment in Ireland of a Data Protection Act. Legislation was needed in order that Ireland could comply with the Council of Europe Convention on Data Protection. The Federal Republic of Germany, France, Norway, Spain, and Sweden had already ratified the Convention, and the United Kingdom planned to do so in 1987, when its own legislation was fully in place.

Mutual recognition of higher education diplomas was a precondition to the extension of international trade in services, as many service industries, including elements of the financial services industry, were based primarily on the exercise of formal professional skills.

Service marks could not be registered in Ireland under the *Trade Marks Act 1963*. Protecting this intellectual property became urgent in the light of the rapid developments in technology and the application of information technology to financial services that resulted in a high level of service product innovation. The number of new service products being developed was likely to increase significantly with intense competition on both home and export markets. Competition was being fuelled, not only by innovations in technology, but also by the erosion of the traditional barriers between the various sectors of the financial services industry. As the number of new services offered to customers increased, it was essential that the public be able to distinguish the new service products from other competitive services, both indigenous and imported. The best way of facilitating this was by the registration of service marks.

Many of the obstacles to the development of international trade in financial services would disappear if there were harmonisation of exchange control regulations within the EEC, and on a broader international basis. World trade in goods and traded services was worth about US$2 trillion in 1984; international capital transactions handled by the financial services industry were estimated at between US$20 trillion and US$50 trillion, all in 1984 dollars.

Only two full members of the EMS did not impose controls on capital movements: the Federal Republic of Germany and the Netherlands. The rest of the EMS contrasted with that position and with the position of currencies such as the US dollar, Sterling, and Yen that were widely traded on an international basis, and that were virtually unrestricted by exchange controls.

There were movements throughout the world to allow linkages between the sectors of the financial services industry. Links between banks and building societies were common in the United Kingdom, links between insurance companies and banks were growing, credit card companies operated in direct partnership with banks, and it was possible for 'outsiders' to buy into stock-broking companies. There was a link between a building society and a Trustee Savings Bank in the UK. It was accepted on a wide basis in the industry in Ireland that there were broad common interests that linked all financial intermediaries and deposit-taking institutions, and all institutions concerned with capital formation in private hands. The financial services industry in Ireland exhibited all the hallmarks of a heavily-regulated industry.

The system of regulation and the code of taxation under which the industry operated gave rise to many distortions in the financial markets. It was, therefore, in the mutual interests of all sectors of the industry to work together towards the achievement of a large measure of deregulation, a prerequisite for a financial services centre.

THE FINANCIAL SERVICES INDUSTRY ASSOCIATION

The economic growth and employment potential of the Irish financial services industry were identified in a number of CII talks in autumn 1982 and spring 1983.[49 to 53] In late 1983, I conceived the idea of establishing, within the CII, a broadly-based representative body to focus the development of the industry, including internationally-traded financial services. A prerequisite was the promotion of political and public awareness of the contribution of financial services to economic development and job creation, so that Government could take the necessary public policy steps to underpin the development of the industry in the national interest. I discussed the proposal with Liam Connellan, Director General of the CII, in the first week in January 1984. He supported the idea, and thus began a process resulting in the establishment of the FSIA, now Financial Services Ireland. My initial step in the political arena was, in early January 1984, to discuss the idea with Ruairí Quinn TD, Minister for Labour, whom I had known since 1969, after which exploratory talks were held with representatives of the financial services industry.[54] Quinn, the relevant Minister for employment and job creation, as an architect, was a practitioner in an internationally-traded service profession, and he immediately identified with the concept. On my suggestion, the Minister was the guest speaker at the CII National Council lunch in April, 1984, when he spoke about economic development issues and his vision for the development of the economy.

Ruairí Quinn supported my initiative from an economic development and job creation perspective and, on my invitation, met with the inaugural FSIA Working Party, prior to the formal establishment of the Association. The first General Meeting of the FSIA was held in Confederation House on 26 November 1984, followed by the formal launch of the FSIA at a CII Press Conference on 10 December 1984.[55] Niall Crowley, Chairman of AIB, was appointed chairman for the initial two years, and I became the Director of the FSIA, while remaining the CII Director of Economic Policy.[1] Ruairí Quinn continued his encouragement and support for the development of the FSIA during 1985, including attending a meeting of the FSIA Council. He was the guest speaker at the FSIA's First Annual General Meeting held in February 1986.[56] Subsequently, European Commissioner Peter Sutherland, in April 1987, acknowledged that Ireland, with the FSIA, was then the only country in the EEC with a single organisation representing the totality of the financial services industry.

THE INTERNATIONAL FINANCIAL SERVICES CENTRE

In October 1983, some months prior to developing the proposal to establish the FSIA, I drafted a submission to Dublin Corporation suggesting that financial services had a role in economic development and job creation in the city of Dublin, along lines similar to the City of London.[57] Following the establishment of the FSIA, I continued to develop proposals for a broadly-based internationally-traded services zone in Dublin. In November 1985, I made a formal proposal to Dublin County Council for the development of internationally-traded financial services in the Council's proposed Enterprise Zone adjacent to Dublin Airport.[58] The

---

[1]   *Irish Independent*, 11 December 1984, 'Financial services body set up': 'The first director of the association is Con Power, the CII's director of economic policy, and generally regarded as being number two in the organisation to Liam Connellan, the director general. Mr Power's appointment to look after the FSIA in its early days is perhaps a measure of the importance of the financial services industry, now undergoing something of a revolution'.

proposal was reinforced by me some days later at a talk to the Irish Corporate Finance Conference in Dublin.[59][¶]

Subsequent to that, twice in March 1986, I discussed with Fergus O'Brien TD, Minister of State at the Department of the Environment with responsibility for Urban Renewal, the possibility of promoting the development of international financial services in Dublin city and, in the same month, I discussed the matter separately with John Boland TD, Minister for the Environment.[60] I developed my discussion with the Minister in a paper given at a conference in April 1986,[61] a copy of which I sent to both Ministers. The conclusion in the talk of April 1986 was:

> 'One very practical step that can be taken is to provide another major physical focus for the development of internationally-traded financial services by giving pride of place to this type of development in the Custom House Docks Area under the terms of the *Urban Development Bill* and of the additional incentives contained in the *Finance Bill 1986*.'

Additional meetings on behalf of the FSIA were held with Fergus O'Brien TD, and with John Boland TD, Minister for the Environment, subsequent to the talk of 21 April 1986, and to high profile radio and television interviews on the same day.[62] In follow-up, the FSIA Council met with the IDA to progress the proposal.[63]

In June 1986, the campaign was brought a step forward in a talk to the Irish Computer Services Association about the possibility of the Custom House Docks area of Dublin being developed as a major International Finance Centre.[64] The proposal received significant news media publicity.[65]

The magazine *Stubbs Business* gave a major impetus to the campaign in July 1986, when it carried as its front cover story the text of my talk to the Irish Computer Services Association in June. *Stubbs Business* gave on the front cover an artist's impression of a developed Custom House Docks site, and overprinted thereon the

---

[¶]   The full text of my talk was distributed to all participants. Additionally, I sent copies to relevant Ministers, Ministers of State, Opposition spokespersons, civil and public servants and financiers. It is worth noting that Mr Dermot Desmond, a practical entrepreneur and man of great vision, took the risk and gave the dynamic leadership that saw these ideas converted into a real bricks and mortar financial services centre.

caption 'Con Power's Plan ... International Finance Centre'.[66] In direct follow-up to the article in *Stubbs Business*, Peter Drew of the Taylor Woodrow Group, London, contacted me early in July 1986, to discuss the proposal and we met in the autumn of 1986.[67]

The FSIA Council had a second meeting with the IDA in October 1986, to outline the FSIA's ideas relative to the development of internationally-traded financial services and to pledge the support of the FSIA members for such a development.[68]

Subsequent to the IDA meeting, I had my final meeting with Fergus O'Brien TD on the proposal to develop internationally-traded financial and professional services at the Custom House Docks in November 1986.[69] The approach was backed by the FSIA Council, with an assurance of the wholehearted backing and participation of the major Irish financial service providers, and with the supportive view of the IDA, given to the FSIA Council at the October meeting. I was accompanied by Peter Drew of Taylor Woodrow, who indicated that his company would be interested in competing to undertake a development of that nature at the Custom House Docks, and based on his experience in London and elsewhere, he was convinced that such a development would be eminently viable. The Minister's thinking for the development of the Custom House Docks at that stage was more along the lines of up-market retail, general commercial, and entertainment, something that he saw as 'an extended Grafton Street, open 24 hours per day'. The Minister did not see internationally-traded financial and professional services as the sole or primary profile of the proposed development at the Custom House Docks, although he did not rule out such services as part of a broader mix.

In a supportive response to the Minister in December 1986, the CII reminded member enterprises of the generous package of tax and rates incentives under the *Urban Renewal Act 1986* and the *Finance Act 1986*, which applied to the Custom House Docks Development for construction projects, commercial buildings, and dwellings, for both owner-occupiers and lessors.[70] Separately, the FSIA, within the CII, undertook a survey among member enterprises to assess interest in the Custom House Docks project among Irish financial services enterprises.[71]

I met again with Charles J Haughey TD in November 1986, to discuss with him the outline suggestion for an International Services Centre at the Custom House Docks, under the terms of the *Urban Renewal Act 1986*, with a special reference to international financial services.[72] I advised Haughey of the support of the CII and of the FSIA and Peter Drew of Taylor Woodrow, who accompanied me, outlined the London docklands developments. Haughey expressed interest, and said that he intended, when returned to Government, to promote the development of internationally-traded service industries, including financial services. As a follow-up, the CII was invited to provide a guest speaker at the Fianna Fáil Business Conference in January 1987, to give the CII's views on development proposals for the economy.[73]

A General Election was held on Tuesday, 17 February 1987. The new Dáil met on Tuesday, 10 March and Haughey was elected Taoiseach. He established an IFSC Committee and appointed me to that Committee. The Committee met for the first time on 9 April 1987. In follow-up to the positive response that he had given us at the meeting in November 1986 (see reference 72), An Taoiseach, Charles J Haughey TD invited Peter Drew of Taylor Woodrow and me to meet with him and Pádraig Flynn TD, Minister for the Environment, in April 1987.[74]

In May 1987, subsequent to the establishment of the IFSC Committee, the CII issued a questionnaire to member enterprises to gauge support for the project. Within three weeks, 58 responses were received, of which 32 were firm expressions of interest from major Irish financial institutions and some international financial services providers with branches or subsidiaries in Ireland.

The CII *Annual Report 1987* referred both to the establishment of the FSIA and to the IFSC as follows:

> 'The Confederation's leadership role in recognising the importance of the financial services industry through the formation of the FSIA in 1984 was rewarded by the decision of Government to establish an international financial services centre in Dublin with EC approval. This sector, which currently employs 45,000 people in the economy, is expected to expand rapidly over the next decade.
>
> 'The Confederation welcomed Government approval for an International Financial Services Centre at the Custom House Docks in Dublin. This was in accord with CII proposals, which were first made in November 1985, regarding the location of such a Centre on land near Dublin Airport. This proposal was amended to embrace the Custom House Docks in April 1986, when the *Urban Renewal Act 1986* was under discussion in the Dáil. The Confederation is represented on the International Financial Services Centre Committee, and the FSIA is separately represented.'

A Special Report in *The Irish Times* in February 1988, contained reference to
the genesis of the IFSC.[1]

IRELAND AS AN INTERNATIONAL EDUCATION CENTRE

Throughout the 1980s, the CII stressed that education was itself a major
international industry. The CRC for the PNR established a Working Group
in July 1989 at the request of the Government, to assess Ireland's
development as an international education centre. The Working Group, of
which I was a member, looked at education services in both the public and
the private sectors at all levels of education. It assessed the position of full-
time and part-time students, and the potential for the Irish education
sector overseas. Work overseas might include the establishment of Irish
campuses in other countries, and also the marketing and franchising of
Irish higher education qualifications and validation systems overseas.
Targets were set in terms of student numbers, jobs to be created, and
income to be earned. The development of private sector education projects
was seen as a new business development area for the IDA, with significant
potential for jobs and for added value in the economy. In 1989, a small
number of projects had already been negotiated, including a Japanese
post-primary school in County Kildare.

I was chairman of the Working Group on Ireland as an International
Education Centre, established under the PESP 1990-1993. One outcome of
that Working Group was the establishment by Government of the
International Education Board – Ireland, to promote Ireland as a centre for
international education. The Board included representatives of the higher
education sector (public and private), English as a Foreign Language (EFL)
schools, Government Departments, and State enterprises.

---

[1]   23 February 1988, *The Irish Times*, Special Report on the CII, *Catering for the fast expanding
services sectors*, in reference to the FSIA and the Custom House Docks: 'One of the often
forgotten contributors to such thinking is the Confederation's own director of economic
policy, Mr Con Power. The CII's director general, Mr Liam Connellan, points out that Mr
Power first made such a proposal for Dublin in November 1985. In various speeches, he
gave wider publicity to the concept, and the cover story of the 4 July 1986 issue of *Stubbs
Business* magazine is *Con Power's plan ... International Finance Centre*. By an amazing
coincidence, the cover illustration shows that his proposal for the centre envisaged new
offices to house the centre on the Custom House Docks site. "We're not concerned about
authorship, but innovation", says Mr Connellan, "we're here to mould opinion". Mr Power
was the founding director of the FSIA, a position now occupied by Mr Greg Byrne.'

TOURISM

The CII promoted tourism as an industry with significant growth potential and with economic links to many other sectors of the economy.[75] Despite the potential and the linkages, the tourist industry was one of the most undervalued industries in terms of both public and political perception. Development of the industry, which at the time gave direct and indirect employment to about 90,000 people, was recognised by Government and the social partners in the PNR 1987, which set a target of 25,000 extra jobs, and an additional IR£500 million (€635 million) *per annum* of foreign tourist revenue.

The CII recognised that a clean environment was an essential prerequisite to the promotion of up-market tourism. That was particularly important for inland fishing, which was in danger of declining as a tourist attraction, due to water pollution. The necessary high-quality leisure craft facilities also needed to be provided by private sector investment in the potentially profitable lake and river cruising business.

In the 1980s, Ireland had a number of major international cultural events such as the Yeats Summer School in Sligo, the Merriman School, the Wexford Opera Festival, and the Waterford International Festival of Light Opera, to name but a few. A special focus was needed on attracting to Ireland people who claimed ethnic Irish descent, and who wished to trace their ethnic roots here. A related activity was the teaching of the English language, particularly to primary and post-primary pupils from other EEC countries, and from further away. Tourism implied having an attraction that others wanted to enjoy and providing the access transport infrastructure to get to that attraction. The latter point, for example, was especially relevant to the Waterford International Festival of Light Opera and similar festivals in the context of road, rail, sea, and air.[76]

There were already about 900 multinational enterprises with manufacturing plants in Ireland and there was scope to encourage them to hold their international conferences here. About 20% of visitors to Ireland were business tourists; the remaining 80% came here for leisure holidays.

In public policy terms, the CII believed that it was essential for the Government to recognise the commercial viability of tourism, and to treat the export tourism sector on the same basis as manufacturing and internationally-traded services for all purposes of taxation and of industrial development. The extension of the Business Expansion Scheme to cover export tourism projects in the *Finance Act 1987*, was a step in the right direction, as was the reduction in 1986 of VAT on meals to 10%.

COMMERCIALISATION OF STATE ENTERPRISES

The CII advocated the commercialisation and development of State enterprises, recognising that, in Ireland, there had not generally been a doctrinaire approach to the use of public enterprise as an instrument of economic policy.[77] In the early 1980s, there were about 30 commercial State enterprises, including Aer Lingus, B & I, Bord na Móna, ESB, Irish Life Assurance Company, Irish Shipping, Irish Steel, Irish Sugar Company, Kilkenny Design Workshops, RTÉ and the VHI. The vast majority of these saw themselves as part of Irish industry and identified with their counterparts in the private sector through membership of the CII. The CII returned to the issue of State enterprise following the 1986 NESC Report and during the social partnership negotiations of 1987.[78 to 81]

The PNR 1987-1990 contained a schedule of job creation projects, mainly for commercial ventures, submitted by State enterprises. Part of the process of review of the State commercial enterprises was the establishment, on 27 March 1990, of a Working Group, under the CRC of the PNR, to assess the economic development and job creation role and contribution of those enterprises. The outcome of the review was the formulation of principles by the Working Group, accepted by the CRC, to reduce constraints on the viable economic development of State enterprises. The principles covered the four broad areas of commercial freedom, funding, social obligations and environmental controls. They were incorporated in the PESP 1991-1993.

During the course of the PNR and the PESP, there were a number of noticeable successes in cost containment of some State enterprises. Airfares for European routes were down in 1990 by over 35% in real terms on the 1986 levels. On a cumulative basis since 1985, Irish electricity prices were reduced by an average of nearly 19% for industrial consumers, 15% for commercial consumers and 12% for domestic consumers. There was an average decrease in prices charged by Telecom Éireann of 3% in 1989 and an average decrease of 2.5% in 1990.

A number of legislative changes facilitated developments within the State enterprises. One example was the establishment of Coillte Teoranta as a new State enterprise, responsible for forestry. Another example was the *Electricity Supply (Amendment) Act 1988*, which allowed the ESB to establish subsidiary companies that facilitated the expansion of external activities. A third example was the legislative change in the *Agricultural*

Credit Act 1988, which allowed the ACC, for the first time, to lend outside the agricultural sector.

Even after the PNR was agreed, the debate on the merits of public enterprises continued. The CII endeavoured to bring balance to the debate and to defend and promote the continued commercialisation of State enterprises, within the public sector.[82 to 84] In personal interventions in February and March 1991, I defended the rationale for State enterprises and advocated wider shareholding in those enterprises; the need for a clear operating mandates; adequate equity capitalisation and access to commercial capital markets; 'above the line' payments by the State for the performance of non-commercial functions; and freedom to follow a commercial pricing policy.[85 & 86]

The State took a number of initiatives to restructure State enterprises. One such example was the Irish Life Assurance Company. The Minister for Finance announced on 12 March 1990 that the Government had decided to proceed with the restructuring of Irish Life, to enable it to develop into an Irish-based international financial services company in the insurance sector.

It was a *sine qua non* that, if the Board of a State enterprise was to be effective, one of the primary considerations for the appointment of directors should be the experience and expertise of the individuals concerned relevant to the particular company. This factor applied irrespective of the method of selection of non-executive members of boards of public enterprises, whether through Government or Ministerial appointment, public service selection, or though some form of competitive selection. Once appointed, the directors of the State enterprise should be allowed to manage the enterprise within the terms of the mandate contained in legislation, and the directors should not be subjected to the hazard of a 'second guess' by the parent Government Department, or a 'third guess' by the Department of Finance.

Commercial criteria related not only to the marketplace, but extended also to personnel and remuneration policy. The dictates of commercial markets meant that top management in State enterprises needed to receive a remuneration package comparable with that of their counterparts in analogous private sector organisations. Commercial realities dictated that the board of the State enterprise should have the same level of commercial freedom relative to pay policy for employees, as was exercised by the boards of private sector enterprises.

The commercial operations of enterprises depended primarily on input costs, the efficiency of operations, and output prices. Input costs for commercial State enterprises should be allowed to follow the normal commercial pattern without the imposition of arbitrary or discriminatory levies and without using the State enterprise as a form of 'hidden tax collector'. An example of a hidden tax was the discriminatory heavy fuel oil levy on the ESB, which was double that imposed on manufacturing industry in general.

State enterprises had complained that pressure was sometimes placed on them to stay within their core business and not to diversify into other areas in competition with the private sector. Those companies claimed that they should neither be discriminated against, nor favoured by, the State in their commercial dealings, solely because the Government was the only or main shareholder. They believed that public and private companies should be treated equally in the marketplace.

The OECD reported in 1990 that, during the previous decade, there was a growing disenchantment with public enterprises in a number of OECD countries, primarily because of their unsatisfactory economic performance.[87] The State enterprises in many OECD countries moved into deficit during the 1970s, and they were very slow to react to changing market conditions and market demand. OECD acknowledged that the slow reaction of State enterprises had been partly due to intervention by Governments, and to the imposition on those enterprises of goals other than the goal of profit maximisation. On the other hand, OECD pointed to a number of studies that indicated that there had been poor management, and that there was an absence of the monitoring discipline of private capital markets.

In response to concerns about the operation of State enterprises, several OECD countries reduced the degree of State involvement through the sale of public enterprises during the 1990s. These countries included the USA, Japan, Germany, France, Italy, United Kingdom, Canada, Austria, Denmark, Netherlands, New Zealand, Norway, Spain, and Turkey. The most dramatic example was in the UK, where almost 60 public enterprises were privatised in the 1990s. In the case of New Zealand, there had been extensive recourse to privatisation with two main objectives: improving efficiency and profitability; and reducing the country's large foreign debt.

The OECD suggested that, on the evidence available, where competition was effective, private enterprises were generally to be preferred to public ownership on both internal efficiency and social welfare grounds. In the case of public utilities, however, the OECD referenced a study by Vickers & Yarrow (1990), which concluded that, from studies of electricity and water industries in the USA, there was no presumption in favour of either public or private regulated ownership. Vickers & Yarrow stated that there was little evidence of gains in efficiency or profitability subsequent to privatisation of utilities in the UK, where the significant improvements in performance took place prior to privatisation and in an environment of regulatory reform. They acknowledged, however, that it was too early to judge the final outcome.

As the CII represented the commercial and economic development interests of enterprises in both the private and State enterprises sectors, it had no doctrinaire view on shareholding, private or public, and was solely concerned to promote a climate favourable to enterprise in terms of legislation, regulation, administration, taxation and the provision of efficient infrastructure networks.[88]

The European Commission was introducing a new monitoring system that would require each State enterprise in the manufacturing sector, that had a turnover of more than 250 million ECUs *per annum*, to make an annual report to the Commission. The objective was to identify when State aid was present in the financial flows between public authorities and publicly-owned manufacturing companies.[89]

The CII, in submissions between 1981 and 1991, recommended to Government that State enterprises be allowed to develop commercially, and proposed operating principles for this to be achieved.[90]¶

¶   The operating principles for State enterprises proposed by CII were: (1) the mandate for
     each State enterprise required definition in legislation. The cost to a State enterprise of
     operating a social or strategic mandate on behalf of Government should be met by an
     above the line transfer from the Exchequer; (2) if a monopoly existed in the market
     served by the State enterprise, the efficiency of the enterprise should be judged by
     reference to appropriate international comparisons; (3) commercial freedom was
     needed for the board of directors, implying that the directors should be appointed
     because of their commercial acumen rather than their political allegiance; (4) the Board
     of Directors of a State enterprise should be allowed to manage the enterprise within the
     terms of the legislative mandate; (5) market dictates meant that top management
     should be remunerated comparably to their counterparts in the private sector; (6) the
     implementation of a programme of expansion by the enterprise required access to the
     commercial capital markets, including freedom to seek a quotation on the Stock
     Exchange, to buy and / or to sell whole businesses or parts thereof, and to enter into
     joint ventures. Commercial freedom implied no guarantees by the State for capital or
     current operations; (7) the State enterprise needed freedom to pursue a commercial
     pricing policy; (8) the capital structure of a State enterprise should permit employee
     shareholding schemes similar to those available in the private sector since 1982; (9)
     input costs to the commercial State enterprises should be allowed to follow the normal
     commercial pattern, without using the enterprise as a form of 'hidden tax collector'.

The record of State commercial enterprises in Ireland was a long and mainly honourable one; there was no reason why those enterprises could not operate profitably, and make a return to the Exchequer. It was vital to ensure that Irish and EEC legislative, fiscal and administrative systems did not discriminate against State enterprises in their commercial operations solely because the Exchequer was the only or the major shareholder.

BUSINESS LINKAGES FOR SMES

During 1990 and 1991, the CII organised a number of presentations by major member enterprises in the public and the private sectors to SMEs to encourage the development of sub-supply of goods and traded services. These presentations were successful. Based on the pilot venture of 1990 and 1991, the CII raised with the CRC of the PESP the issue of sub-supply by SMEs as an economic development and job creation project.

February 1993: presentation of An Taoiseach's Business Linkage Awards: (left to right) Donal Downing, Aer Lingus; Alan McCarthy, An Bord Tráchtála; Albert Reynolds TD, An Taoiseach; Kieran McGowan, Managing Director, IDA; Con Power, Department of the Taoiseach.

The CRC endorsed the validity of the approach and asked the State Companies Linkage Group under the PESP, which I chaired, to prepare a scheme for An Taoiseach's Business Linkage Awards to be funded by the

Department of the Taoiseach. The Awards were both for State enterprises and for SMEs. I collaborated with the IDA and An Bórd Tráchtála to structure the scheme, which was launched on 2 October 1992. A National Adjudication Committee selected the winners, and An Taoiseach, Albert Reynolds TD presented awards at a function in Dublin Castle on 22 February 1993.

SUMMARY

◊ The CII undertook an extensive information campaign to promote public and political awareness and understanding of the nature of the economic difficulties that faced Ireland in the early and mid-1980s. This was one prerequisite to the establishment and subsequent success of social partnership.

◊ I researched and promoted high added-value business areas, including international financial services, knowledge as a traded commodity, Ireland as an international education centre, tourism, the further encouragement of foreign direct investment, the identification of Irish business opportunities in Eastern Europe and the strategic positioning of Ireland as an international hub between North America, Europe and the Near, Middle and Far East.

◊ Details are given of my key role in the conception, foundation and initial direction of the FSIA (now Financial Services Ireland) in December 1984, and of a series of papers by the author, between 1985 and 1987, that proposed the establishment of, and helped to lay the foundation for, the IFSC in Dublin.

◊ I also researched and promoted the further commercialisation of State enterprises within the public sector and the promotion of business linkages between major public and private sector enterprises and SMEs.

CHAPTER 13
WINNING WITH EUROPE

EEC MEMBERSHIP & PUBLIC EXPENDITURE

Chapter 2, *The Evolution of National Policy*, records that the CII actively campaigned for Ireland's membership of the EEC. The CII, then the FII, formally adopted a free trade policy in 1968, reversing its previous protectionist policy. On a broader political and societal front, preparation for EEC membership was somewhat imbalanced, as the pro-EEC political campaign for the referendum in 1972 placed too narrow a focus on income support and grants from the EEC.

In my view, the electorate and interest groups were led to believe that there would be significant transfers to Ireland of EEC resources, which they would not have to earn. Understandably, that approach led, in turn, to popular demands for additional public services immediately after joining the EEC. Those public services could not be provided out of the proceeds of taxation and successive Governments borrowed at home and abroad to fund delivery of their promises and meet popular expectations. The story of public expenditure is told in **Chapter 3**, *The Economy: Warts & All!* Suffice it to say here that the EBR rose sharply from 6.4% of GNP in 1972, the year prior to Ireland joining the EEC, to a peak of 15.7% in 1981 and was 9.1% in 1987.[1] The National Debt in 1972 was IR£1,451 million (€1,842 million), or 56% of Irish GNP, of which less than 9% was borrowed abroad, so that the external debt servicing drain on the Irish economy was small.[2] The National Debt as a percentage of GNP rose to 85.7% in 1981 and peaked at 117.6% in 1987, amounting to IR£30,085 million (€38,200 million), of which 41% had been borrowed abroad. The foreign debt element as a percentage of the total had peaked in 1983 at 48%. Comparative figures for the National Debt / GDP ratio for all 12 Member States of the EC in 1989, when Ireland submitted the *National Development Plan 1989-1993*, ranged from 6% for Luxembourg, 22% for Germany, to 120% for Portugal, with Ireland at 106.8%.

Servicing the National Debt consumed 25.4% of net Government current expenditure in 1987, or 32.6% of total tax revenue. In many of the years of the mid- to late 1980s and early to mid-1990s, Irish foreign debt servicing exceeded the value of transfers to Ireland from the EC Structural Funds.

The CII constantly emphasised the reality that a sovereign State must earn its own jobs and living standards through its own real economic output; borrowing to provide current public services was unsustainable! Membership of a wider international group, such as the EEC, could help by way of resource transfers in the short-term, provided the transfers were invested in improving the capacity of the poorer country to earn an enhanced economic output. Investment in a nation's capacity to earn more jobs and higher living standards primarily means investment in infrastructure to conserve and enhance the natural environment, develop the built economic infrastructure, including the transport infrastructure, and enhance the human resources infrastructure through education and training. In the long-term, economic development was led by the market, and necessarily depended on improved market penetration for products and traded services. That, in turn, required enhanced market access, which, to the CII, was the major benefit of EEC membership.

THE EXTENT OF THE CHALLENGE

Against the background of the challenges of economic recovery, in August 1989 the NESC stated the view of the social partners, including the CII, that it was 'absolutely clear that Ireland's future lies in the fullest participation in the European Community'.[3] The NESC added that it was 'well aware of the problems and difficulties that have been, and will be, experienced in the process of integration'. The NESC concluded that there were two prime requirements for Ireland:

♦ A clear national strategy for European integration, which would provide a guide to external negotiations and domestic decision-making.
♦ Continued consensus among the social partners, at a national level, and at the level of each individual enterprise, to ensure a swift and flexible response, conducive to the objectives of fuller employment, higher living standards and a better social framework.

Based on past performance, Ireland's ability to grow at a rate high enough to reach EC average living standards within a realistic timescale needed to be seriously questioned. The major Government priorities in the EEC, since joining in 1973, were the protection of the CAP and securing the maximum funding from the European Structural Funds. Ireland was the largest net *per capita* beneficiary from those Funds in the pre-Celtic Tiger days. The programme of European Structural Funds, for the five years 1989 to 1993, provided Ireland with about IR£3 billion (€3.8 billion) of aid, which was double the *per capita* aid given to the other less-developed regions. Ireland, with only about 5% of the population of the less-developed regions, received over 10% of the allocation to those regions.

Despite the transfer of EEC resources since 1973, Ireland had made slow progress towards the achievement of economic and social cohesion within the EC. Irish GDP *per capita* was almost 61% the EEC average in 1960, when the modernisation of the economy got under way, following the 1958 Programme for Economic Development. GDP *per capita* had fallen to 59% of the EEC average in 1973, when Ireland joined the Community. By 1987, Irish GDP *per capita* was still only 64% of the EC, after 14 years membership.[4]

The progress of the Irish economy during the period from 1960, when modern Irish industrialisation gathered pace, to 1992, the year of completion of the European Single Market, was poor in comparison with the other three, less-developed, Member States of the EEC. A comparison published by the European Commission early in 1992 illustrated the point:

Table 13.1: % EEC *per capita* average GNP in less-developed Member States, 1960 & 1992

Country	1960 %	1992 %
Ireland	62.0	61.2
Greece	39.2	52.1
Portugal	38.6	56.7
Spain	59.9	80.3

Source: European Commission, 1992.

During the 20 years from 1960 to 1979, Irish GNP growth at 4.2% *per annum* on average was 0.1% less than the EC annual average of 4.3%. The situation deteriorated during the next decade, 1980 to 1989, when the Irish annual average GNP growth was 1.6%, significantly less than the 2.1% achieved by the EC on average. During that latter decade, Irish GNP growth had been only 0.2% *per annum* on average over the period 1980-

1986, increasing to an average of 3.6% *per annum* in the period 1987-1989. Using another measure of international comparison, Irish living standards, calculated as GDP *per capita* in purchasing power terms, amounted to 64.5% of the EC average in 1980, and this had only advanced to 68.8% by 1990. Irish GNP growth in the years 1989 and 1990 exceeded the EC average, with out-turns of 5% and 5.7%, respectively, compared with 3.5% and 2.9%, but, at that stage, it looked as if that favourable differential could not be sustained in the immediate future.

The pace of EC economic cohesion was far too slow for Ireland. The Government, in the *National Development Plan 1989-1993*, calculated that Ireland would need incremental growth of 1.8% *per annum* on average above the EC average for a sustained period of 25 years to reach EC average living standards at the end of that period. If the incremental growth rate were only 1.0% *per annum* on average above the EC average, Ireland would take 40 years to achieve the catching-up process.[5]

Unemployment was a related area in which Ireland failed to make progress within the EEC. Irish unemployment averaged 4.7% *per annum* during the period 1960 to 1973. The annual unemployment rate increased sharply to 8.1% in the period 1974 to 1980. By 1987, the PNR acknowledged an unemployment rate of 18.5% and stated that the unemployed numbered 242,000, of whom 73,000 were under 25 years of age, representing one of the highest unemployment rates in the EC. Indeed, for most of the period, from 1960 to 1992, Ireland's unemployment rate was almost double the EEC average, despite significant transfers from the EEC under the CAP and from the Structural Funds, the relative success in attracting FDI, and the accumulation of an enormous National Debt. Ireland was the only EC Member State not to have recovered its employment level of 1980 by 1990. The conclusion was inescapable: the policies followed had not been successful, as was confirmed in the *Culliton Report* of 1992:[6]

> 'The lesson that Ireland's problem of inadequate employment growth cannot be solved by large-scale spending programmes has been hard learnt. Instead of trying to create jobs directly in that way, it is clear that the approach must be to create the conditions in which ability and enterprise can be translated into employment opportunities.'

With living standards so much less than the EC average, and unemployment so much higher than the average, Ireland needed to address with urgency the formulation of strategic, economic development policies, better suited to the promotion of Ireland's own development interests within the EC.

The imperative for the future was that Ireland needed to solve its own problems, albeit with help from the richer Member States of the EC. Ireland needed to concentrate more sharply than heretofore on identifying and promoting economic activities with objective, long-term, relative advantages, such as knowledge-based industries, internationally-traded services, and natural resources. A less-developed region in a political union could not rely on being sustained indefinitely by income support and aid transfers from elsewhere within the union. Neither could a less-developed region rely on the indefinite use of cash and fiscal incentive packages to provide positive discrimination in favour of business location within the region, although both economic resource transfers and business location incentives could, and did, help in the short-term.

THE BUSINESS VOICE IN EUROPE

In 1972, the CII, in partnership with the FUE and the ACCI, established the Irish Business Bureau in Brussels. Subsequently, the CII established a comprehensive network of contact with the European Commission, the European Parliament, and the institutions of the European Community. The CII became an active member of UNICE. On a broad basis, each of the CII's central policy functions and each of the almost 80 affiliated federations, associations and groups was involved in European affairs.[¶] By way of example, a small number of areas are mentioned relating to the impact of the EEC on aspects of the CII's economic policy.

The CII was represented on the Economic & Financial Affairs Committee of UNICE in the years leading up to the Celtic Tiger.[7] This included membership of the Macroeconomic Working Party under the European Union Social Dialogue between the European Commission, UNICE and the European Trade Union Confederation (ETUC). In collaboration with the Director of the Irish Business Bureau in Brussels, a

---

[¶] In outline, the CII central policy functions dealt with Company Affairs – economics & taxation, business law, competition, innovation, and human resources; Infrastructure – transport, national roads, energy, environment; Regional Councils, with regional meetings in 15 centres throughout the country; International – foreign trade, bilateral business associations – of which there were 11 by 1990, and the Irish Business Bureau in Brussels. The sectors represented the interests of producers of goods and of traded services in both the private and the public sectors. They are named in **Appendix I**.

number of annual visits were arranged to the European Commission for representatives of the CII Economics & Taxation Policy Committee. Topics discussed with European Commissioners, members of Cabinets, and senior officials of the Commission, for example, in 1992 included State aids and economic and social cohesion, indirect tax harmonisation, European Structural Funds, and the then moves towards European Monetary Union.

On a wider European geographic basis, the CII was represented on the Free Enterprise Information Group (FEIG) of the CEIF.[8] The involvement was particularly relevant to sharing views and experiences with colleagues from other European Industrial Federations, on topics such as the making of strategic policy inputs to Government and public authorities, the promotion of economic awareness in the general community, and a range of public affairs issues. The FEIG promoted the production and use of industrial film and video and organised the Annual International Industrial Film & Video Congress, which the CII hosted in Dublin in 1989.

In 1980, the European Council of Ministers for Labour adopted guidelines for a European Labour Market Policy.[9] The CII responded to the guidelines in January 1981. The CII supported the emphasis by the Council of Ministers on dissemination of knowledge of the labour market, vocational guidance, training and re-training, and job placement services. Many of the initiatives contained in the policy reflected projects implemented by the CII since 1979. The CII was concerned that the European Council did not refer to the need to eliminate the 'black economy'. The CII view was that unrecorded employment was a growing phenomenon in Ireland and in some other EEC Member States and that action was required to eliminate the black economy in the interests of legitimate business and of the protection of taxation base.

CII representation on the Committee of the ESF of the European Commission facilitated a European involvement in education and training issues.[10] The Committee was structured on a tripartite basis, with representatives of Government, trade unions, and employers / industry from each Member State. Senior officials of the Department of Labour represented the Government, ICTU nominated the trade union representatives, and the CII and the Irish Employers' Confederation (the FIE and the CIF) nominated the employer and industry representatives. The Irish representatives from all three backgrounds met together prior to each meeting of the European Committee and agreed on a common national approach. Ireland benefited significantly from the ESF, both in terms of the quantum of funding and the economic development focus of programmes, ranging from the facilitation of the transition from agriculture to industry and traded services to the development of skills required by knowledge-based industries. On a wider geographic basis, the CII was represented on an Education Advisory Committee to the OECD, which involved participation in an industry / education forum for all industrial developed countries.[11]

The CII advocated the enhancement of mechanisms for employee information and consultation, in the context of proposals developed by the European Commission from 1980 onwards, initially as a company law initiative, and subsequently as a social affairs issue. Against the background of the continuing European debate, early in 1984, Ruairí Quinn TD, Minister for Labour, referred to the need for a continuous flow of information between management and workers at enterprise level, as a means of increasing communication and promoting greater harmony in industrial relations. The Minister stressed that he regarded this as a priority issue and that he would continue to exhort managers, workers, and their representative organisations to develop mechanisms for information sharing and communication. As mentioned in **Chapter 5**, in response to Minister Ruairí Quinn, the CII, in 1984, drafted guidelines for a *Code of Practice on Employee Information & Consultation*.[12]

The CII participated in a number of the initiatives that were proposed and implemented by the EC for the poorer regions, including Ireland, in the context of the completion of the European Single Market by 1992. As mentioned in **Chapter 12**, to some extent, the initiatives to promote the development of traded services were anticipated by the establishment of the FSIA within the CII in 1984, and by the CII proposals to Government for the establishment of an International Traded Services Zone.[13]

The CII was involved on a continuing basis in promoting the European dimension of Ireland's national roads network, regional development, local government issues, and environmental issues through, and in collaboration with, the Irish Business Bureau in Brussels.[14] This led, as mentioned in **Chapter 7**, *The Road to Tomorrow*, to my appointment as Executive Chairman of the interim NRA within the Department of the Environment,[15] and as a member of the Co-ordinating Committee for the National Programme of European Community Interest (Roads), funded with the aid of the ERDF 1986-1990.[16]

Involvement in various aspects of European affairs on behalf of the CII led directly to my collaboration with Brendan Halligan in recruiting many of the initial founding members to underpin the early viability of the

Institute of European Affairs, subsequently the Institute of International & European Affairs.[1]

April 1991, at the launch of the Institute of European Affairs, members of the organising committee: (left to right) Terry Stewart, Director of the European Commission Office; Derry O'Hegarty, Senior Partner, Deloitte & Touche; Con Power, CII Director of Economic Policy; and Brendan Halligan, Chairman, Bord na Móna. (Photo: © *The Irish Times*)

THE EUROPEAN STRUCTURAL FUNDS

The objective of the European Structural Funds was to help the poorer regions to become economically self-reliant and, thus, ensure that they could earn more jobs and higher living standards through self-sustaining activities. While transfers from the Structural Funds were high in absolute terms in the years leading up to the Celtic Tiger, the total resources allocated, in aggregate, to the less-developed regions of the Community (Objective 1 Regions) for the five years 1989-1993 amounted to only one-

---

[1]   I was a founding member of the Board of Directors of the Institute of European Affairs and was its first Vice-Chairperson, as well as a Member of Council, of the Executive Committee, and of the Finance & Administration Committee. The Institute was registered under the Companies Acts on 26 March 1991 and was launched at a press conference in Dublin on 23 April 1991. The eleven founding directors were Billy Attley, Tony Brown, Brendan Halligan, Brigid Laffan, Con Lucey, Maurice Manning, Stephen O'Byrnes, Derry O'Hegarty, Con Power, Terry Stewart and Frank Wall.

third of one per cent of the aggregate GDP of the European Community. The figure was 0.2% in 1988 and was projected to rise to 0.33% by 1993. It was likely that a transfer of between 0.2% and 0.33% of the aggregate GDP of the EC, *per annum*, over a five-year period would not be sufficient to achieve anything remotely resembling social and economic convergence for the less-developed regions of the EC. The European Commission described the inadequacy of the transfers from the Structural Funds in its *Annual Report 1987* concerning the ERDF:

> '... the trend differences in GDP and population growth imply that in the period immediately ahead no more than a small reduction in the disparity of average *per capita* income can be envisaged ... in 1992, average *per capita* GDP in the four poorest countries will still represent only some 65% of average *per capita* GDP in the four richest countries.'

The European Economic & Social Committee, in a commentary on the Commission's *Annual Report 1987*, stated that the doubling of the EC Structural Funds for the Objective 1 Regions could only have a minimal effect on achieving economic convergence for the less-developed regions of the Community.[18] The Commission's *Annual Report 1987* underlined the glaring disparities not only between Member States, but, more especially, between regions and sub-regions within those Member States, in terms of employment and of living standards.

The aid that Ireland received from the Structural Funds focused on: Agriculture, fisheries, tourism and rural development; industry, services and supporting infrastructure; overcoming the problems of geographic peripherality, especially by improving the transport infrastructure with special reference to the network of national roads; and human resource development.

Priorities, suggested by the CII, during the discussions that led to the preparation by the Government of the National Development Plan 1989-1993, included five infrastructure development areas and three economic sector development areas. The five infrastructure areas were transport; energy; education; environment; and telecommunications. Investments were made in each of the first four areas, but no Structural Funds were allocated to the completion of the telecommunications network during the period 1989-1993. The three sectoral development areas recommended by the CII were the food industry; forestry; and the tourism infrastructure. Investment was made in all three areas, particularly in tourism, including private sector projects.

Difficulties in Irish public finances resulted in a significant proportion of the funds being used for income support purposes, rather than for investment. Evidence of that was seen in the manner in which investment in the transport infrastructure was treated. The Government acknowledged that transport costs for Irish exporters to Europe accounted for between 9% and 10% of export sales values, and that the costs were approximately twice those incurred by EC countries, trading with one another on the European mainland. Notwithstanding the acknowledgement of the significant cost penalty placed on Irish business, and the acknowledgement that the condition of the network of national roads was one of the few remaining seriously deficient areas of national infrastructure, financial allocations for improving the network addressed less than 20% of the problems, in the five years 1989-1992. Investment in all modes of the transport infrastructure (road, rail, sea and air) amounted to 17% of the combined EC and Irish Government funds for all programmes in the Community Support Framework 1989-1993.

EU transfers to Ireland, although strategically important and focused in a number of key areas such as agriculture, infrastructure development (including the transport infrastructure), and human resource development, never exceeded 5% of Irish GDP *per annum*.

THE EUROPEAN SINGLE MARKET, 1992

The CII, together with other pro-European Community organisations, including the Institute of European Affairs, played an exceptionally active role in the referendum campaign in support of the *Single European Act 1986*, and claimed that this had a significant impact in achieving the 69.9% vote in favour,[19] despite a vociferous campaign against the *Single European Act* and considerable apathy, which resulted in the very low turnout of 44.1%.

Following the adoption of the *Single European Act*, the CII welcomed the historic agreement reached at the European Council in 1988, having as twin pillars the completion of the European Single Market by 1992, and the doubling of the Structural Funds in order to accelerate the development of the weaker regions of the EEC, including Ireland.[20] The CII's view was that the opening of the European market was very much in Ireland's interests, and the CII saw the opportunities of this new home market as underwriting Ireland's potential to create more jobs and earn higher living standards. The principle of the Single Market was supported by freedom of movement of people, goods, services and capital.

The view of the European Commission was that the introduction of the Single European Act (SEA) in 1987 gave a major boost to Ireland at a time when 'its economy was, in 1987, on the brink of economic disaster'. The Commission regarded this development as 'the most important factor in the recovery and rehabilitation of the Irish economy'. The Commission's belief was that the SEA forced a change in Irish business strategy and refined corporate Ireland's 'commercial prowess'.[21]

During 1988, the year after the enactment of the SEA, much of the CII's energies were concentrated on raising Irish industry's awareness of the implications of 1992, realising that most major measures affecting the business environment would already be in place long before 1992. The CII's message to its members was that the European Single Market would affect all enterprises, irrespective of size, not just because of the abolition of frontiers, but also because of important new developments in technical standards, legislation, patents, trademarks, company law, and freedom of establishment. Throughout the second half of 1988, the CII organised many briefings and seminars on each aspect of the Internal Market that impacted on Irish enterprises, irrespective of size, that manufactured goods or performed traded services in both the private and the public sectors.[22]

Through ratification of the Treaty on European Unions (Maastricht Treaty) by referendum on 8 June 1992, Ireland ensured strategic positioning at the core of a rapidly-evolving European Union.[23] The turnout at the referendum was 57.3% and the vote in favour was 69.1%. The Maastricht Treaty opened the way to political integration through the creation of three pillars:[24] the concept of European citizenship; the powers of the European Parliament; and economic and monetary union (EMU). Under the Treaty, the EEC formally became the European Community (EC).

A new European order was taking shape, and Ireland needed a strategic response. My personal view, given at an invited trade union lecture in Dublin in April 1992, was the following:[25]

> 'Full participation by Ireland in the European Union is the only way to ensure the economic, monetary and social progress essential to enhance access to markets; improve inward business investment flows; maintain low inflation and fiscal disciplines; reduce costs and interest rates; and consolidate Ireland as an ideally situated location for mobile international business investment.'

> 'Ratification by Ireland of the Maastricht Treaty must be accompanied by a pragmatic reorientation of domestic attitudes, policies and practices to develop an enterprise culture geared to earning more jobs and higher living standards by dramatically developing those manufacturing, services and natural resource areas in which we have a real comparative

> economic advantage over our international competitors on home and
> international markets … Success in the international marketplace also
> requires that Ireland must promote an image of self-confidence based on
> a reinstatement of, and an economic redefinition of, our national pride.'

By way of postscript, ratification of the Amsterdam Treaty was approved by referendum on 22 May 1998, with a turnout of 56.2% and a vote of 61.7% in favour. Ratification of the Treaty of Nice was rejected by referendum on 7 June 2001, with a turnout of 34.8% and a vote of 53.9% against. The Treaty of Nice was put to referendum a second time on 19 October 2002, after the insertion of a protocol clarifying the issue of neutrality. Ratification of the revised Treaty of Nice was approved at the second referendum, with a turnout of 49.5% and a vote in favour of 62.9%.

ECONOMIC & MONETARY UNION

Ireland joined the EMS in March 1979, and the Irish Pound broke its one-for-one parity with Sterling, which had obtained since the *Act of Union* in 1801. The CII supported the decision to join the EMS, as it offered the prospect of lower inflation, lower interest rates, and more effective control of development policy, while deepening Ireland's commitment to the EC.[26] During the first year of operation, the EMS proved to be a zone of monetary stability in a world where major currencies fluctuated violently. The Irish Pound held its value within the EMS and the CII supported the policy of the Central Bank regarding the management of Ireland's external reserves.

The first of three stages for full EMU began in July 1990, and Stage Two was scheduled to occupy the period between 1994 and 1997. The move to full EMU would take place as soon as seven EC Member States were willing to make the move, and to meet the full criteria. The CII strongly urged that Ireland be in the initial group of participating Member States.

Two major considerations arose from an Irish viewpoint relative to the criteria that would apply to each EC Member State in terms of eligibility for full membership of EMU. The first was the achievement of a high degree of price stability, in terms of a rate of inflation being close to that of the three best-performing Member States. The second major consideration of Ireland was the requirement to have a sustainable Government financial position. That would become apparent from having achieved budgetary positions within a deficit that met specific criteria. The two criteria relative to the Government deficit were:

- The ratio of the planned or actual deficit to GDP should not exceed a ceiling of probably not more than 3% of GDP.
- The ratio of National Debt to GDP could only exceed a reference value – the EC discussion was then centring around 60% – if the ratio was diminishing at a sufficiently rapid rate, and was steadily approaching the reference value.

The CII, for many years, had campaigned against excessive Government spending and the accumulation of National Debt. That campaign was meeting with success and the first of the criteria could be readily met. The EBR, which rose rapidly from 6.4% of GNP in 1972 to a peak of 15.9% in 1981, had since fallen steadily, and was 2% in 1990. The stated aim of Government was not to exceed an EBR of 1.9% in 1992, and, thereafter, to eliminate the EBR within a short period of years.

The situation was not quite as positive relative to the ratio of National Debt to GDP and GNP. The National Debt / GNP ratio in Ireland reached a peak of 130% in 1986,[1] but was on target be reduced to around 109% at the end of 1991, and the objective of Government was to reduce it to 100% by 1993. That would still be considerably in excess of the possible limit of 60%, but Ireland would validly claim that the ratio was diminishing significantly, and steadily approaching the reference value.

In addition to the two major considerations, from an Irish viewpoint, of price stability and Government finances, each participating Member State would be required to have respected the normal fluctuation margins provided for by the ERM of the EMS for at least two years without devaluing against any other Member State currency. The Irish pound was then firmly placed within the ERM of the EMS, and would have no difficulty in meeting the test.

Finally, the durability of convergence achieved by the Member State, and of its participation in the ERM of the EMS, would require to be reflected in the long-term interest rate levels. Irish interest rates depended greatly on movements in the country's external reserves. The announcement of a further relaxation in exchange controls, to take effect in 1992, helped sentiment in the financial markets and would benefit short-term interest

---

[1] The National Debt / GNP ratios for various years have been subsequently recalculated on a number of occasions by the Department of Finance, whose *Budget & Economic Statistics 2007* shows a ratio of 115.1% in 1986, with a peak of 117.6% in 1987. The ratio fell below 100% in 1990, when it reached 99.4%. The revised figure for 1991 was 96.0% and for 1993, 93.5%. The ratio went below the reference value of 60% in 1998, when it reached 54.6% and it fell each year thereafter until it reached 24.1% in 2006.

rates. Irish interest rates were close to the ECU rates, and the CII had consistently advocated control of public finances to ensure that the risk premium element of interest rates was reduced to a minimum. It was confidently expected that Ireland would be able to meet the test in relation to interest rates.

The view of Irish business was that Ireland should do everything possible to meet all four criteria for full participation in the final stage of EMU, on the grounds that being in the lower tier of a two-tier European Community would not be in Ireland's interests. History records that Ireland succeeded!

The CII supported the movement towards full EMU and, at an early stage joined the Association for the Monetary Union of Europe (AMUE).[#] In March 1991, the CII, jointly with the AMUE, organised a conference in Dublin on the topic of *Economic & Monetary Union.*[27] At that conference, I evidenced the Government's public support for the movement towards full EMU by quoting An Taoiseach, Charles J Haughey TD, who, on 9 March 1991, stated that before the end of the 1990s, the ECU would be the common currency in the EC and there would be a common economic and financial regime.[28] I also quoted an opinion poll sponsored by the AMUE in autumn 1990, that showed a 74% Irish support for a single currency.[29] My personal view was that the focus for Ireland within the emerging EMU needed to be more sharply on economic development aspects rather than on monetary aspects, where the richer and more powerful EC Member States would set the agenda. I observed that Ireland's aim should be real economic convergence within the EC and the pursuit of Ireland's economic advantage through enhancement of overall national competitiveness.

The second stage of EMU began on 1 January 1994. It provided for the establishment of a European Monetary Institute (EMI) responsible for strengthening monetary policy coordination, with special reference to price stability, making the necessary preparations for the establishment of the European System of Central Banks (ESCB) and monitoring the development of the European Currency Unit (later to become the Euro).

The third stage began on 1 January 1999, including the irrevocable fixing of the exchange rates between the national currencies and the ECU

[#]   Founded in 1987 by leading European industrialists, the AMUE supported the achievement of monetary union and the introduction of a single currency in the EC. It was an independent organisation, whose membership comprised mainly enterprises and business organisations, and it collaborated with research institutions and public authorities in the then 15 EEC Member States.

and the subsequent replacement of the national currencies of the participating Member States by the Euro. Strict economic convergence criteria were set for participating Member States, including criteria relative to price stability, public finances, participation in the EMS exchange-rate mechanism and long-term interest rates. Ireland met the criteria to participate in the third stage, *ab initio*.

Euro notes and coins were introduced on 1 January 2002, and Ireland's transition to the single currency was satisfactorily achieved within a very short period.[1]

SECTORAL DEVELOPMENT

In addition to monetary issues, Ireland needed to address the future of the main economic sectors, noting that the importance of agriculture in the economy had diminished considerably in each decade since the foundation of the State. Notwithstanding the decline, agriculture in Ireland in 1991 still employed about 15% of the workforce, in contrast to the EC average of 6.8%, and in contrast to the dramatically low figures for some other Member States such as the UK (2.2%) and the Netherlands (4.8%). Irish agricultural output contributed 9.7% of gross added value in the economy, more than three times the EC average of 3.1%. An international consultancy report indicated that agricultural land in Ireland was of a technical quality, among the best in Europe.[30] The CII argued that Ireland's search for a solution to high unemployment should include effective use of land and other natural resources, including alternative land uses, such as forestry and agri-tourism.

A major problem remained, as there was a continual decline in European demand for Ireland's two foremost agricultural products: beef and milk fat. Within the EC, butter fat consumption fell by 9% in 1989 and the demand for beef fell by 10%. The net result was that about 60% of beef output in Ireland was put into EC intervention, rather than sold to consumers. Ireland needed to focus on producing high added-value food products for final consumers, implying the need for a radical reform of the

---

[1]   Of the EU 27 Member States, 15 were in the Euro Zone by 2008: Austria, Belgium, Cyprus, Finland, France, Germany, Greece, Ireland, Italy, Luxembourg, Malta, the Netherlands, Portugal, Slovenia and Spain. 10 Member States resolved to join: 2009, Slovakia; 2010, Lithuania; 2011, Estonia; 2012 or later, Bulgaria, Czech Republic, Hungary, Latvia, Poland, Romania and Sweden. The remaining two Member States have not yet decided: Denmark and the United Kingdom.

CAP, then structured to militate against high added-value production. There was a notable absence of strategic thinking about alternative markets and products in the Irish agricultural sector. Irish agriculture faced other problems, including the high age structure of farmers, with more than 45% over the age of 50 years and with the very small size of many farms. Only 15% of farms were considered fully commercial, with a further 30% of farms having the potential for development. That meant that 55% of farms were marginal in an economic sense.

The shape of Irish industry altered dramatically in the years prior to 1991. Industry, for Irish statistical purposes, was divided into the sub-sectors of manufacturing; building and construction; mining, quarrying & turf; and electricity, gas and water. The major sub-sector within industry was manufacturing. Manufacturing employment, as a percentage of the total number at work, doubled between 1926 and 1989, from 10% to 20%. This doubling masked the true position, however, because the growth was very rapid between 1926 and 1951, from 10% to 15%; the figure of 17% was reached in 1958, and the percentage remained almost static at 20% since the 1970s. Meanwhile, the structure of Irish industry had changed. There was, in 1991, a far greater emphasis on high technology, knowledge-based industries and on multinationals. There were, for example, about 1,000 manufacturing multinationals in Ireland. They came from more than 25 overseas countries, with the greatest number from any single country from the USA. In 1991, there were about 350 USA manufacturing multinationals in Ireland, and between them, they directly employed about 47,000 people. USA manufacturing multinationals accounted for about 50% of all overseas manufacturing jobs, and almost 25% of total manufacturing employment!

Traditional low added-value sectors were in decline, but there was significant growth in areas such as chemicals, pharmaceuticals, healthcare products, precision engineering and electronics.

The Telesis Consultancy Group, a US consultancy, prepared a major report for the NESC in the early 1980s.[31] Telesis recommended a reallocation of public expenditure on industrial promotion in favour of internationally-trading indigenous industry and skilled sub-supply firms. The NESC, in 1989, confirmed that the change in direction had occurred,[32] and stated that the Telesis review 'confirms the correctness of the basic thrust of Ireland's industrial policy in recent years, *viz.* the placing of emphasis on indigenous enterprises rather than the attraction of mobile foreign investment'.

Telesis recommended that there should be a substantial reduction in the level of grants offered to new foreign firms, for two main reasons. Firstly, it estimated that Ireland offered considerably higher incentives than other comparable locations for average projects, and, secondly, it believed that funds could be better used in the development of indigenous industry. The CII, on the other hand, argued that there was a grave misunderstanding in relation to grants offered in Ireland. The report of the EC Commission on State Aids for the period 1986-1988 showed that State aid *per capita* of general population in Ireland, at €198, was significantly lower than the average for the then 12 EC Member States of €254. Luxembourg headed the list with €538, followed by Belgium, Germany, Italy and France, all of which were above the EC average. State aid to industry in Ireland was supplemented by Structural Funds grants given in the Industry & Services Operational Programme. The fact was that the poorer Member States faced unfair competition in terms of the high sums that richer Member States offered by way of direct cash grants to industry. The poorer Member States supported the EC Commission in its efforts to target aid to the less-developed regions, and to dismantle expensive and economically unnecessary aid programmes in the richer Member States.

A third major recommendation by Telesis related to improving control of the process of industrial development, and there followed a significant restructuring in the mechanisms of industrial promotion in Ireland over the years immediately prior to 1991.

Ireland, as a small island, suffered from access transport cost disadvantages. The integration of the EC, and of a wider Europe, provided a new challenge and a new opportunity for Ireland. The challenge was to place a far greater emphasis on skills as well as on the development of natural resources.

Three areas of internationally-traded services merit mention: internationally-traded financial services; internationally-traded education services; and software services. All three had been vigorously advocated by the CII since the early 1980s, with the vision that Ireland should develop the concept of the 'global office', which could apply to a wide range of professional services such as finance, engineering, architecture, graphic design, and any other sector where the skills of people could be translated into service products that could be transmitted on international telecommunications networks.

INDIRECT TAX HARMONISATION

Harmonisation of indirect taxes took place in the context of the EC Internal Market Programme, with the first two legal texts adopted in 1991. They were a Directive setting down the basic operating rules for the new VAT system from 1 January 1993, and a Regulation on co-operation between the EU Member States. Lobbying by UNICE was successful in having the statistical burden on small enterprises reduced.[33]

The CII's focus on the need to begin to bring Irish rates of VAT and Excise into line with other EC Member States began in the pre-Budget submission for 1989.[34] At that stage, the submission was to reduce the 25% standard VAT rate by extending the VAT base, at no net cost to the Exchequer. That was repeated in the submission for the 1990 Budget, when the CII pointed out that, in Ireland, VAT covered only about 35% of private consumption; the figure for the United Kingdom being 44%, whereas in most other EC Member States the VAT base covered about 90% of private consumption.[35] The CII's view on indirect tax harmonisation was conveyed in a submission to the European Commission in August 1989, copied to the Irish Government. The submission covered framework issues relative to VAT rates, VAT structures, Excise Duties, duty free facilities, and travellers' allowances.[36]

The CII, in its 1991 pre-Budget submission, urged Government to continue reducing the standard rate of VAT, which in 1990 had come down from 25% to 23%. The submission made detailed points about the sale of certain electronics goods.[37]

In its 1992 pre-Budget submission, the CII dealt with four operational elements.[38] The first was that VAT rates in Ireland be brought as closely as possible into line with corresponding rates in Britain to ensure that there would be no loss of trade in Ireland and no consequential loss to the Exchequer arising from a differential in favour of the United Kingdom, including cross-border trade with Northern Ireland driven by tax differentials rather than valid commercial imperatives. The second was that excise duties should be minimal on products and services that impacted on input costs in manufacturing and service industries. The third was that EC institutions adopt rates of duty on alcoholic beverages directly proportional to the alcoholic strength of each beverage, along the lines of principles established by the European Court of Justice. The fourth expressed concern at the complexity of interim proposals for the regulation of co-operation between Member States on indirect taxes, subject to the need to combat fraud.

DIRECT TAX HARMONISATION

FDI was facilitated mainly by the IDA, which was established in 1949 as an agency within the then Department of Industry & Commerce, and became an autonomous State-sponsored body in April 1970, under the *Industrial Development Act 1969*. One of the significant factors in enhancing Ireland's attractiveness as a location for foreign inward investment was a low corporate tax regime, initially zero for profits arising from certain export earnings, then moving to a 10% rate for manufacturing and certain traded services, and ultimately to 12.5% as a general fiscal measure.

The European Commission raised the question of enterprise taxation on many occasions, including in 1975 and 1984, but particularly from 1987 onwards.[39] The Commission's 1987 document had the objective of introducing a modern system of enterprise taxation, which would encourage economic efficiency and facilitate both investment and innovation. The Commission recognised that tax rates on enterprise profits within the EC needed to be reduced; tax systems had become too complicated; special tax allowances had accumulated; the creation of tax shelters, itself undesirable, frustrated the making of true economic decisions; and there was a built-in bias in favour of substituting capital for labour.

The CII strongly supported the Government's stance on the retention of Member State sovereignty in a number of tax areas, including enterprise taxation. Little progress, if any, had been made up to the commencement of the Celtic Tiger years, and the low Irish corporate tax regime continues, to the benefit of FDI. This point is still relevant and very topical in 2008!

IRELAND: EUROPE'S SUCCESS STORY

By the end of 1989, the preconditions for economic growth already existed in Ireland and the broad social partnership consensus on economic issues had done much over the previous three years to strengthen the environment of economic development.[40] Development depended on people who had the skills and abilities to produce and successfully market goods and services. It remained for the Irish to prove that, through a co-operative approach, economic success and social cohesion could be achieved on a scale that had eluded Ireland in the past. The success of the Celtic Tiger years, in retrospect, validates that view. An informed view from abroad was that of the Australian Trade Commission,[41] whose 2006 article noted that the Irish economy outperformed all other EU economies in the 1990s, recording an economic growth rate throughout the period that was three times the EU average. The article gives four reasons for success:

♦ Human capital, due to Ireland's investment in skills, education and training, notably in engineering, science and information technology from the 1960s.

♦ Excellent knowledge transfers between commerce and education, coupled with the Social Partnership Agreements.

♦ The promotion of close links between universities and business, with industry clustering, technology transfer and supply chain business linkages.

♦ An economy open both to trade and inward investment.

The article acknowledged that EU membership and assistance had helped Ireland. Importantly, it concluded that 'it was Ireland's own reforms, particularly in education and training, which were the key drivers of Ireland's economic success'.

In terms of economic statistics, the annual average growth rate of 6.9% in the 1990s was achieved with a modest contribution to this figure of 0.5% from European Union transfers. Without the transfers and the consequential focus on infrastructural and development projects, it is doubtful that the figure would have been as high as 6.4%! Admittedly, the EU transfers were mainly in key areas such as education, training, and economic infrastructure, and they acted as a significant catalyst for development. Fundamentally, access to the huge European Union market was an essential ingredient to the attraction of much foreign inward investment. European economic, social and fiscal legislation played a key role in creating the climate for enterprise.

SUMMARY

◊ Ireland's GDP *per capita* was only 59% of the EEC average in 1973, when Ireland joined the EC and was still only 64% of that average when the PNR was adopted by Government and the social partners in 1987.

◊ Subsequent to joining the EEC, each of the central policy functions of the CII and each of the almost 80 affiliated federations, associations and groups was actively involved in European affairs. Issues pursued included use of the European Structural Funds for infrastructural projects in education and

     training, energy, environment, telecommunications and
     transport.

◊ I played an active role in policy areas such as the completion of
     the European Single Market, EMU, sectoral development,
     indirect tax harmonisation and direct tax issues.

◊ European economic, social and fiscal legislation were key
     factors in creating the environment for enterprise in Ireland
     and access to the huge EU market was an essential ingredient
     in attracting foreign inward investment.

CHAPTER 14
IRELAND ON THE
WORLD STAGE

THE ISLAND OF IRELAND

On the world stage, the island of Ireland is a single geographic entity, despite the political division between the Republic of Ireland and Northern Ireland. However, in the early 1990s, the CII and the Confederation of British Industry (CBI) in Northern Ireland, in surveys among their members, found that there was a lack of knowledge on each side of the border about the market on the other side. Lack of market knowledge was accompanied by a concern about the risks of doing business in the other jurisdiction, particularly among enterprises in the Republic of Ireland, together with the practical problem arising from long delays for commercial vehicles crossing the customs and security-controlled border. Comparing Ireland with Denmark, which had a similar size population, the CII and the CBI Northern Ireland concluded that the sale of goods manufactured on the island of Ireland could be increased by at least 50% in aggregate within the two jurisdictions, were the island treated as a single economic market entity. Survey results showed that manufacturers in the Republic of Ireland were selling only one-third as much *per capita* in Northern Ireland as in the Republic, while manufacturers in Northern Ireland were only selling one-sixth as much *per capita* in the Republic as in Northern Ireland.

The CII and CBI NI established the Joint Business Council in 1991, with the objective of doubling trade between the two parts of the island within five to six years. The work of the Council received a significant impetus from a speech by Sir George Quigley in 1992, in which he urged enterprises, North and South, to give substance, on the island of Ireland, to the completion of the Single European Market.[1] The CII identified tourism as a business sector that, especially in Northern Ireland, would benefit significantly if peace was restored and with full cooperation within the sector, North and South. The work of the Joint Business Council was so successful that trade in both directions on the island of Ireland doubled from about €1,420 million to about €2,840 million between 1993, when CII merged with the FIE to form IBEC, and 2000, when Inter*Trade*Ireland began operations.[2]

One background development to the expansion of North / South trade was the establishment, in 1990, of a link between the CII and Kompass Ireland, publishers of business directories and databases.[3] A similar link existed between the CBI and Kompass UK. Appointment as chairman of Kompass Ireland led me to propose the publication of an *All-Ireland Business Directory*, having made many of the initial Northern Ireland business contacts, through on-going professional accountancy involvements.[4] The first *All-Ireland Business Directory* was launched by Desmond O'Malley TD, Minister for Industry & Commerce, in March 1992.[5] The directory gave comprehensive profiles of 14,000 enterprises on the island of Ireland, including the top 2,000 enterprises in Northern Ireland. The Minister observed that the *All-Ireland Directory* complemented the establishment of the CII / CBI NI Joint Council and the appointment by both organisations of executives to promote trade between the two parts of the island of Ireland.

A STRATEGIC RESPONSE TO THE NEW EUROPEAN ORDER

By the beginning of the 1990s, a New European Order was rapidly evolving, which was economic, cultural, social, monetary and political in nature.[6] In 1991, some of the more dramatic political events in the USSR and Central and Eastern Europe may have seemed remote from an Irish viewpoint, but it would have been foolhardy for Ireland to imagine it possible to escape the consequences of fundamental changes. An announcement was made on 22 October 1991 of an agreement between the EC and EFTA to establish the world's largest economic zone of 380 million people in 19 countries from 1 January 1993.

Considerable progress had been made towards the integration of the EC by the completion of the Single European Market at the end of 1992 and by the positive outcomes of the two intergovernmental conferences on *EMU* and *Political Union*.

Events in the early 1990s seemed to be moving rapidly towards an even more integrated form of political union: the ultimate shape of that political union was still unclear but, from an Irish viewpoint, it was imperative that Ireland put its own house in order, rather than accept as inevitable a long-term institutionalisation in the new structures as a permanently less-developed region. Ireland needed to concentrate on identifying and promoting economic activities with long-term economic advantages, learning from successful small countries both within the EC and on the wider world stage.[7]

EUROPE'S ECONOMIC SHIFT TO THE EAST

By 1990, two developments of direct relevance to Ireland were having a dramatic impact on the economic structure of Europe; the countries at the centre of the EC were becoming even relatively stronger and some of the Eastern and Central European countries were fast becoming significant international competitors, initially in the food industry, but ultimately the competition would extend across the full spectrum of business and industry. The economic, social, cultural, and political shift to the Centre and to the East had begun; Ireland needed urgently to address the strategic question of how to improve national competitiveness and enhance economic growth in the face of intense international competition.

More fundamental was the need to make strategic decisions about the sectors of business in which Ireland had comparative strengths, to make strategic international investment and trade alliances and to put in place all of the legislative, administrative, regulatory, fiscal, and infrastructural mechanisms and structures essential to provide a positive framework for enterprise.

GERMANY WITHIN THE EUROPEAN COMMUNITY

The former Federal Republic of Germany had extensive commercial links with the Western industrialised nations, which accounted for 86% of exports and 83% of imports. The Federal Republic made massive outward investments, of which over 80% were in the Western industrialised nations, half within the EC.

The history of the previous four decades supported the belief that Germany's external economic policy would remain oriented towards the maintenance and development of international trade and investment, and that Germany would remain firmly anchored within the EC and the West.

What Thomas Mann said in 1953 was still true in the early 1990s: 'We want not a German Europe but a European Germany'.[1]

The former German Democratic Republic (GDR) had the advantage of integration with the Federal Republic of Germany, with which it shared kinship, ties of history, personal relationships, culture and language. There were, however, short-term challenges. The modernisation of the former GDR would cost trillions of DMs and German industrialists believed that investments of that magnitude would far exceed the country's resources. The Federation of German Industries stated that finance, goods and expertise from Germany's Western economic partners would be necessary. Most of the business investment would have to come from the private sector, but the financing of infrastructures and the initial financing of the social insurance system would have to come from public funds. That had potential implications for Ireland in terms of the continuity and the quantum of the EC Structural Funds post-1993.[8] Following an analysis by the European Commission of the impact of the assimilation of the GDR into EC membership, the forecast was that the extra cost to the EC arising out of German integration would amount to no more than 500 million ECUs *per annum* until 1993. The Commission believed, however, that the process of German unification would require additional finance up to 2,000 million ECUs *per annum* for three years thereafter and this would have to come primarily from a redeployment of German funds, otherwise available for investment elsewhere.

There was a view within German industry that the problems faced by the former GDR in terms of rapidly increasing unemployment, social security and the cost of environmental repair would be far greater than originally envisaged. In addition, the initial assessment of the European Commission was that 30% of the former GDR fell within the definition of a less-developed region for the purposes of the Structural Funds, and that would place an additional demand on aid from EC Funds post-1993.

The unification of Germany necessarily interposed an additional step on the road to EC economic, monetary, and political union. There were some indications from within Germany that there might be a slowdown in the move towards EMU. Helmut Schlesinger, Bundesbank Vice-President, said on 3 October 1990, the day of German unification, that the Bundesbank saw little use in setting a firmer timetable for monetary integration within the EC. That was followed by the publication of a

---

[1]   Thomas Mann (1875-1955), the German writer who received a Nobel Prize in 1929 for his novel, *Buddenbrooks*, first published in 1901.

confidential report drafted by Hans Tietmeyer of the Bundesbank that *inter alia* outlined very stiff conditions for the transition to the second stage of EMU, including:

- The EC needed to have completed the European Single Market, including the elimination of all border controls.
- All currencies within the EC must have joined the narrow band of the ERM.
- The treaties on EMU must have been ratified by all of the EC Member States.
- The financing of public deficits by monetary measures must have been banned in all of the EC Member States.
- All national legislation must have provided that governors of Central Banks would not be subject to instructions that would undermine their independence.
- The convergence of anti-inflation policy among all EC Member States must have *progressed substantially*.

The report of the Bundesbank set down stringent conditions for the transition to the Third Stage of EMU: inflation must have been very largely eliminated in all EC Member States; budget deficits must have been reduced to levels that were not problematic; the process of convergence must have been accepted by the markets in the form of harmonisation of capital market rates; and the Central Banks of Member States must have become politically independent. It was likely that those stiff conditions for both the second and third phases of EMU would sharpen the focus of discussions. That could well have been in Ireland's interests, as it was likely that the problems faced by Germany in the integration of the former GDR would give Germany first-hand practical experience of dealing with a disadvantaged less-developed region within its own national territory.

OPPORTUNITIES, ADVANTAGES & THREATS

The integration of the European Internal Market provided a new challenge and a new opportunity for Ireland. The challenge was to place a far greater emphasis on skills and on the development of natural resources, which would bring sharply into focus the fact that industrial development policy needed to be based on ascertaining and promoting those business sectors in which Ireland had a competitive advantage on home and export markets. When the Internal Market was ultimately completed, resources would naturally move freely to the geographic regions of best comparative economic advantage: Ireland needed to identify and exploit to the full its own strengths, not only to earn Ireland's *place in the sun*, but even to *keep Irish heads above water*.[9]

The areas in which Central and Eastern Europe needed skills inputs, financed mainly by the West and particularly by the EC, were high technology, high added-value products and services; human resource development, including education and training; environmental protection; financial services; public administration; and other intellect-based activities. Irish management consultants and members of a wide range of practising professions were well-placed to obtain contracts for people development and infrastructure development in Central and Eastern Europe. Emphasis would be placed on the international languages of trade, marketing, technology, consumer attitudes, and the development of entrepreneurial skills.

Ireland had significant experience in the areas of education and training, both in the public and the private sectors, and could play a major part in projects operated under the aegis of the European Training Foundation. Education and training projects in which Ireland had comparative advantages included not only all of the technical and business disciplines, but also the teaching of English, which was a major requirement in all of the countries of Central and Eastern Europe. Opportunities existed through the European Bank for Reconstruction & Development (EBRD), which had been established in 1991, with headquarters in London. This was when communism was crumbling in Central and Eastern Europe and when the former soviet countries needed support to nurture the emerging private sector in a democratic environment.

The main thrust of the activities of the EBRD from the beginning was assisting the development of a competitive productive sector in each of the countries receiving assistance, mainly in collaboration with commercial partners. At least 60% of the loans made by the EBRD were to finance private initiatives; the balance of the loans could be used to finance the public infrastructures required for the activities of the private sector, including telecommunications and transport infrastructures. That meant, from the beginning, that there was considerable scope for participation by Irish telecommunications, civil engineering, and transport professionals in the projects financed by those loans. The EBRD became the largest single investor in Central and Eastern Europe and it mobilised significant foreign direct investment in addition to its own financing. In 2008, 61 countries own the EBRD, including Ireland, together with two intergovernmental institutions. Its Governors include Brian Lenihan TD, Minister for Finance, and David Doyle, Secretary General, Department of Finance.

Within the Single European Market, and on the wider European and world stage, opportunities would arise across a very wide economic development spectrum, but success would come only to those countries and those enterprises willing to invest time and effort to develop potentially exciting new markets.[¶]

For Irish industrialists to dismiss the potential competitive challenge from the countries of Central and Eastern Europe would have been a serious mistake. That was particularly true in the case of the former GDR, which had a long and deeply rooted industrial tradition that could develop very rapidly. Leipzig, Dresden, and other cities could again appear on the international business map. The Eastern *Lander* of Germany undoubtedly would be an attractive location for potential investors and traders, because of consumer market size and development potential.

THE RISK OF MARGINALISATION

The EC recognised that, in a Single European Market, there was a danger that the peripheral less-developed regions, including Ireland, could become increasingly marginalised unless there was a significant transfer of resources to such regions, to support the development of the physical and human resources infrastructures.[10] Such a transfer could only be short-term; Ireland would be required eventually to generate its own self-sustaining economic advancement. The danger of increased

---

[¶] The range of opportunities for Ireland could include education and training, banking, insurance, agri-business, airplane leasing, aircraft maintenance, tourism, precision engineering, electronics and informatics, computer services, software, distributive services, communications, auditing, management consultancy, and a wide range of products and services of knowledge-based industries and professional practices. On the other hand, some of the countries of Central and Eastern Europe would be competitors of Ireland in terms of the geographic location and market size advantages, which they could offer to internationally-mobile investment in heavy production facilities. Ireland suffers the serious access transport cost disadvantages associated with geographic location as a small island on the western periphery of Continental Europe, together with the relatively high unit transport cost of distribution to the geographically-dispersed small home market population.

marginalisation could grow with the inevitable unification of markets within the existing continental Member States of the EC, with Central and Eastern Europe. DRT International, of which Deloitte & Touche was the Irish member firm, surveyed many of its major clients in September 1990, and found that the former East Germany and Hungary were the two most favoured countries for investment, followed by the USSR and the then Czechoslovakia, later to become the Czech Republic and Slovakia. While there were still problems of prohibitive trade and investment regulations, DRT International's conclusion was that investment commitments of between US$20 billion and US$50 billion were probably in the pipeline for Eastern Europe from big international corporations. Although developments during 1991 may have been slower than some people expected, mainly because of the need to put into place the necessary legislation relating to banking, property ownership and business law, nevertheless, overseas investment was expected to amount to US$1 billion each in Czechoslovakia and Hungary that year!

THE DEVELOPMENT OF TRADE ALLIANCES

The CII undertook representational and operational activities to promote foreign trade. The first formal step in outward orientation was when a delegation from the then Federation of Irish Manufacturers (FIM) visited the CBI in London in 1947 and established a valuable and lasting liaison.[11] The following year, the Irish Government invited the President and the Secretary of the FIM to make themselves available in London for consultation during the talks that led to the signing of the Anglo-Irish Trade Agreement. During the 1950s, the FIM organised a number of international trade missions, including one to the Cologne Fair, Germany, in February 1958.

By 1979, the beginning of the formative years of the Celtic Tiger, the CII Director of Transport & Foreign Trade, John Kenna, was responsible *inter alia* for the CII Export Committee and the CII Developing Countries Group. The CII *Annual Report 1979* gives details of technical assistance projects awarded to Irish enterprises under the LOME Convention;[12] liaison with Córas Tráchtála on export issues; the promotion of trade and investment between Ireland and Japan in collaboration with the Japan External Trade Organisation (JETRO) which, in 1979, established its Irish offices in Confederation House; discussions with delegations from Greece, Yugoslavia, Turkey, and the USSR, together with discussions under the

GATT. A highlight of the annual lunch held in conjunction with the CII Annual General Meeting was the hosting of Ambassadors from all countries accredited to Ireland that traded with CII member enterprises.

In 1982, the CII actively promoted, among its members, the Employment Support Scheme, administered by Córas Tráchtála, to facilitate the recruitment and training of export salespersons.[13] That year, the CII added a special focus on Eastern European markets.

In 1986, the CII established a US Policy Group, under the chairmanship of Dr TP Hardiman, a past president of the CII, to focus on economic relations with the USA, including trade, investment, and industrial co-operation.

The Office of the Hungarian Chamber of Commerce, part of the Hungarian Ministry of International Economic Relations, was established in Confederation House in 1987, headed by a Counsellor. The Czechoslovak Trade Office followed quickly, also established in Confederation House.

By 1989, in addition to the foreign trade activities, the CII *Annual Report* recorded that the CII maintained a network of 1,200 Irish export sales executives resident abroad with whom the CII liaised through circulation of the CII International Newsletter, *Irish Business Focus*. At that stage, nine international bilateral business associations in Ireland were affiliated to the CII.[14] Liaison with the bilateral associations was co-ordinated by Donal Murphy, CII Director of Development. The Irish-Italian Business Association affiliated to the CII in March 1990.

Primary responsibility for Irish trade promotion with the European Union rested with the Irish Business Bureau in Brussels, which annually processed hundreds of enquiries from CII member enterprises.

In 1988, in association with the CII Annual Conference, the Confederation published a booklet that briefly traced some of the relationships between Ireland and other countries of Western Europe.[15]

In addition to the direct trade-related issues, Liam Connellan, CII Director General, and I visited the USA in 1988 to discuss taxation and investment issues, and we visited Poland in 1991 to assess potential trade and investment opportunities for CII member enterprises. I visited Hungary in 1990 and Russia in 1992 to discuss economic and trade relations and I discussed economic relations with other countries.[16]

COMPETITION FROM LOW WAGE ECONOMIES

Ireland was not, and could not be, in the long-term, a low wage economy, as it was far too open an international trading nation to maintain such a position. The expectations and aspirations of the Irish workforce were to enjoy living standards on a par with the richer EC Member States. Irish people saw the riches of other EC Member States, and legitimately sought similar levels for themselves. Highly-skilled Irish people spoke the world's most important business language – English – and were highly mobile internationally. If the expectations and aspirations of highly educated, internationally mobile, young people could not be met at home, they would undoubtedly seek, and ultimately find, opportunities elsewhere. Ireland, therefore, could not depend on low added-value industries with a wage rate differential below the EC average to compensate for transport and other infrastructural cost disadvantages that were imposed by its geographic position, small size and demographic structure.

Irish wage levels, gross before deduction of tax and social security, were, in 1991, over 91% of the EC average, and were rising. The Irish high dependency ratio of more than two persons depending on each member of the workforce, in contrast to one to one-and-a-half in the EC on average, distorted the *per capita* wage rate comparison. Wage rates fast approaching the EC average, coupled with some infrastructure cost disadvantages, notably access and inland transport costs, indicated that Ireland would be obliged to pursue more vigorously than previously the development of high added-value specialisations.

HIGH ADDED–VALUE SPECIALISATIONS

Ireland, with less than 0.9% of the population of the EC 27 and about 0.06% of world population (2007 figures), would need to win and retain only a tiny proportion of overseas markets in order to earn high levels of employment and living standards. This small size gave Ireland the potential to go up-market for its share of international trade, thus the need to *think smart* rather than *think big*! A fundamental prerequisite to action was the need to realise that high unemployment and relatively low living standards were symptoms of a disease, which was fundamentally attitudinal. The symptoms were under-utilisation of resources and lack of overall national competitiveness, not only in terms of input costs and output prices, but also in terms of the business sectors that Ireland had failed to adequately foster in the past. It was paradoxical that, in the past, the Irish had to travel to other countries to exploit their innate entrepreneurial skills and business acumen. The message for now was that knowledge-based industries, which depended primarily on the development of intellectual skills, did not necessarily suffer from infrastructure cost disadvantages: Irish people could at last develop their entrepreneurial skills and business acumen at home!

The primary objective, therefore, needed to be the development of people with the skills and motivation to produce new and improved products, processes and traded services, and with the ability to bring those developments to fruition in the marketplace, both at home and overseas. The emphasis on people needed to be the pivotal point in a corporate marketing strategy for Ireland, which would include factors such as high added-value; quality; up-market development; specialist niches; customer service; and all of the other dynamics of the market. Those factors constituted an integrated and comprehensive national marketing strategy, although it remained important to apply the strategy to specific enterprise sectors in the product, process and service areas. An opportunity existed to reorient Irish industrial development through strategic initiatives and structural adjustments.

A presentation that I made in November 1988[17] revealed that the growth rate in value of Ireland's exports of goods and services during the six years 1979 to 1984 was relatively the highest in the EC and was the sixth highest in all OECD countries. Ireland, Belgium / Luxembourg, and Malaysia each engaged in international trade amounting to between 110% and 120% of their national output, in contrast to countries, such as the USA, France and Japan, where international trade only equalled between 15% and 40% of national output. This showed that Ireland could dramatically market itself as a trading nation, recognised as such by the international community.

Table 14.1: Irish Exports *per capita* to Selected Countries, 1986[1]

Country	IR£	€
Northern Ireland	383	486
Great Britain	46	58
Belgium / Luxembourg	44	56
Netherlands	39	49
Germany (FR)	17	21
France	16	20
USA	3	3.8
Japan	1	1.3

The scope for further expansion in target markets was demonstrated by the small extent to which Ireland had penetrated some of those markets. The table above, taken from my presentation in November 1988, gives the value of Irish sales per person in each of a number of selected overseas markets in 1986. It appeared from the examples given that there could be significant scope for increased market penetration in most of Ireland's overseas markets.

STRATEGIC CENTRALITY

Ireland needed to identify the business sectors in which it had long-term real economic advantages and it needed to pursue strategic trade and investment alliances. A Euro-centric view of Irish peripherality was a one-sided and negative concept; a more balanced picture emerged by looking to the West as well as to the East.[18]

An indication of how Ireland could be strategically positioned to gain from interaction with the West, as well as with the East, could be gleaned by examining the position of Denmark. The Danes, living at the north-eastern periphery of the EC, depended partly for their economic wellbeing on their interaction with their Nordic neighbours: Finland, Norway and Sweden. Denmark was a member of the EC, but it also joined with her neighbours in the Nordic Union. Similarly, could Ireland join in a mutually

---

[1]   The table shows, for example, that Irish sales of goods and services to Great Britain in 1986 amounted to IR£46 (€58) per British inhabitant, whereas sales to the USA amounted to only IR£3 (€3.8) per US inhabitant.

advantageous trading arrangement, such as a North Atlantic Union with the USA, Canada and possibly Mexico, while remaining firmly within the EC? Ireland has much to bring to such an arrangement, as a trading nation that already exported 80% of the goods that were manufactured here. Ireland was uniquely the trading nation of the periphery of Europe, proportionately on a par with Belgium and Luxembourg, the traders geographically at the centre of the EC.

The view painted on the broad world canvas placed Ireland strategically at the centre between North America and continental Europe. That was a much more positive approach than the negative view of peripherality off the western extremity of continental Europe. The positive view of Ireland on the wider world stage could change the national perception of geography, and could point the way to transform Ireland into a wealthy, developed international trading economy.

TRADE & INVESTMENT LINKS WITH THE USA

Ireland was singularly successful in attracting inward investment from US multinationals. At the beginning of the 1990s, about 350 USA business operations in Ireland employed approximately 43,000 people. US investment accounted for 49% of overseas manufacturing jobs in Ireland, and 23% of total manufacturing employment in Ireland. Ireland had at least four major long-term economic advantages to offer the USA, in addition to the very important, but necessarily short-term, fiscal and other business location incentives:

♦ English was the spoken language, so that the Irish subsidiary or branch would have no difficulty in communicating with the parent company in the USA. On the other hand, Irish marketing graduates, proficient in continental European languages, could be the US sales force in Europe.

♦ Ireland, relatively, had an abundance of highly qualified young people, particularly graduates, whose reputation among the US multinationals was extremely high.

♦ Ireland did not have the substantial industrial infrastructure of other larger Member States of the EC, so that a US subsidiary or branch in Ireland would necessarily continue to source a significant proportion of raw materials and components from the USA. Thus, the benefits of increased production were shared between Ireland and the USA, not least with extra jobs arising in both countries. This contrasted with the position of establishing a US subsidiary or branch in one of the more industrially-developed Member States of the EC, where raw materials and components would be readily sourced locally. By the early 1990s, the economic activities of the US multinationals in Ireland directly resulted in the creation of 25,000 jobs in the USA, according to a report published by the US Congress, and it resulted in the USA having a trade surplus of US$ 1,000 million *per annum* with Ireland.

♦ Ireland was an EC Member State so that there was direct access to the large EC market for goods and traded services produced by US subsidiaries and branches located here.

The link between Ireland and the USA was even more important for Ireland, viewed against the background of the completion of the European Single Market, but also on a far broader basis across the whole of continental Europe.[18] There was ample scope to develop a similar mutually beneficial trade and investment relationship with Canada. Developments in Mexico, in the early 1990s, indicated that it might not be long before Ireland and Mexico could start to develop mutually beneficial strategic trade relationships.

The extent of the beneficial trade and investment links between Ireland and the USA is graphically demonstrated in the 2007 figures published by the American Chamber of Commerce Ireland.[19] The following sample statistics for 2007 illustrate the point:

♦ There were over 580 US enterprises in Ireland, representing 70% of all IDA-sponsored FDI employment.

♦ They directly employed 100,000 persons and indirectly employed more than 200,000 others.

♦ Investment in those enterprises amounted cumulatively to US$87 billion.

♦ This investment represented 6.3% of all US investment in the EU 27 and 3.1% of all overseas US investment worldwide.

♦ US enterprises located here exported €60 billion worth of products and services from Ireland in 2007.

♦ US enterprises in Ireland paid 40% of the total Irish Corporation Tax 'take'.

♦ The US is one of Ireland's top trading partners, with bilateral trade in both directions amounting to €23 billion.

♦ In reciprocal terms, Irish enterprises in the US employed 80,000
  persons and cumulative Irish investment in those enterprises
  amounted to €33.5 billion.

IRELAND AS A GLOBAL OFFICE

The link between Ireland and the USA has deepened with time and
extended to the internationally-traded services sector.[20] The combination of
highly qualified and skilled people, together with modern
telecommunications infrastructure, meant that Ireland was a desirable
location for US financial service providers wishing to locate in Europe.

By mid-October 1991, 180 projects were certified for the IFSC at the
Custom House Docks in Dublin.[1] The USA was the source for 27 of the
projects, which was the largest national contingent after the 42 Irish
projects and just ahead of the 26 projects from Germany. As
internationally-traded services did not necessarily suffer from the
infrastructure cost disadvantages associated with a small island location,
the *global office* was viable in any place in which skilled people located,
provided there was a high quality communications network to support
trade. US companies that wanted to engage in international financial
services and other database services could use Ireland as a strategically-
located office to beam into all of continental Europe, with the advantage
that Ireland could work for the US during the US off-peak hours, because
of the time differential between Ireland and the US. There was no reason
why an equally beneficial time link could not be forged with the entirety of
North, Central and South America.

The concept of the *global office* could, of course, apply to a wide range of
professional services such as engineering, architecture, graphic design, or
any area where the skills of people could be translated into service
products, capable of transmission on international telecommunications
networks; the concept was not narrowly confined to financial services and
information databases.[21]

---

[1]   In 2007, more than 430 international operations were approved to trade in the IFSC,
      and a further 700 managed entities were approved to carry on business under the IFSC
      programme. From 1 January 2006, companies in the IFSC pay the standard national
      corporation tax rate of 12½% (*IPA Administration Yearbook & Diary 2008*).

SUMMARY

◊ The completion of the European Single Market and the political and economic liberalisation processes in Central and Eastern Europe opened up new opportunities for sales and investment.

◊ Equally, there were movements towards the international relocation of certain production facilities. The centralisation of production facilities in the most favourable locations went hand-in-hand with the decentralisation of services and distribution.

◊ Ireland needs to focus on areas of comparative advantage, including high technology industries, knowledge-based industries, internationally traded professional services, financial services, and education and training services.

◊ Ireland needs also to overcome problems of geographic peripherality through infrastructure improvements and strategic trade and investment alliances, particularly with North America.

CHAPTER 15
LESSONS OF CONTINUING RELEVANCE

A number of conclusions and recommendations arise from Ireland's experience during the formative years of the Celtic Tiger. These are of continuing relevance to sustaining the momentum of Ireland's social and economic progress, particularly in times of national and international economic turbulence.

♦ There is a continuing need for holistic, integrated and iterative long-term planning, which addresses the management of change and responds on the same timescale as the rapid evolution of the global knowledge economy. The process needs to be complementary to the necessarily shorter-term horizon of parliamentary politics. This requires national consultative processes. Critically, the need cannot be fulfilled through reliance on the structures of Government and the public service alone, as was evidenced by the history of social and economic developments in Ireland during the period 1979 to 1993. (**Chapter 1**, *The Context*)

♦ There is a need for a continuing focus on the control of Government expenditure, borrowing, and the accumulation and servicing of National Debt, as well as for the achievement of value-for-money in public expenditure. Public expenditure, if allowed to get out of control, erodes national competitiveness, with the resultant loss of markets, loss of jobs, business closures and lowering of living standards. (**Chapter 3**, *The Economy: Warts & All!*)

♦ The importance of the role of the social partners is paramount: without their active participation, the watershed NESC report *A Strategy for Development 1986-1990: Growth, Employment & Fiscal Balance*, of November 1986, could not have been produced. That report was the catalyst for the negotiation of the PNR, October 1987, and for setting the parameters within which it was possible for Government to chart and manage the regeneration of the economy in the context of the completion of the European Single Market. (**Chapter 4**, *Failed 'Solutions'* and **Chapter 5**, *The Turning Point*)

♦ Employee participation in enterprise should be facilitated and promoted at national level and at the level of each enterprise, in terms of employee shareholding, information and consultation, and wider employee involvement in areas such as health and safety programmes. (**Chapter 5**, *The Turning Point*)

♦ Personal taxes should not exceed the capacity and tolerance of the taxpayers and business taxes should reflect the need to promote Irish enterprise within the global business environment in terms of economic development and job creation. (**Chapter 6**, *Room for Improvement*)

♦ Government should focus on the creation of an environment for enterprise that covers all relevant legislative, regulatory, administrative, fiscal and infrastructural areas appropriate to national governance. This is required to underpin business competitiveness in order to stimulate job creation, the enhancement of living standards, and economic growth. Specific areas for attention include regulation of the financial markets, development of a national energy policy, and cost control in regulated utility industries. (**Chapter 6**, *Room for Improvement*)

♦ The legislative, regulatory, and administrative environment needs to be periodically reviewed and up-dated to support public and private enterprise, including with reference to emerging threats to international competitiveness. (**Chapter 6**, *Room for Improvement*)

♦ Ireland requires internationally competitive infrastructure networks for transport and related elements of the built environment. While much has been done to improve the transport infrastructure, a lot remains to be completed in terms of each of the transport modes: road, rail, sea and air; in terms of the integration of those transport modes, as appropriate, and in terms of the continuing development needs of public transport. Little progress has been made to put in place a national waste management infrastructure for all types of waste, domestic, commercial and industrial, including toxic and hazardous waste. (**Chapter 7**, *The Road to Tomorrow* and **Chapter 8**, *Keep it Clean*)

♦ A focus is required on the role, funding, and functions of local authorities, and on correcting the hazards of imbalanced regional development. Little progress has been made in terms of the strengthening of local government or in the achievement of more balanced regional development since the CII campaign on both issues during the late 1970s, the 1980s and the 1990s. (**Chapter 9**, *Share is Fair*)

♦ Government and the social partners need to remain vigilant to ensure that the economy remains internationally competitive, including internationally-competitive business input costs and inflation no higher than in our international trading partners. (**Chapter 10**, *The Money Illusion*)

♦ Education and training needs to be continuously up-dated in the light of national and international economic developments, including a focus on education for high added-value employment. Such a focus should not sacrifice the nation's cultural heritage through lack of support for the arts and humanities, which are, in the long run, just as important as economic success. (**Chapter 11**, *Back to Basics*)

♦ There is a need to promote economic awareness continuously among the general population. Government and the social partners have a role to play in this, as has the education system. The vital nature of economic development needs to be recognised in terms of the output of and purchasing power over products and services. (**Chapter 12**, *A New Dawn*)

♦ National economic strategy requires continuous review to identify and up-date key economic growth sectors, public and private, in which Ireland possesses relative economic advantages. (**Chapter 12**, *A New Dawn*)

♦ Ireland needs to pursue an appropriate national development strategy within the European Union and internationally, having regard to growing competition from Central and Eastern Europe, China, India, and elsewhere, as identified in **Chapters 13** and **14**, *Winning with Europe* and *Ireland on the World Stage*.

APPENDIX I
THE CONFEDERATION OF IRISH INDUSTRY (CII)

WHAT WAS THE CII?

The CII was founded in November 1932 as the FII. Incorporated as the Federation of Saorstát Industries in May 1934, the name was changed to the FIM in 1938. It reverted to the original FII name in 1958. In 1969, the name was changed to the CII, to reflect a significant widening in the membership base.[1] The CII merged with the FIE in 1993 to form IBEC.

A voluntary representative body, the CII was funded by membership subscriptions. Members were drawn from manufacturing industry and commercially traded services, in both the private and public sectors. Expansion of membership beyond manufacturing commenced in July 1969, when the major banks and a number of State enterprises joined, followed by other services sectors, such as insurance, computer services, management consultancy, and patent and trademark agencies.

The CII represented its members in core business areas such as competition policy, economics, education and training, energy, the environment, infrastructure development, legal affairs, planning and development, taxation, transport and trade.

The CII acted both centrally as a confederation and through each of the almost 80 affiliated associations, federations and groups that catered for the interests of specific industries, commercial sectors and trade groups.

The work included representations to the Government, Government Departments, public authorities, institutions of the EU and international organisations. Public affairs programmes were aimed at the general public and at key target groups. The CII maintained a well-resourced Press & Publications Office.

The representational work was informed and facilitated by the CII's membership of about 120 official bodies in Ireland, the EU, the OECD, and on a wider international front. In many cases, its affiliated organisations had their own memberships of official bodies. In relation to the European Union, the CII, in partnership with the FIE and the ACCI, maintained the

Irish Business Bureau in Brussels. The CII was a member of the three industrial representative bodies: UNICE, CEIF and the Business & Industry Advisory Committee to OECD (BIAC).

THE STRUCTURE OF THE CII

A National Council, elected by the member enterprises, with a President elected biannually at the Annual General Meeting, governed the CII. The Council comprised members elected by the general body of ordinary members; members appointed by affiliated federations, associations and groups; and co-opted members. The National Council elected from among its members a National Executive Committee and a Finance & General Purposes Committee. A Round Table of appointed members considered global policy issues.

The CII was managed by a full-time Director General, appointed by the National Council. In turn, the Director General appointed other executive staff, including the Director of Economic Policy, the Director of Industrial Policy and the Secretary / Financial Controller.

CII Policy Committees in 1992, immediately prior to the formation of IBEC, were:

- **Company Affairs**: Economics & Taxation, Business Law, Competition, Innovation and Human Resources.
- **Infrastructure:** Transport, National Roads, Energy and Environment.
- **Bilateral Business Associations:** Ireland with Britain, Belgium, France, Germany, Italy, Japan, Korea, Poland, Spain, Sweden and Taiwan.
- **Regional Councils:** Cork, North Dublin, Mid West, North West and South East.

Sectoral Members in 1992 were divided as follows:

GOODS PRODUCING SECTORS
- **Agri-Business**: The Food Drink & Tobacco Federation, with its affiliates; Irish Dairy Industry Association; Irish Association of Pigmeat Processors; CII Alcohol Group; Eau De Vie; Food Processors & Suppliers Group; Irish Bread Bakers Association; Irish Flour Millers Association; Irish Refrigeration Enterprises; Irish Tobacco Manufacturers Advisory Committee; Margarine Manufacturers

Association of Ireland; Pet Food Manufacturers Association; Ground Limestone Producers Association; and the Irish Forest Industry Chain.

- **Building Materials**: Building Materials Federation, with its affiliates; Concrete Manufacturers Association of Ireland; Irish Plastic Pipe Manufacturers Association; and Polystyrene Moulders Association.
- **Clothing:** Apparel Industries Association.
- **Electronics & Informatics**: Federation of Electronic & Informatic Industries, with its affiliate, the Irish Transformer Manufacturers Association; and the Telecommunications Industry Association.
- **Engineering**: Engineering Industry Association, with its affiliates; the Irish Agricultural Machinery Manufacturers Association; Irish Foundry Services Ltd; and the Irish Cable & Wire Association.
- **Mining**: Irish Mining & Exploration Group.
- **Plastics**: Plastics Industry Association, with its affiliate the Federation of Print Paper & Board Industries.
- **Small Firms**: Small Firms Association.
- **Textiles:** Irish Textiles Federation.

SERVICES SECTORS
- **Computing Services**: The Information & Computing Services Association; and the Irish Computer Aided Design Association.
- **Consultancy:** Association of Management Consultant Organisations.
- **Distribution**: The Article Number Association of Ireland; Consumer Electronics Distributors Association; Electrical All Industry Committee.
- **Financial Services**: Financial Services Industry Association.
- **Marine and Offshore**: The Irish Federation of Marine Industries; Irish Offshore Services Association; and the Irish Fisheries Federation.

EXTERNAL REPRESENTATION

The CII was represented on almost 120 Governmental, public authority and trade associations in Ireland, in the EU, in the OECD and on a wider international basis.

CII ECONOMIC POLICY DIVISION
(1979–1993)[2]

During my years as Director of Economic Policy, the responsibilities of the
Economic Policy Division were:

CENTRAL POLICY AREAS:

♦ Competition Policy (established 1990).

♦ Business Law (from 1982).

♦ Economics & Taxation (re-structured 1981).

♦ Energy (from 1982).

♦ Environment (initiated by me in 1980).

♦ Human Resources: Education, Training & the Labour Market
  (established 1979).

♦ National Roads, Physical Planning & the Built Infrastructure
  (established 1979).

♦ The CII Education College (initiated by me in 1983 and incorporated
  in 1984).

SECTORS & TRADE GROUPS

♦ Financial Services Industry Association (initiated by me in 1984).

♦ Ground Limestone Producers Association (from 1982).

♦ Irish Mining and Exploration Group (from 1982).

♦ Irish Waste Contractors Federation (initiated by me in 1981).

♦ Patents, Trademarks and Licensing (from 1982).

♦ Small Firms Association (from 1982).

CII CENTRAL SERVICES

♦ Press & Publications Office.

♦ Galway Regional Office.

♦ Limerick Regional Office.

POSTSCRIPT

I was appointed the first Director, Economic Affairs, of IBEC, following the merger of the FIE and the CII, effective from 1 January 1993.

Understandably, the remit of the former CII Economic Policy Division was altered by IBEC, with many of the sectoral and central policy functions that I had developed over the years being reassigned elsewhere within the new organisation. Furthermore, my secondment by the CII to the Department of the Taoiseach, which would have continued had I remained an employee of IBEC, would undoubtedly have given rise to difficulties both for that organisation and for me, on my subsequent re-entry to IBEC, following my absence during the key formative years of the merged organisation.

In the circumstances, I decided that the time was opportune for me to resign and to pursue my own career in the wider business context that I developed during my 14 years in the CII. I resigned from IBEC at the end of April 1993, resulting automatically in termination of my secondment to the Department of the Taoiseach, and established an economic and public affairs consultancy practice, DCP Consultants Limited, together with Mary Hickey, who had been a colleague in the CII since 1980.

DCP Consultants undertook economic assignments in areas such as regional development, spatial planning, energy, environment, financial services, higher education, healthcare, international trade, intellectual property and transport. The practice also prepared legislative, fiscal, administrative and regulatory submissions to Government and other public authorities, including in areas of negotiations strategy, on behalf of Irish and overseas clients in both the public and the private sectors. Additionally, it offered my services as a non-executive director in the business information, construction, financial services, healthcare, industrial automation and news media sectors. The consultancy continued until my retirement in 2005 at age 66.

APPENDIX II
MEMBERSHIP OF GOVERNING AUTHORITIES, COMMISSIONS & COMMITTEES (CON POWER)

Department of Education & Science

♦ National Council for Educational Awards: Member of the Council, the Executive Committee of the Council, and of various Committees and Working Parties of the Council, January 1976 to July 1985; and Member of the Board of Business Studies, the Construction Studies Board, and Chairperson of the Art & Design Board of Studies, at various stages from February 1974 to March 1992.

♦ Governing Body of the National Institute for Higher Education, Limerick, July 1975 to June 1981 (NIHE Limerick became the University of Limerick in June 1989).

♦ Educational Broadcasting Committee, December 1980 to October 1982.

♦ Commission on Adult Education, October 1981 to June 1983.

♦ Steering Committee on Recreation Management, April 1983 to August 1985.

♦ Governing Body of Dublin City University, October 1987 to September 1990.

Department of Enterprise, Trade & Employment

♦ Manpower Consultative Committee and four sub-committees thereof, January 1981 to August 1984.

♦ Council of AnCO, May 1982 to December 1987.

♦ National Youth Policy Committee, September 1983 to October 1984.

Department of the Environment & Local Government

♦ Co-ordinating Committee for the National Programme of European Community Interest (Roads), funded with the aid of the ERDF 1986-1990, May 1988 to June 1990.

♦ Chairman of the interim National Roads Authority within the Department of the Environment & Local Government, July 1988 to December 1993 (including Executive Chairman on part-time secondment to the Department, July 1988 to December 1989).

Department of Finance
♦ Chairperson, Financial Services Ombudsman Council, a statutory body established under the *Central Bank & Financial Services Authority of Ireland Act 2004*, from the inauguration of the Council on 1 October 2004, to 16 October 2008.

Department of Justice, Equality & Law Reform
♦ Garda Síochána Advisory Group, May 1988 to December 1991.

Department of the Taoiseach
♦ National Economic & Social Council, May 1979 to June 1984; Regional Policy Committee, May 1979 to April 1981; Social Policy Committee, April 1981 to June 1984.
♦ Monitoring Committee for the First National Understanding, 1979.
♦ Monitoring Committee for the Second National Understanding, 1980.
♦ Central Review Committee for the Programme for National Recovery, October 1987 to December 1990; Secretariat Group of the CRC; Education Centre Working Party of the CRC, established June 1989; CRC Working Group on State Companies, established May 1990.
♦ International Financial Services Centre Committee, April 1987 to January 1989.
♦ Central Review Committee for the Programme for Economic & Social Progress, January 1991 to December 1993; Chairman of each of three Working Groups: Ireland as an International Education Centre, State Companies Linkages, and Telemarketing & Direct Marketing; full-time secondment to the Department of the Taoiseach 1 March 1992 to 30 April 1993.

Central Statistics Office
♦ Inter-Departmental Committee on Construction Industry Statistics, October 1970 to February 1972.

British / Irish Organisation

♦ British-Irish ENCOUNTER, an independent organisation, established by the British and Irish Governments in July 1983, to contribute to the improvement of relations between the peoples of these islands in areas of economic, social, cultural and other matters of common concern. ENCOUNTER was funded by the British and Irish Governments, and related also to the Administrations in Northern Ireland, Scotland, and Wales. Board Member, 1 January 2004 to 14 November 2006.

European Union & OECD

♦ Free Enterprise Information Group of the Council of European Industrial Federations, September 1979 to August 1988.

♦ Committee of the European Social Fund of the Commission of the European Union, November 1980 to November 1988.

♦ Economic and Financial Affairs Committee of UNICE; of the Macroeconomic Working Party under the European Union Social Dialogue between the EU Commission, UNICE and the ETUC; and of the Statistics Working Group, October 1985 to March 1992.

♦ Education Committee of the Business & Industry Advisory Committee to the OECD, October 1985 to March 1992.

Professional Bodies: Accountancy & Company Secretarial Bodies

♦ Dublin Branch Council, Institute of Chartered Secretaries & Administrators, November 1984 to February 1988.

♦ Consultative Committee of Accountancy Bodies in Ireland, Industrial & Commercial Members Committee, May 1987 to March 1992, including Chairman 1988/1989 and member of the main CCAB-Ireland Committee that year.

♦ Chair of the Development Committee of the Association of Chartered Certified Accountants, 1990 / 1991.

♦ Chairman, Professional Practice Committee of the Chartered Institute of Management Accountants, Republic of Ireland Region (CIMA), April 1994 to September 1996 and *ex-officio* member of the Republic of Ireland Regional Council.

♦ Consultative Committee of Accountancy Bodies, Business Law Committee, South, April 1996 to June 2003.

♦ Committee of the ACCA Ireland Business Leaders' Forum, September 1998 to date.

◆ Member of the Panel for the Admissions & Licensing, Disciplinary, and Appeal Committees of the Association of Chartered Certified Accountants, London, February 1999 to date.

◆ Member of the ACCA Ambassador programme, Association of Chartered Certified Accountants, January 2009 to date.

Institution of Engineers of Ireland

◆ Transportation Policy Committee of the Institution of Engineers of Ireland (now Engineers Ireland), September 1994 to June 2001.

Independent Hospital Association of Ireland

◆ Chairman, 1 March 1999 to 28 April 2002, including Executive Chairman from 1 June 2001 to 28 April 2002.

Academic & Learned Societies

◆ Committee of the Statistical & Social Inquiry Society of Ireland, 1979 to 1992.

◆ Irish National Board of Advisors, *Association Internationale des Étudiants en Sciences Economique et Commerciales*, February 1981 to September 1988.

◆ Committee of the Foundation for Fiscal Studies, 1986 to 1992.

◆ Board of Patrons of the Institute of Community Health Nursing, December 1986 to September 1988.

◆ President, Irish Science Teachers' Association, May 1988 to April 1990.

◆ Committee of the UCD Service Industries Research Centre, 1990 to 1992.

◆ Institute of European Affairs (subsequently, Institute of International & European Affairs), founding member of the Board of Directors and Vice-Chairperson, Member of Council, Finance & Administration Committee, and Executive Committee, March 1991 to June 1993; Council Member, March 1991 to date.

◆ Academic Board of the Dublin Business School, April 1991 to June 1994.

REFERENCES

CHAPTER 1: THE CONTEXT

1. *National Debt of Ireland 1923-2006*, NTMA, Dublin, July 2007.
2. *Quarterly Bulletin No.4, 2006*, Central Bank of Ireland, Dublin.
3. *Quarterly Economic Commentary, Winter 2006*, ESRI, Dublin.
4. *Quarterly Economic Commentary, Winter 2007*, ESRI, Dublin.
5. *Programme for National Recovery*, Stationery Office, Dublin, October 1987.
6. *A Strategy for Development 1986-1990: Growth, Employment & Fiscal Balance*, Report No.83, NESC, Dublin, November 1986.
7. O'Hagan, JW & Foley, GJ, Department of Economics, Trinity College, Dublin, *The Confederation of Irish Industry: The First Fifty Years 1932-1982*, CII, March 1982.
8. 'The 1982 Budget', *CII Newsletter*, Vol.36, No.6, 22 December 1981.
9. 'The 1987 Budget', *CII Newsletter*, Vol.46, No.1, 11 November 1986.
10. Power, C, CII briefing meetings with Charles J Haughey TD, Leader of Fianna Fáil, 28 October 1987 and 1 November 1987.
11. *Programme for National Recovery*, Fianna Fáil 1987 General Election Manifesto, not dated, received in CII Library, 29 January 1987.
12. See reference 6 above.

CHAPTER 2: THE EVOLUTION OF NATIONAL POLICY

1. Kennedy, KA, Giblin, T & McHugh, D, *The Economic Development of Ireland in the Twentieth Century*, Rutledge, London & New York, 1988.
2. O'Mahony, D, *The Irish Economy: An Introductory Description*, Cork University Press, 1964.
3. See reference 1.
4. *Parliamentary Debates, Dáil Éireann*, Vol.6, Stationery Office, Dublin, 16 January 1924.
5. *Parliamentary Debates, Dáil Éireann*, Vol.7, Stationery Office, Dublin, 6 May 1924.
6. *Parliamentary Debates, Dáil Éireann*, Vol.8, Stationery Office, Dublin, 17 July 1924.
7. *Tariff Commission Act 1926*, No.40 of 1926, Stationery Office, Dublin, 31 July 1926.
8. *Customs Duties (Provisional Imposition) Act 1931*, No.38 of 1931, Stationery Office, Dublin, 5 November 1931.

9. *Control of Manufactures Act 1932*, No.21 of 1932, Stationery Office, Dublin, 29 October 1932.

10. See reference 1.

11. *Emergency Imposition of Duties Act 1932*, No.16 of 1932, Stationery Office, Dublin, 23 July 1932.

12. *Control of Imports Act 1934*, No.12 of 1934, 24 March 1934, and *Control of Imports (Amendment) Act 1937*, No.8 of 1937, Stationery Office, Dublin, 12 March 1937.

13. *Finance (Agreement with United Kingdom) Act 1938*, No.12 of 1938, and *Agreement with United Kingdom (Capital Sum) Act 1938*, No.13 of 1938, Stationery Office, Dublin, 16 May 1938.

14. *Imposition of Duties (Confirmation of Orders) Act 1939*, No.20 of 1939, Stationery Office, Dublin, 19 July 1939.

15. *Emergency Powers Act 1939*, No.28 of 1939, Stationery Office, Dublin, 2 September 1939.

16. See references 1 and 2.

17. The US Congress established the *Marshall Plan*, named after the US Secretary of State, General George Marshall, in April 1948. It ended in 1951. The countries that shared in this US$ 12.7 billion aid plan, with the amounts received by each, were: Austria $488m; Belgium & Luxembourg $777m; Denmark $385m; France $2,296m; Federal Republic of Germany $1,448m; Greece $366m; Iceland $43m; Ireland $133m; Italy $1,204m; Netherlands $1,128m; Norway $372m; Portugal $70m; Sweden $347m; Switzerland $250m; Turkey $137m; and UK $3,297m.

18. *Programme for Economic Expansion*, Stationery Office, Dublin, November 1958.

19. Whitaker, TK, *Retrospect 2006-1916*, IPA, Dublin, 2006.

20. McBrierty, VJ, *Ernest Thomas Sinton Walton 1903-1995, The Irish Scientist*, Trinity College Dublin Press and Physics Department of Trinity College Dublin, 2003.

21. *Second Programme for Economic Expansion*, Part I, Stationery Office, Dublin, August 1963.

22. *Second Programme for Economic Expansion*, Part II, Stationery Office, Dublin, July 1964.

23. *Third Programme: Economic & Social Development*, Stationery Office, Dublin, 1968.

24. *Report to the Minister for Education on Regional Technical Colleges*, Steering Committee on Technical Education, Stationery Office, Dublin, February 1967.

25. *National Development 1977-1980*, White Paper, Stationery Office, Dublin, January 1978.

26. O'Hagan, JW & Foley, GJ, Department of Economics, Trinity College, Dublin, *The Confederation of Irish Industry: The First Fifty Years 1932-1982*, CII, Dublin, March 1982.

27. The six CII personnel who died in the air disaster at Staines, near Heathrow Airport, London, on Monday, 18 June 1972, were: Con Smith, President; Edward (Ned) Gray, Director General; Guy Jackson, Member of the National Executive and a former President; Michael Rigby Jones, Member of the National Executive; Michael Sweetman, Director of Business Policy; and Fergus Mooney, Trade Officer.

28. Power, C, European memberships on behalf of the CII: (a) Free Enterprise Information Group (FEIG) of the Council of European Industrial Federations (CEIF), September 1979 to August 1988; (b) Committee of the European Social Fund of the Commission of the European Union, November 1980 to November 1988; (c) Economic & Financial Affairs Committee of UNICE, October 1985 to March 1992; (d) Macroeconomic Working Party under the European Union Social Dialogue between the European Commission, UNICE and ETUC, October 1985 to March 1992.

29. *National Debt of Ireland 1923-2006*, NTMA, Dublin, 2007.

30. Power, C, *The European Monetary System*, talk to the IMI North-West Region, Sligo, 11 December 1978.

31. Power, C, *The Agenda for Economic Recovery*, Garda Síochána Training Centre, Templemore, County Tipperary, 7 July 1982.

32. *Development for Full Employment*, Green Paper, Stationery Office, Dublin, June 1978.

33. Power, C, *Contribution to a Debate on the Irish Economy*, Philosophical Society, University College Cork, 5 March 1983.

34. See reference 25.

35. *Ireland's Economic Prospects in the 1980s*, talk at the Chairman's Annual Dinner, IMI North-West Region, Sligo, 4 May 1979.

CHAPTER 3: THE ECONOMY: WARTS & ALL!

1. *Programme for National Recovery*, Stationery Office, Dublin, October 1987.

2. Power, C, *Public Expenditure & Economic Growth: A Negative Correlation*, Irish Corporate Finance Conference 1986, organised by Business Research International, Dublin, 24 / 25 November 1986; 'Public debt stifles economic growth', *CII Newsletter*, Vol.46, No.3, 25 November 1986; 'Lenders may doubt capacity to repay', *The Irish Times*, 26 November 1986; 'National Debt inaction to destroy jobs', *Irish Independent*, 26 November 1986; 'Foreign lenders will begin to question our ability to service and repay debt', *The Irish Times*, 29 November 1986.

3. 'The 1987 Budget', *CII Newsletter*, Vol.46, No.1, 11 November 1986.

4. *A Strategy for Development 1986-1990: Growth, Employment & Fiscal Balance*, Report No. 83, NESC, Dublin, November 1986.

5. 'Financial Statement, Budget 1972, Official Report of the Minister for Finance, *Parliamentary Debates, Dáil Éireann*, Vol.260, Stationery Office, Dublin, 19 April 1972.

6. 'Employment in Industries & Composition of Labour Force', *Administration Yearbook & Diary*, IPA, Dublin, 1988.

7. 'The Main Problems Remain: The 1986 Budget', *CII Newsletter*, Vol.44, No.15, 18 February 1986.

8. *National Debt of Ireland 1923-2006*, NTMA, Dublin, 2007.

9. 'The 1982 Budget', *CII Newsletter*, Vol.36, No.6, 22 December 1981.

10. 'The 1983 Budget', *CII Newsletter*, Vol.38, No.5, 30 November 1982.

11. Dukes, A, TD, 'Financial Statement, Budget 1983: Official Report of the Minister for Finance', *Parliamentary Debates, Dáil Éireann*, Vol.339, Stationery Office, Dublin, 9 February 1983.

12. 'The 1984 Budget', *CII Newsletter*, Vol.39, Nos.22 & 23, 25 October 1983.

13. 'The 1985 Budget', *CII Newsletter*, Vol.42, No.10, 8 January 1985.

14. 'The 1986 Budget', *CII Newsletter*, Vol.44, No.5, 3 December 1985.

15. See reference 3 above.

16. See reference 2 above.

17. 'Public Debt Stifles Economic Growth', *CII Newsletter*, Vol.46, No.3, 25 November 1986.

18. *Irish Social Policies: Priorities for Future Development*, Report No.61, NESC, Dublin, November 1981.

19. Power, C, *The Social Dimensions of Economic Problems*, talk to the Kilkenny Rotary Club, 4 October 1982; 'Plea for review of State spending', *The Irish Times*, 5 October 1982; 'State aid is "indiscriminate"', *Irish Independent*, 5 October 1982; 'State spends £118 a week for every person working' and 'Cut in State spending urged', *Irish Press*, 5 October 1982; 'Yes, it's true' and 'Lack of focus leads to overspending', *Kilkenny People*, 8 October 1982; 'State Aid is Indiscriminate', *CII Newsletter*, Vol. 37, No. 23, 12 October 1982; 'Government spending – wasteful says economist', *Kilkenny People*, 15 October 1982; 'Today we live in difficult times', *Sligo Champion*, 29 October 1982.

20. *Annual Report 1972-1973*, Central Bank of Ireland, Dublin, 1973.

21. *Databank of Economic Time Series*, Research Paper 1/87, Department of Finance, Dublin, December 1987.

22. Power, C, *Ireland Limited: The Case for More Effective Administration*, AGM of the Republic of Ireland Region, ICSA, Council Chamber, City Hall, Cork, 14 September 1985; *Let's Make the Right Comparisons*, CII Mid-West Region, Limerick, 7 November 1985; 'Government & the Economy: International Comparisons', *CII Newsletter*, Vol. 44, No. 8, 24 December 1985.

23. Dukes, A, TD, 'Financial Statement, Budget 1986: Official Report of the Minister for Finance', *Parliamentary Debates, Dáil Éireann*, Vol.363, Stationery Office, Dublin, 29 January 1986.

24. 'Countdown to the city's tax march', *Sunday Press*, 10 April 1983.

25. Power, C, 'Tax: Why we're on the bottom line', News Analysis, *Irish Independent*, Dublin, 8 April 1983.

26. Power, C, 'Our industry must return to reality', News Analysis, *Irish Independent*, Dublin, 25 April 1983.

27. Power, C, 'Lack of balance in tax debate could prove dangerous', Business & Finance, *The Irish Times*, 2 May 1983.

28. *Reports of the Commission on Taxation: First, Direct Taxation*, July 1982; Second, *Direct Taxation: The Role of Incentives*, March 1984; Third, *Indirect Taxation*, June

1984; Fourth, *Special Taxation*, May 1985; Fifth, *Tax Administration*, October 1985, Stationery Office, Dublin.

CHAPTER 4: FAILED 'SOLUTIONS'

1. The Governments formed during this period, and the Taoiseach in each case, were: (1) 21st Dáil: Fianna Fáil, 5 July 1977, Jack Lynch; (2) 21st Dáil: Fianna Fáil, 11 December 1979, Charles J Haughey, following a change in leadership of Fianna Fáil during the lifetime of the 21st Dáil; (3) 22nd Dáil: Fine Gael and the Labour Party, 30 June 1981, Dr Garret FitzGerald; (4) 23rd Dáil: minority Fianna Fáil, 9 March 1982, Charles J Haughey; (5) 24th Dáil: Fine Gael and the Labour Party, 14 December 1982, Dr Garret FitzGerald.
2. *National Development 1977-1980*, White Paper, Stationery Office, Dublin, January 1978.
3. *Development for Full Employment*, Green Paper, Stationery Office, Dublin, June 1978.
4. *Programme for National Development 1978-1981*, White Paper, Stationery Office, Dublin, January 1979.
5. Power, C, *Ireland's Economic Prospects in the 1980s*, talk at the Chairman's Annual Dinner, IMI North-West Region, Sligo, 4 May 1979; 'Challenge of enlarged EEC', *Irish Independent*, 5 May 1979; 'Schools must take account of growing industrial economy – economist', *Sligo Champion*, 18 May 1979.
6. FitzGerald, G, TD, on the nomination of Charles J Haughey TD as Taoiseach, *Parliamentary Debates, Dáil Éireann*, Vol.333, Stationery Office, Dublin, 9 March 1982.
7. *National Economic Plan: Building on Reality 1984-1987*, Stationery Office, Dublin, 2 October 1984.
8. '1985 Budget', *CII Newsletter*, Vol.42, No.10, 8 January 1985.
9. *A Strategy for Development 1986-1990: Growth, Employment & Fiscal Balance*, Report No.83, NESC, Dublin, November 1986.

CHAPTER 5: THE TURNING POINT

1. 'The European Challenge: No Alternative to Strong Industrial Growth – CII Annual Conference 1986', *CII Newsletter*, Vol.44, No.16, 25 February 1986.
2. Power, C, *Strategy for Economic Development*, guest speaker at the Marley Branch, Fine Gael, South County Dublin, 25 February 1986. Reported as 'Power's 10 Point Plan', *Stubbs Business*, Vol.XCVI, No.9, 5 March 1986.
3. *A Strategy for Development 1986-1990: Growth, Employment & Fiscal Balance*, Report No.83, NESC, Dublin, November 1986.
4. Hastings, T, Sheehan, B & Yeates, P, *Saving the Future: How Social Partnership Shaped Ireland's Economic Success*, Blackhall Publishing, Dublin, 2007.

5. 'The 1987 Budget', *CII Newsletter*, Vol.46, No.1, 11 November 1986.

6. 'A Question of Hats', *The Irish Times*, 20 January 1987 and 'Keynote Speakers', *The Irish Times*, 27 January 1987

7. Fitzgerald, G, TD, Leader of Fine Gael, *Dáil Éireann Report*, Vol.371, 10 March 1987.

8. Dukes, A, TD, Leader of Fine Gael, *The Tallaght Strategy – Two Decades On*, Business Breakfast Briefing, South Dublin Chamber, 23 February 2007.

9. *Programme for National Recovery*, Stationery Office, Dublin, October 1987.

10. *Parliamentary Debates, Dáil Éireann*, Vol.389, Stationery Office, Dublin, 26 April 1989.

11. *Programme for Economic & Social Progress*, Stationery Office, Dublin, January 1991.

12. See reference 4 above.

13. Treacy, N, TD, Minister of State, 'Finance Bill 2005, Second Stage (Resumed)', *Dáil Éireann Report*, Vol.597, 9 February 2005.

14. Ahern, B, TD, An Taoiseach, WEF Annual Meeting, Davos, Switzerland, 25 January 2007.

15. Ahern, B, TD, An Taoiseach, 2007 Conference for the Regions, CIPFA, Dublin Castle, 13 September 2007.

16. EEC Document Reference COM (80) 186 final, Commission to the Council of Labour Ministers, 5 May 1980.

17. Walsh, B & Nolan, S, *Jobs & the Workforce*, 1981, and summarised in *CII Newsletter*, 2 February 1982.

18. 'Enterprise Allowance Scheme', *CII Newsletter*, Vol.41, No.3, 8 May 1984.

19. 'Business Help for Enterprise Allowance Scheme', *CII Newsletter*, Vol.42, No.1, 30 October 1984.

20. 'The Implementation of the Social Guarantee for Young People', *CII Newsletter*, Vol.42, No.3, 13 November 1984.

21. *CII Supports the Government's Manpower White Paper*, Press Release, 16 October 1986.

22. *CII Newsletter*, Vol.45, No.13, 29 July 1986, reporting on a submission made to Government on 17 July 1986.

23. 'CII Views on Commission on Social Welfare', *CII Newsletter*, Vol.45, No.24, 28 October 1986.

24. 'Employment of Disabled Persons', *CII Newsletter*, Vol.45, No.10, 8 July 1986.

25. 'The 1986 Budget', *CII Newsletter*, Vol.44, No.5, 3 December 1985.

26. *Employee Communications*, The Labour / Management Service, IPC, Dublin, 1980.

27. 'CII warning on disclosure plan by EEC', *Evening Press*, Dublin, 14 August 1984; 'CII slams plan to open firms' books', *Irish Press*, Dublin, 15 August 1984.

28. Power, C, *The Importance of Employee Information & Consultation*, Rotary Club of Cork, 8 October 1984.

29. Power, C, *The Economic Development Viewpoint on the Importance of Employee Information & Consultation*, IPM and IPC, Dublin, 10 December 1984.

30. 'Employers say information law would hit jobs', *Irish Independent*, 11 December 1984; 'CII accused of fostering secrecy on company data', *The Irish Times*, 11 December 1984.

31. 'Bosses urged to keep employees informed', *Irish Independent*, 11 December 1984.

32. Recommendation 129, Annual Conference, ILO, Geneva, Switzerland, 1967.

33. Power, C, *Reporting to Employees*, talk to the ICMA and ICSA, IMI, Dublin, 24 January 1985.

34. 'Urges less secrecy in firms', *Irish Independent*, 25 January 1985.

35. Report No.19, Joint Oireachtas Committee on the Secondary Legislation of the EEC, Dublin, 3 September 1985.

36. 'Employee Information & Consultation (Vredeling)', *CII Newsletter*, Vol.43, No.19, 17 September 1985.

37. *The establishment of a European Works Council or procedure in Community-scale undertakings and Community-scale groups of undertakings for the purposes of informing and consulting employees*, European Council Directive 94/45/EC, Brussels, 22 September 1994.

CHAPTER 6: ROOM FOR IMPROVEMENT

1. *Programme for National Recovery*, Stationery Office, Dublin, October 1987.

2. 'The 1988 Budget', *CII Newsletter*, Vol.48, No.4, 1 December 1987; 'Favourable response given by business to Budget measures', *The Irish Times*, 28 January 1988.

3. Power, C, *Development Strategy for Success: How a Small Island Beats International Competition*, 5th Irish Corporate Finance Conference, Business Research International, Dublin, 15 November 1988.

4. 'The 1989 Budget', *CII Newsletter*, Vol.50, No.4, 6 December 1988; 'CII seek £150m to ease tax', *Irish Press*, 7 December 1988; 'CII call on spending cuts', *Irish Independent*, 7 December 1988; 'CII speaks on the budget', *Strategy*, 16 December 1988.

5. *Budget 1989 – CII Response*, Press Release, 25 January 1989; 'Budget '89 – CII Speaks Out', *Industry & Commerce*, January 1989.

6. 'The 1990 Budget', *CII Newsletter*, Vol.51, No.24, 26 October 1989; 'CII calls for zero borrowing', *Sunday Independent*, 8 October 1989; 'CII's Budget', Editorial, *Irish Independent*, 7 November 1989.

7. *Medium-Term Review 1989/1994*, No.3, ESRI, Dublin, June 1989.

8. *Ireland*, OECD Economic Surveys 1988/1989, OECD, Paris, June 1989.

9. Power, C, *CII Budget Priority: Cut Borrowing*, talk to CII Mid-West Region, University of Limerick, 15 January 1990.

10. 'The 1991 Budget', *CII Newsletter*, Vol.53, No.24, 30 October 1990.

11. Power, C, *Budget Must Promote Development*, Pre-Budget seminar, Foundation for Fiscal Studies, Dublin, 23 January 1991; 'Call on EBR', *Irish Independent*, 24 January 1991.

12. 'The 1992 Budget – Submission to Government', *CII Newsletter*, Vol.55, No.16, 5 November 1991; Power, C, *Reducing Debt is Top Budget Priority*, Superintendents' Development Course, Garda Síochána College, Templemore, County Tipperary, 20 January 1992; 'Zero EBR top priority: CII', *Irish Independent*, 21 January 1992.

13. 'Budget's Missed Opportunities', *IBEC News*, Vol.1, No.3, 15 March 1993.

14. Quinn, R, TD, 'Financial Statement, Budget 1997: Official Report of the Minister for Finance', *Parliamentary Debates, Dáil Éireann*, Vol.473, 22 January 1997.

15. Dukes, A, TD, 'Financial Statement, Budget 1983: Official Report of the Minister for Finance', *Parliamentary Debates, Dáil Éireann*, Vol.339, 9 February 1983.

16. *Comprehensive Public Expenditure Programmes*, Stationery Office, Dublin, July 1983.

17. Power, C, 'Analysis of Public Expenditure', *CII Newsletter*, Vol.40, No.14, 31 January 1984.

18. MacSharry, R, TD, Minister for Finance, 'Oral Answers – Public Expenditure Programmes, *Parliamentary Debates, Dáil Éireann*, Vol.376, 9 December 1987.

19. Power, C, *Credit Management: Essential for the Functioning of the Economy*, Institute of Credit Management, Dublin, 23 October 1984.

20. 'Report on Industrial Competitiveness', *CII Newsletter*, Vol.36, No. 20, 30 March 1982.

21. 'Report on International Industrial Competitiveness', *CII Newsletter*, Vol.41, No. 5, 22 May 1983.

22. 'High Costs Put Jobs at Risk', *CII Newsletter*, Vol.46, No.17, 3 March 1987.

23. *Working Party on the Cost Environment for Enterprise*, comprised of representatives of the CII, FUE, Department of Industry & Commerce, Department of Finance, Department of Labour, and Department of the Taoiseach, inaugural meeting, 5 June 1987.

24. Ahern, B, TD, An Taoiseach, *Parliamentary Reports, Dáil Éireann*, Vol.480, 30 September 1997.

25. 'The 1986 Budget', *CII Newsletter*, Vol.44, No.5, 3 December 1985.

26. 'The 1987 Budget', *CII Newsletter*, Vol.46 No.1, 11 November 1986.

27. 'The 1988 Budget', *CII Newsletter*, Vol.48, No.4, 1 December 1987.

28. See reference 27.

29. 'The 1989 Budget', *CII Newsletter*, Vol.50, No. 4, 6 December 1988.

30. 'The 1990 Budget', *CII Newsletter*, Vol.51, No.24, 26 October 1989.

31. 'The 1991 Budget', *CII Newsletter*, Vol.53, No.24, 30 October 1990.

32. 'The 1992 Budget – Submission to Government', *CII Newsletter*, Vol.55, No.16, 5 November 1991.

33. Power, C, 'Corporation Tax Rise Poses Threat to Investment', *CII Newsletter*, Vol.54, No.11, 22 January 1991.

34. *Second Survey on State Aids in the European Community in the Manufacturing & Certain Other Sectors*, SEC (90) 1165/3, European Commission, Brussels, 10 July 1990.

35. *OECD Report on Ireland*, OECD, Paris, June 1991.

36. Power, C, 'OECD Report on Corporate Tax is Naïve', *CII Newsletter*, Vol.55, No.7, 2 July, 1991.

37. *OECD Economic Outlook No.48*, OECD, Paris, December 1990.

38. Power, C, 'US Tax & Investment – Four Key Issues', *CII Newsletter*, Vol.51, No.20, 3 October 1989; 'US Bill on PFICs Introduced', *CII Newsletter*, Vol.50, No.16, 28 February 1989; 'US Tax Update', *CII Newsletter*, Vol.51, No.6, 13 June 1989; 'US Taxation – PFICs', *CII Newsletter*, Vol.54, No.11, 22 January 1991.

39. Power, C, *Warning on Proposed Company Law Changes*, CII Dublin Regional Meeting, 1 October 1984, and ICPAI, Dublin, 28 June 1985.

40. Power, C, *Directors are not All Equal*, CII North East Region, Dundalk, 17 February 1987 and CII North Dublin Region, 28 June 1990.

41. *Companies (Amendment) Bill, 1985*, CII Press Release, 6 February 1986, and *Companies (Amendment) Bill, 1990*, CII Press Release, 28 August 1990.

42. 'Companies under Court Protection', *CII Newsletter*, Vol.54, No.10, 15 January 1991.

43. 'Freedom of Information & Data Protection', *CII Newsletter*, Vol.43, No.20, 24 September 1985.

44. *Review of EC Fourth Directive on Annual Accounts*, CII Submission to the Company Law (Legislation / EEC) Branch, Department of Industry & Commerce, 15 August 1989.

45. 'Companies (Amendment) Bill 1985', *CII Newsletter*, Vol.43, No.12, 16 July 1985.

46. 'The 1990 Budget', *CII Newsletter*, Vol.53, No.24, 30 October 1990; 'The 1992 Budget – Submission to Government', *CII Newsletter*, Vol.55, No.16, 5 November 1991.

CHAPTER 7: THE ROAD TO TOMORROW

1. *Roads Needs Survey*, An Foras Forbartha, Dublin, 1974.

2. *Response to the Green Paper on Development for Full Employment*, CII Economic Review No.2, CII, Dublin, 1978.

3. Power, C, 'Response to the Road Development Plan for the 1980s', *CII Newsletter*, Vol.31, No.1, 22 May 1979.

4. *Road Development Plan for the 1980s*, Stationery Office, Dublin, May 1979; launched by the Minister for the Environment on 4 May 1979.

5. The CII met with Sylvester Barrett TD, Minister for the Environment and senior officials in the Department to discuss the CII response to the *Road Development Plan for the 1980s* on 17 July 1979. The CII deputation comprised the President, the immediate past-President, the Director General, and Power, C, as Director of Economic Policy.

6. *CII Roads Policy Committee* inaugural meeting on 24 July 1979.

7. 'CII worried by lack of road development', *The Irish Times*, 9 April 1980; 'Road plans criticised', *Irish Press*, 9 April 1980; 'Poor roads "handicap industrial

progress"', *Irish Independent*, 17 April 1980; 'Road spending needs to be doubled – CII', 13 August 1980; 'Roads gone to pot', *Cork Examiner*, 13 August 1980; '"Colossal expenditure" on roads needed in 1980s – CII', *Irish Independent*, 13 August 1980; '£4,000m road investment urged', *The Irish Times*, 13 August 1980; 'Irish road plan not the answer', *Sunday Independent*, 9 November 1980.

8. Power, C, 'The Importance of Transport Infrastructure – Industry's Case for Roads', *CII Newsletter*, Vol.33, No.21, 21 October 1980.

9. 'CII urges roads agency', *Irish Independent*, 20 July 1983; 'New body needed to finance roads', *Evening Herald*, 20 July 1983.

10. *'Minister announces new roads authority*, Announcement by Liam Kavanagh, TD, Minister for Labour that *a roads authority would be set up in the life of the present Dáil*, welcomed by Power, C', *Irish Press*, 8 November 1983.

11. 'Launch of Junior Chamber Ireland 'Roads for a Better Future' Campaign', *Irish Independent*, 1 May 1984.

12. *Integrated Policy & Planning for Transport in a New Ireland* (New Ireland Forum sectoral studies), Stationery Office, Dublin 1984.

13. *Transport as a Bottleneck to Economic Growth in Ireland*, Regional Policy and Transport Series No.14, European Parliament, Strasbourg, France, 1986.

14. *Proposed National Roads Authority*, submission to the Minister for the Environment, 19 October 1987, published as Information Sheet No.6, *Roads - Key to Economic Development*, CII, Dublin, March 1988.

15. Power, C, 'National Roads Authority – Key to Major European Finance', *CII Newsletter*, Vol.49, No.12, 26 July 1988.

16. *Ireland - Road Development 1989 to 1993*, Operational Programme, submitted by the Irish Government to the European Commission on 30 March 1989 and launched by the Minister for the Environment on 7 June 1989.

17. Power, C, *Implementing the Road Plan 1989-1993*, Annual Conference 1989 of the Institution of Engineers of Ireland, Dundalk, County Louth, 29 September 1989, published in the *CII Newsletter*, Vol.51, No.22, 17 October 1989; *Ireland's Transport Problems as a Peripheral Region within the EC*, Southern Section, Chartered Institute of Transport in Ireland, Dublin, 21 November 1989.

18. *Ireland's Transport Problems as a Peripheral Region with the European Community*, Communication from the European Commission, 20 September 1989.

19. *National Development Plan 1989-1993*, submitted by the Government to the European Commission on 22 March 1989, Stationery Office, Dublin, 31 March 1989.

20. Power, C, *Ireland Needs Efficient Infrastructure*, National Conference on Aspects of the Irish Infrastructure – Past Condition & Future Needs, University College Dublin, 3 & 4 April 1990, published by the Department of Civil Engineering, UCD, July 1991.

21. Power, C, *Roads & the Environment*, Seminar on Planning & the Environment, County Meath Constituency Executive, Fine Gael, Navan, County Meath, 17 July 1990; 'Electric trams urged as solution to traffic congestion, pollution', *The Irish Times*, 16 July 1990; 'Trams: pollution solution', *Cork Examiner*, 18 July 1990;

'Light tramway advocated for Dublin', *The Irish Times*, 18 July 1990; 'Tramway scheme mooted', *Cork Evening Echo*, 18 July 1990; 'Dublin needs to see return of trams', *Cork Evening Echo*, 23 July 1990.

CHAPTER 8: KEEP IT CLEAN

1. *National Survey of Air & Water Pollution in Ireland*, summary of survey undertaken by IIRS / Industrial Development Authority (IDA), Dublin, 1976.
2. Power, C, Industrial Waste Management, *CII Newsletter*, Vol.36, No.2, incorporating the CII response to the national strategy for waste disposal announced by the Minister for the Environment on 18 May 1981, newsletter published 23 November 1981.
3. *Irish Waste Contractors' Federation*, CII Press Release of the inaugural meeting held on 24 February 1982.
4. *Recommendation of the Council on Guiding Principles Concerning International Economic Aspects of Environmental Policies*, Council Document No. C (72)128. OECD, Paris, May, 1972.
5. *Protect our Water Resources: A Guide for Industrialists*, Water Pollution Advisory Council, 1982.
6. 'Water Pollution Control', *CII Newsletter*, Vol.37, No.7, 22 June 1982.
7. 'Effluent Discharge Charging Schemes', *CII Newsletter*, Vol.37, No.19, 14 September 1982, incorporating a CII submission made to the Minister for the Environment on 21 April 1982, and discussed with senior officials of the Department on 20 May 1982.
8. *Local Government (Water Pollution) Regulations 1978*, Stationery Office, Dublin, Statutory Instrument No 108/1978.
9. 'European Communities (Toxic & Dangerous Waste) Regulations 1982', *CII Newsletter*, Vol.38, No.10, 4 January 1983.
10. 'The 1982 Budget', *CII Newsletter*, Vol.36, No.6, 22 December 1981, and 'The 1983 Budget', *CII Newsletter*, Vol.38, No.5, 30 November 1982.

CHAPTER 9: SHARE IS FAIR

1. *The Financing of Local Authorities*, Report No.80, NESC, Dublin, May 1985.
2. *Fourth Report of the Commission on Taxation: Special Taxation – CII Submission to the Minister for Finance*, CII, 23 July 1985.
3. Power, C, *Local Government & Economic Development: A Role for Public / Private Partnership*, talk to the Annual Conference of the General Council of County Councils, Ballybunion, County Kerry, 6 June 1986, summarised as 'Local Authorities & Industry', *CII Newsletter*, Vol.45, No.11, 15 July 1986. Power, C, 'The Vital Role of Financing Local Authorities', *Stubbs Business*, 11 September 1987. 'Local Authorities have a Vital Role', *CII Newsletter*, Vol.47, No.22, 13

October 1987. Power, C, '1992 – A New Lease of Life for Local Authorities', *Local Authority News*, No.6, 1989.

4. 'Boost house market with joint owners plan – CII', *Irish Independent*, 7 June 1986; 'Councils urged to use land for private housing', *The Irish Times*, 7 June 1986; 'Local Authorities have a development role', *Sligo Champion*, 13 June 1986; 'Local Authorities have a development role', *Western People*, 11 June 1986.

5. *CII Submission on Subsidiarity, Local Government Structures, Regional Authorities, Local Government Finance & Related Issues*, to the Advisory Expert Committee on Local Government Reorganisation & Reform, CII, Dublin, 20 September 1990; 'Local Government Reorganisation & Reform', *CII Newsletter*, Vol.54, No.1, 13 November 1990.

6. 'Valuation Bill 1985', *CII Newsletter*, Vol.43, No.21, 1 October 1985; Power, C, 'Why Pay Rates?', *Business & Finance*, 31 October 1985; 'Up-date on Valuation Bill', *CII Newsletter*, Vol.44, No.13, 4 February 1986; 'Valuation Act 1986', *CII Newsletter*, Vol. 44, No.20, 25 March 1986; *Rates & the Valuation of Industrial Premises*, CII Information Sheet No.5, November 1986; 'Valuation Bill 1987', *CII Newsletter*, Vol.48, No.7, 22 December 1987; 'Increase in Industrial & Commercial Rates', *CII Newsletter*, Vol.53, No.12, 24 July 1990.

7. *Regional Development in Ireland*, Colin Buchanan & Partners, in association with Economic Consultants Limited, and with assistance of staff from An Foras Forbartha, An Foras Forbartha, Dublin, 1968.

8. *East Region Settlement Strategy 2011*, ERDO, Dublin, 1985; Power, C, *Regional Development & Infrastructure Provision: A Serious Imbalance in favour of the East Region*, talk to CII Western Region, Castlebar, County Mayo, 8 July 1985; 'Warning of Serious Problems', *Western People*, 17 July 1985; 'Con Power on regional development', *Stubbs Business*, 18 July 1985; mention in *Connaught Telegraph*, 24 July 1985, and *Donegal Democrat*, 26 July 1985.

9. Power, C, *Can Ireland Afford a New Pale?*, talk at a Conference of the Mid-West RDO, Limerick, 26 / 27 November 1986, published November 1987; Hazards of Imbalanced Regional Development, *CII Newsletter*, Vol.46, No.11, 20 January 1987.

10. 'Integrated Regional Programmes – Main Focus for EC Investment', *CII Newsletter*, Vol.49, No.10, 12 July 1988; Power, C, 'Strategy & Infrastructure', *Irish Exporter*, August 1988; 'Infrastructure Investment to Boost Competitiveness', *ACCA Digest*, Irish Region, Vol.11, No.4, December 1988; Power, C, 'EC Funds present opportunities to build competitive infrastructures', *Carlow Nationalist*, 13 January 1989.

11. Haughey, CJ, TD, An Taoiseach, speaking at the CII Annual Conference, Dublin, 26 February 1988.

12. Power, C, *Shannon: The Hub between West & East*, CII Mid-West Region, University Club, University of Limerick, 28 November 1991; 'Shannon can be gateway for tourism', *Cork Examiner*, 29 November 1991; 'CII leader pinpoints airport growth', *Limerick Leader*, 30 November 1991; 'Shannon: A one-stop shop for Eurocargo clearance?', *Evening Press*, 6 December 1991; 'Industry backing',

Limerick Post, 7 December 1991; 'Confederation of Irish Industry Backs Shannon', *Limerick Tribune,* 7 December 1991; 'Airport Status "uncontestable"', *Clare Champion,* 13 December 1991; 'Flights "dirty tricks" threat to jobs', *Irish Independent,* 27 December 1991; '1992 is "make or break" for Shannon', *Cork Examiner,* 31 December 1991; 'Shannon: Warning on "hijack"', *Evening Herald,* 6 January 1992; 'Shannon must unite against "dirty tricks"', *Limerick Leader,* 4 January 1992; 'Industrial Review Group Support for Shannon Strategies', *Clare Champion,* 17 January 1992; 'Shannon move would threaten jobs in Sligo', *Sligo Champion,* 28 February 1992.

CHAPTER 10: THE MONEY ILLUSION

1. *Inflation in the Irish Economy: A Contemporary Perspective,* edited by McAleese, D & Ryan, WJL, with 14 essays by invited experts on different aspects of inflation, CII and Helicon Press, Dublin, 1982.
2. *Inflation: A Public Awareness film,* a Louis Marcus Production commissioned by CII, Dublin, launched 9 November 1983 (producer and director, Louis Marcus; camera, Robert Monks; location sound, Liam Suarin; studio sound, Pat Gibbons; animation, Aidan Hickey; narrator, Bill Golding).
3. 'Financial Statement, Budget 1972: Official Report', *Parliamentary Debates, Dáil Éireann,* Vol.260, Stationery Office, Dublin, 19 April 1972.
4. 'The 1982 Budget', *CII Newsletter,* Vol.36, No.6, 22 December 1981.
5. 'The 1983 Budget', *CII Newsletter,* Vol.38 No.5, 30 November 1982.
6. 'The 1984 Budget', *CII Newsletter,* Vol.39 No.22 & 23, 25 October 1983.
7. 'The 1986 Budget', *CII Newsletter,* Vol.44 No.5, 3 December 1985.
8. 'The 1989 Budget', *CII Newsletter,* Vol.50, No.4, 6 December 1988.
9. Power, C, *Industrial Development: Business Costs & EC Structural Funds,* with a Press Release, *Warning on Inflation & Borrowing,* 4th Annual Business Studies Conference, organised by CII in association with BSTAI, Carysfort College, Blackrock, County Dublin, 7 October 1989.
10. 'The 1990 Budget', *CII Newsletter,* Vol.51, No.24, 26 October 1989.
11. 'The 1991 Budget', *CII Newsletter,* Vol.53, No.24, 30 October 1990.
12. 'The 1992 Budget – Submission to Government', *CII Newsletter,* Vol.55, No.16, 5 November 1991.
13. 'Exchange Rate Guarantees', *CII Newsletter,* Vol.36, No.20, 30 March 1982.
14. See reference 6.
15. *The Role of the Financial System in Financing the Traded Sectors,* Report No.76, NESC, Dublin, October 1984.
16. 'Interest Rates', *CII Newsletter,* Vol.42, No.6, 4 December 1984.
17. 'High Interest Rates Causing Unemployment', *CII Newsletter,* Vol.46, No.12, 27 January 1987.
18. 'High costs put jobs at risk', *CII Newsletter,* Vol.46, No.17, 3 March 1987.
19. Power, C, *Interest Rate Cut Overdue,* CII South Dublin Region, 15 June 1987.

20. 'The 1988 Budget', *CII Newsletter*, Vol.48, No.4, 1 December 1987.
21. See reference 11.
22. Reynolds, A, TD, Minister for Finance, at the Annual Meetings of the IMF and the World Bank, Washington, 26 September 1990.
23. See reference 12.
24. 'Expenditure Priorities', *CII Newsletter*, Vol.31, No.21, 16 October 1979.
25. Wyse, P, Minister of State at the Department of Finance, *Parliamentary Reports, Dáil Éireann*, Vol.317, Stationery Office, Dublin, 5 December 1979.
26. O'Kennedy, M, Minister for Finance & O'Malley, D, Minister for Industry, Commerce & Tourism, *Parliamentary Reports, Dáil Éireann*, Vol.319, Stationery Office, Dublin, 16 April 1980.
27. Power, C, *Inflation, Public Expenditure & the Exchange Rate*, CII South East Region, Waterford, 7 July 1982.
28. *EMS Realignment*, CII Press Release, 18 March 1983.
29. Power, C, *Exchange Rates & Industrial Costs*, CII Midlands Region, Mullingar, County Westmeath, 1 May 1986.
30. Power, C, *Exchange Rate Policy & Industrial Competitiveness*, Staff Seminar, College of Business, NIHE Limerick, 21 January 1987.
31. *The Economist*, 6 December 1986.

CHAPTER 11: BACK TO BASICS

1. Power, C, 'Education & the Needs of Industry', *COMPASS – Journal of the Irish Association for Curriculum Development*, Vol.9, No.1, 1980; 'Schools / Industry Links', *CII Newsletter*, Vol.32, No.25, 13 May 1980.
2. 'Response to White Paper on Educational Development', *CII Newsletter*, Vol.34, No.10, 3 February 1981.
3. Power, C, *Man at Work & Play in the 80s*, In-service course for teachers, Sport & Youth Section, Department of Education, Waterford, 19 October 1981 and *CII Newsletter*, Vol.35, No.24, 3 November 1981.
4. 'Public Expenditure Estimates: CII Submission to Government: CII Proposals for Reducing Public Expenditure', *CII Newsletter*, Vol.45, No.13, 29 July 1986.
5. 'The 1991 Budget: Increased Participation in Education', *CII Newsletter*, Vol.53, No.24, 30 October 1990.
6. Ó Murchú, U, *Careers in Industry for the 1980s*, a 20-minute slide / tape presentation commissioned by the CII.
7. *The CII Education College*, an Education Trust, was incorporated as a company limited by guarantee on 19 December 1984, CRO No.104935. The Revenue Commissioners granted charitable status, together with educational covenant status. The name was changed to the *IBEC Centre for Educational Research & Development* on 2 July 1993.
8. CII / ISTA projects included five chemistry booklets published 1987-1990: *Rate of Reaction & Equilibrium, Oxidation-reduction Reactions, The Extraction of Metals,*

Industrial Chemistry, and *Organic Chemicals in Everyday Life*. A polymer kit was produced containing 14 polymers suitable for both the Leaving Certificate and Junior Certificate syllabuses. Physics videos were prepared, including: *Electromagnetic Induction* and *Waves, Electrostatics & Simple Harmonic Motion*. In recognition of the CII's support, Con Power was elected President of ISTA 1988-1990.

9. *Strategy for Industrial Innovation: The Role of the Third Level Institutions*, CII, Dublin, 7 April 1981.

10. *Innovation Report 1981*, proceedings of a conference held on 15 April 1981, Business Series No.10, CII, Dublin, January 1982.

11. Power, C, *Educational resources must be used to contribute to Industrial Growth*, Industry / Higher Education Seminar organised by NBST and IDA, Sligo Regional Technical College, 9 December 1983.

12. Power, C, 'In-depth management structure is vital to RTCs', *Technology Ireland*, Dublin, May 1979.

13. *Technological Education & a Technological University*, submission by CII on invitation from the Study Group established by the Minister for Education, 16 February 1987.

14. 'Industrial Design Education', *CII Newsletter*, Vol.33, No.1, 20 May 1980.

15. Power, C, 'Art, Design & Economic Growth', *CII Newsletter*, Vol.42, No.7, 11 December 1984.

16. Power, C, 'Design is the Key to Export Success', *CII Newsletter*, Vol.48, No.9, 5 January 1988.

17. 'European Orientation Programme', *CII Newsletter*, Vol.43, No.8, 18 June 1985.

18. 'The 1986 Budget', *CII Newsletter*, Vol.44, No.5, 3 December 1985.

19. *Innovation Policy in Ireland*, OECD, Paris, restricted publication, 18 September 1985.

20. *White Paper on Industrial Development*, Stationery Office, Dublin, July 1984.

21. 'Apprenticeship', *CII Newsletter*, Vol.34, No.3, 9 December 1980.

22. 'Training within Industry', *CII Newsletter*, Vol.36, No.12, 2 February 1982. As a follow-up at the request of the CII, AnCO arranged a series of information sessions for industrialists, held in AnCO Training Centres in Cork, Dublin, Dundalk, Galway, Shannon, Sligo, and Waterford, January to March 1983.

23. 'Training Contracts to Boost Recruitment', *CII Newsletter*, Vol.47, No.2, 12 May 1987.

24. *Proposal for a European Council Directive on a General System for the Recognition of Higher Education Diplomas*, Ref. COM (85) 355 final, European Commission, Brussels, 22 July 1985.

25. 'Shannon Aerospace Training Initiative', *CII Newsletter*, Vol.53, No.2, 15 May 1990.

26. *Safety in Industry Act 1980 (Commencement) Order 1981*, SI No.59/1981.

27. 'Safety at Work', *CII Newsletter*, Vol.35, No.5, 23 June 1981.

28. 'Absenteeism in Industry', *CII Newsletter*, Vol.44, No.14, 11 February 1986.

29. 'Health Programme Needed for Industry', *CII Newsletter*, Vol.49, No.4, 23 May 1988.
30. Hughes, G, *Disability Benefit Reform: Rationalisation or Subsidisation?*, Policy Research Series No.8, ESRI, March 1988.
31. 'Health – The Wider Dimensions', *CII Newsletter*, Vol.46, No.22, 7 April 1987.
32. Power, C, 'Promotion of Health at the Workplace', *Occupational Health & Safety Newsletter*, No.46, Department of Labour, October, 1988; 'The Value of Health Promotion', *Health & Safety*, August 1989; 'The Value of Health Promotion', *Industry & Commerce*, September, 1989.
33. *Safety, Health & Welfare at Work Act 1989*, No.7 of 1989, Stationery Office, Dublin, 1989.

CHAPTER 12: A NEW DAWN

1. O'Hagan, JW & Foley, GJ, *The Confederation of Irish Industry: The First Fifty Years 1932 – 1982*, CII, Dublin, March 1982.
2. 'Job Attitudes Among Young People', *CII Newsletter*, Vol.31, No.21, 16 October 1979.
3. '21st International Industrial Film Festival', *CII Newsletter*, Vol.33, No.7, 1 July 1980.
4. 'Film Festival Award', *CII Newsletter*, Vol.33, No.25, 18 November 1980.
5. Power, C, 'The Challenge of Economic & Social Development', *AONTAS Review*, Vol.3, No.1, 1981, and *Guideline*, September 1981.
6. 'CII Film Premiere: The Voice of Industry', *CII Newsletter*, Vol.35, No.22, 20 October 1981.
7. Power, C, *Industrialisation & Social Change*, First Anniversary Booklet of An Garda Síochána College, Templemore, County Tipperary, 22 February 1982.
8. 'Industrial Films & Videos', *CII Newsletter*, Vol.36, No.15, 23 February 1983.
9. 'The Irish Film Board', *CII Newsletter*, Vol.36, No.23, 20 April 1922.
10. Power, C, 'The Consumer is King', *Science & Technology*, May 1982, and *Industry & Commerce*, November / December 1982.
11. Power, C, 'The Environment for Enterprise', *Business Studies for Leaving Certificate Students (Part 2)*, School & College Publishing Limited, Dublin, 1983.
12. 'Industrial Film', *CII Newsletter*, Vol.38, No.12, 18 January 1983.
13. Power, C, 'It's a Question of Economics', *Industry & Commerce*, February / March 1983.
14. Power, C, *Response to Unemployment: A View from Industry*, Proceedings of the 31st Annual Summer School of the Social Study Conference, 'Young Ireland: Realism & Vision', Dungarvan, County Waterford, 30 July to 6 August 1983.
15. Power, C, 'An Environment for Enterprise & Job Creation', *Education Ireland*, Vol.1, No.2, February / March 1984.
16. Power, C, 'Pay '84: Let's Face Real Facts', News Analysis, *Irish Independent*, Dublin, 9 March 1984.

17. 'Industrial Film & Video', *CII Newsletter*, Vol.41, No.24, 15 October 1984.

18. Power, C, 'The Consumer as the Creator of Jobs', *Energy Saver*, 16 November 1984.

19. 'Young People Need to Know about Business', *CII Newsletter*, Vol.42, No.6, 4 December 1984.

20. 'Industrial Film & Video Congress', *CII Newsletter*, Vol.44, No.20, 25 March 1986.

21. Power, C, 'Poverty in Ireland: What is the Solution?', *CII Newsletter*, Vol.52, No.3, 22 May 1990.

22. 'Communication – A Missing Link', *CII Newsletter*, Vol.55, No.8, 16 July 1991.

23. Power, C, *The Place of Irish Industry in the Community*, ICTU course, The People's College, Dublin, 18 July 1979.

24. Power, C, *The Irish Economy*, and related economic awareness presentations to public meetings of Parents' Associations in post-primary schools, higher education institutions, training bodies, and to other community, professional and business groups: Coláiste Mhuire, Dublin, 14 November 1979; Vocational School, Thomastown, County Kilkenny, 26 November 1979; St Anne's Secondary School, Dublin, 9 January 1980; AnCO, Dublin, 8 April 1980; Irish Countrywomen's Association, Termonfeckin, County Louth, 9 April 1980; St Joseph's Secondary School, Rush, County Dublin, 24 September 1980; College of Marketing & Design, Dublin, 16 February 1982; Rotary Club, Waterford, 15 March 1982; IEI and IEE (Irish Branch), Dublin, 22 April 1982; Coláiste Bhríde, Clondalkin, Dublin, 19 October 1982; Wesley College, Dublin, 11 November 1982; The High School, Dublin, 25 January 1983; The 70s Club, Dublin, 9 May 1983; Our Lady's School, Templeogue, Dublin, 17 January 1984; Loreto Secondary School, Clonmel, County Tipperary, 22 February 1984; Mount St Anne's Secondary School, Milltown, Dublin, 13 March 1984; Drogheda Chamber of Commerce, 16 April 1984; Institute of Bankers, Tralee, County Kerry, 26 April 1984; Residents' Association, Ballyboden, Dublin, 1 May 1984; AnCO, Dublin, 17 October 1984; Post-Graduate Guidance Counselling Class, UCD, 19 November 1984; Loreto Secondary School, Fermoy, County Cork, 29 November 1984; IPA, Dublin, 8 November 1985; Ardee Town Commissioners, County Louth, 24 April 1986; BSTAI, Dublin, 2 May 1986; Combined Post-Primary Parents' Councils, Portlaoise, County Laois, 9 May 1986; Community Association, Ardee, County Louth, 2 September 1986; Coláiste Odhráin CBS, Tramore, County Waterford, 25 February 1987; PRII, Dublin, 7 December 1987; MII, Galway Branch, 9 October 1989; Pastoral Centre, Donamon, County Roscommon, 10 October 1989; IITD, Galway, 30 & 31 March 1990; IABC, Dublin, 26 June 1991; Terenure College, Dublin, 12 March 1992; CIMA, Waterford, 23 September 1994.

25. Power, C, *The Challenge of Economic & Social Development*, 12th Annual Conference, AONTAS, Waterford, 2 May 1981.

26. *Inflation*, Press Release, CII, 9 November 1983.

27. Power, C, *The Role of Industry in Building an Economy for All Our People*, RDS Extension Lecture, Sligo Regional Technical College, 27 January 1982; County

Longford VEC, Longford, 15 February 1982; and Tralee Regional Technical College, 11 March 1982.

28. Power, C, *The Economic Background to Unemployment: Some Pointers towards a Solution*, seminar on Unemployment, Young Fine Gael National Seminar, Sligo, 2 October 1982.

29. Power, C, *The Social Dimensions of Economic Problems*, Kilkenny Rotary Club, 4 October 1982.

30. Power, C, *Our Economic Future is Mainly in Our Own Hands*, Faculty of Commerce, UCD, 3 December 1982; and Annual Business Conference, Commerce & Economics Society, UCG, 11 March 1983.

31. Power, C, *Enterprise: The Key to National Recovery*, Dublin South County Constituency Executive, Fine Gael, 22 February 1983.

32. Power, C, *A Positive View of Economic Prospects*, Leixlip Chamber of Commerce, Leixlip, County Kildare, 24 March 1987.

33. See reference 2 above.

34. See reference 6 above.

35. See reference 26 above.

36. Dukes, A, TD, Minister for Finance, *Budget 1984*, Dáil Éireann, Wednesday, 25 January 1984.

37. CII Public Affairs Publications 1981: *Strategy for Industrial Innovation: Discussion Document for the CII Conference on Strategy for Industrial Innovation*, April 1981; *Innovation Report 1981*, proceedings of the CII Conference on 'Strategy for Industrial Innovation', April 1981; *Industry 1981*; *Industry Report 1981*, proceedings of the CII 10th Annual Economic Conference; *Jobs & the Workforce* by Prof Brendan Walsh (ESRI) and Sean Nolan; and *The evolution of manufacturing industry in Ireland* by John O'Hagan & Kyran McStay (Trinity College Dublin).

38. The *EMF World Competitiveness Report*, Geneva, Switzerland, assessed the competitiveness of 22 OECD countries and nine developing countries under each of 340 criteria. Of those criteria, 234 related to official statistical data, and the remaining 106 criteria related to responses to questionnaires issued to a wide range of business executives in each country.

39. Power, C, *Programme for National Recovery: Pragmatism & Action*, Institute of Bankers and Sligo Chamber of Commerce, Sligo, 30 November 1987; published in the *Journal of the Institute of Bankers in Ireland*, Vol.89, No.1, Spring 1988.

40. Power, C, *Industrial Growth & Jobs: The Need for a Sharper Focus on Marketing Our Strengths*, and a Press Release, *Growth Industries with Employment Potential*, CII 8th Annual Careers in Industry Conference, in association with IGC, Dublin, 19 September 1986.

41. *Industrial Policy for the 1990s*, Confederation of Irish Industry, June 1987.

42. *Completing the Internal Market*, White Paper from the Commission to the European Council at Milan on 28 & 29 June 1985, Com (85) 310 final, 14 June 1985.

43. Talks in the *Uruguay Round* of GATT opened in Geneva on 23 February 1987. Trade in services was included in the agenda for the first time since GATT was established in 1947.

44. *A Report of the Telecommunications Action Programme*, from the Commission to the European Council of Industry Ministers, Luxembourg, 9 June 1986.

45. *The European Electronics & Information Technology Industry: State of Play, Issues at Stake & Proposals for Action*, Commission of the European Communities, Brussels, 3 April 1991.

46. Power, C, *1992: A New Dawn for Knowledge-based Industries in Ireland*, International Seminar, The Bolton Trust, Royal Hospital Kilmainham, Dublin, 28 February 1990.

47. The EC Third Framework Programme for Science & Technology 1990-1994 provided 5.6 billion ECUs, and was formally adopted by European Community Research Ministers during the Irish Presidency on 26 February 1990.

48. *Common Market for Services*, Chapter IV of *Completing the Internal Market*, see reference 42 above.

49. Power, C, *The Economic Background to Unemployment & Some Pointers towards a Solution*, Young Fine Gael Seminar on Unemployment, Sligo, 2 October 1982.

50. Power, C, *Employment & Economic Growth*, AGM of the Parents' Association, Coláiste Bhríde, Clondalkin, Dublin, 19 October 1982.

51. Power, C, *Jobs for the 1980s*, Careers Fortnight 1982, Careers & Appointments Office, UCD, 8 November 1982.

52. Power, C, *The Road to Employment & Economic Growth*, Parents' Association, The High School, Dublin, 25 January 1983.

53. Power, C, *Employment Prospects are Mainly in Our Own Hands*, Annual Business Conference, Commerce & Economics Society, UCG, 11 March 1983.

54. Power, C, and Quinn, R, TD, Minister for Labour, meetings to discuss the development of internationally-traded financial services, 12 January and 7 March 1984.

55. 'Money men's new body', *Irish Press*, 11 December 1984; 'New financial body formed by institutions', *The Irish Times*, 11 December 1984; 'Financial services body set up – FSIA', *Irish Independent*, 11 December 1984; 'FSIA clarifies its objectives', *The Irish Times*, 14 December 1984; 'Mr Spring, the CII and the bank levy', *Irish Independent*, 15 December 1984 – including the reference that Con Power conceived the idea of a financial services association about a year ago; the launch of the FSIA was also reported in *Marketing Opinion*, January 1985; *Success*, January 1985; *Stubbs Gazette*, 2 January 1985; and *Business & Finance*, 3 January 1985.

56. Quinn, R, TD, Minister for Labour, Guest Speaker at the FSIA First Annual General Meeting Lunch, Burlington Hotel, Dublin, 24 February 1986.

57. *City of Dublin*, CII submission to the Special & Permanent Development Team of Dublin Corporation, drafted by Power, C, and made through the CII representative on the Team, Dan McInerney, 19 October 1983.

58. Power, C, *The Irish Financial Services Industry in an International Context*, proposal to the Enterprise & Employment Committee of Dublin County Council for the inclusion of internationally-traded financial services in the Enterprise Zone proposed by the Council on land adjacent to Dublin Airport, 12 November 1985.

59. Power, C, *Liberalisation of International Trade in Financial Services: The Impact on Ireland*, with a Press Release, *Ireland's Strong Financial Services Industry has Massive Growth Potential*, Irish Corporate Finance Conference, Business Research International, Dublin, 18 November 1985.

60. Power, C, and O'Brien, F, TD, Minister of State, Department of the Environment, with responsibility for Urban Affairs, Housing & Local Government, meeting on 24 & 26 March 1986, and separately with Boland, J, TD, Minister for the Environment on 26 March 1986.

61. Power, C, *Call for International Traded Services Zone in Dublin*, at a seminar on Completing the Internal Market, organised jointly by FSIA and ICEM, Dublin, 21 April 1986.

62. Power, C, interview on *Morning Ireland*, RTE Radio 1, on the topic of the proposed International Traded Services Zone in Dublin, 21 April 1986 and on the RTÉ 1 TV News at 9.00 p.m. on the same day.

63. FSIA Council met with the IDA to discuss the proposal to establish an International Traded Service Zone as an IDA Business Park at the Custom House Docks in Dublin, 3 June, 1986.

64. Power, C, *Dublin can be a major International Finance Centre*, Irish Computer Services Association, Dublin, 24 June, 1986.

65. Power, C, interview on *News at One*, RTÉ Radio 1, on the topic of an International Finance Centre at the Custom House Docks, 24 June, 1986; 'Dublin can be a major finance centre', *Evening Press*, 24 June 1986; 'CII Plan for using Custom House site', *The Irish Times*, 25 June 1986; 'Custom House site "ideal"', *Irish Independent*, 25 June 1986; 'Custom House Docks a major finance centre?', *Irish Independent*, 25 June 1986.

66. 'International Finance Centre – Con Power's Plan', *Stubbs Business*, Vol.XVCI, No.26, 4 July 1986.

67. Drew, P, was chairman & managing director of St Katharine by the Tower Limited, a subsidiary of Taylor Woodrow, and was responsible for leading the London docklands revival. He joined Taylor Woodrow in 1965, and became a director in 1979. He was chairman of Taylor Woodrow from 1989 until he retired in 1992.

68. Following initial discussions between Power, C, and the IDA, the Council of the FSIA met the IDA to explore the possibilities for the development of international financial services in Ireland and pledged the support and involvement of the FSIA members.

69. Power, C and Drew, P, met with O'Brien, F, Minister of State at the Department of the Environment, on 17 November 1986.

70. 'Incentives for Docks Development', *CII Newsletter*, Vol.46, No.6, 16 December 1986.

71. Power, C, had an initial meeting with Benson, F, chairman, CHDDA, on 23 February 1987, to discuss business interest in developing projects under the *Urban Renewal Act 1986*, and to give the initial results of expressions of interest from member enterprises of FSIA. Subsequently, collaboration was ongoing between

FSIA and CHDDA, including the organisation in conjunction with the IDA of a seminar for financial services companies in New York on 16 March 1989.

72. Power, C and Drew, P, met with Haughey, CJ, TD, Leader of Fianna Fáil, in Leinster House on 17 November 1986.

73. Power, C, spoke as a representative of the CII on management of the economy; development policies, including the promotion of internationally-traded financial and professional services; and economic infrastructure development, including the network of national roads, at the Fianna Fáil Business Conference, Burlington Hotel, Dublin, 18 January 1987.

74. Power, C and Drew, P, met with Haughey, CJ, TD, An Taoiseach, and Flynn, P, TD, Minister for the Environment, at Abbeville, Kinsealy, County Dublin, on 21 April 1987.

75. 'Tourism has Enormous Potential', CII Newsletter, Vol.42, No.13, 29 January 1985 and 'Tourism – Significant Key to National Recovery', CII Newsletter, Vol.48, No.11, 19 January 1988.

76. Power, C, Cultural Tourism: The Benefits of Repeat Business, official opening of the 32nd Waterford International Festival of Light Opera, Theatre Royal, Waterford, 17 September 1990.

77. Power, C, The Complementary Roles of Public & Private Enterprise, RDS Extension Lecture, Sligo Regional Technical College, 24 March 1982 and CII Newsletter, Vol.36, No.22, 13 April 1982.

78. Power, C, 'Jobs Need both Public & Private Enterprise', Newsletter of the Dublin Student Society of ICSA, February 1987.

79. 'Private Investment in State Companies', CII Newsletter, Vol.46, No.12, 27 January 1987.

80. 'Participation in State Enterprise', CII Newsletter, Vol.46, No.16, 24 February 1987.

81. 'Swedish Example backs State Participation Case', CII Newsletter, Vol.46, No.25, 28 April 1987.

82. Power, C, State Companies: Enterprise, not Dogma, Department of Public Administration, UCC, 15 March 1990; 'Irish Life: ICTU asks for meeting', Irish Independent, 14 March 1990; 'State enterprise versus public enterprise', Munster Express, 23 March 1990.

83. Power, C, 'A Pragmatic Argument for Privatisation in Ireland', in Public Expenditure & the Private Sector, edited by Mulreany, M & St John Devlin, L, IPA, Dublin, 1988.

84. '1992 – The Challenge for State-sponsored Enterprises', CII Newsletter, Vol.52, No.7, 26 December 1989.

85. Power, C, 'The Privatisation Debate', Business & Finance, Dublin, 7 February 1991.

86. Power, C, Importance of State Companies and Press Release, Clear Mandate Needed for State Companies, Department of Public Administration, UCC, 14 March 1991.

87. The Public Sector: Issues for the 1990s, Working Paper No.90, Department of Economics & Statistics, OECD, Paris, December 1990.

88. Power, C, *State-sponsored Commercial Enterprises*, talk at the *Privatisation Debate*, CPSU, Dublin, 11 October 1991.

89. The legislative basis for the move by the European Commission was contained in Articles 1 and 5 of Directive 80/723/EEC, published in full in the EC *Official Journal*, reference OJ LI95, 29 July 1980.

90. 'The Budget 1991', *CII Newsletter*, Vol.53, No.24, 30 October 1990.

CHAPTER 13: WINNING WITH EUROPE

1. Department of Finance, *Budget & Economic Statistics 2003* and *2007*.

2. *National Debt of Ireland 1923-2007*, NTMA, website http://www.ntma.ie, November 2008.

3. *Ireland in the European Community: Performance, Prospects & Strategy*, Report No.88, NESC, Dublin, August 1989.

4. *Programme for National Recovery*, Stationery Office, Dublin, October 1987.

5. *Ireland – National Development Plan 1989-1993*, Stationery Office, Dublin, 1989, and presented by the Government to the European Commission in March 1989.

6. *A Time for Change: Industrial Policy for the 1990s*, Report of the Industrial Policy Review Group (Culliton Report), Stationery Office, Dublin, January 1992; Power, C, *Enterprise Culture Needed*, Department of Management & Marketing, UCC, 21 February 1992.

7. Power, C, represented the CII on the Economic & Financial Affairs Committee of UNICE, including on the Macroeconomic Working Party under the European Community Social Dialogue between the European Commission, UNICE and ETUC, October 1985 to March 1992.

8. Power, C, represented the CII on the FEIG of the CEIF, September 1979 to August 1988.

9. Submission to the European Commission on the Communication from the Commission to the Council of Ministers for Labour regarding *Guidelines for a Community Labour Market Policy*, 5 May 1980, and the Resolution of the Council of Ministers for Labour, 27 June 1980, submission dated 17 February 1981.

10. Power, C, was a member of the Committee of the European Social Fund, appointed by the European Commission on the nomination of the CII made through the Irish Department of Labour, November 1980 to November 1988.

11. Power, C, represented the CII on the Education Committee of BIAC, October 1985 to March 1992.

12. *Employee Involvement* section in *Chapter 5: The Turning Point*.

13. *International Financial Services* and *The FSIA & the IFSC* sections in **Chapter 12**: *A New Dawn*.

14. **Chapter 7**: *The Road to Tomorrow*.

15. Power, C, chairman of the interim NRA within the Department of the Environment & Local Government, July 1988 to December 1992, including

executive chairman on part-time secondment from the CII to the Department, July 1988 to December 1989.

16. Power, C, Member of the Co-ordinating Committee for the National Programme of European Community Interest (Roads) 1986-1990, funded with aid from ERDF, May 1988 to June 1990.

17. Power, C, Institute of European Affairs, founding member of the Board of Directors and Vice-Chairperson, Member of Council, Finance & Administration Committee and Executive Committee from March 1991 to May 1993. Member of the Council of the Institute, March 1991, to date.

18. *Opinion on the Annual Report 1987 of the European Commission on the European Regional Development Fund*, European Economic & Social Committee, Brussels, 12 July 1989.

19. *Annual Report 1987*, CII, Dublin.

20. European Council, Brussels Summit 1988, Brussels, 11 to 13 February 1988.

21. *The EU in Ireland*, website of the European Commission, January 2008.

22. *Annual Report 1988*, CII, Dublin.

23. The *Treaty on European Union* ('the Maastricht Treaty')was signed in Maastricht, Netherlands, on 7 February 1992, and entered into force on 1 November 1993.

24. The three pillars of the Maastricht Treaty are the European Communities, the Common Foreign & Security Policy, and police and judicial cooperation in criminal matters.

25. Power, C, *New European Order: Ireland's Strategic Response,* lecture in tribute to the late Ruaidhrí Roberts, former General Secretary, ICTU, organised by The People's College, The Larkin Hall, ICTU Training Centre, Dublin, 9 April 1992.

26. *Annual Report 1979*, CII, Dublin.

27. *Conference on Economic & Monetary Union,* CII / AMUE, Dublin, 21 March 1991; chairman, Con Power, CII Director of Economic Policy; speakers: Maurice O'Connell, Second Secretary General, Department of Finance; Paddy McEvoy, Chief Executive, Irish Intercontinental Bank; Brian O'Loghlen, European Commission; Brian Garraway, Deputy Chairman, BAT Industries & Board Member, AMUE; and David Croughan, CII Chief Economist.

28. Power, C, *EMU: The Road to Political Union,* CII / AMUE Conference, Dublin, 12 March 1991 – see reference 27.

29. *Opinion Poll on a European Single Currency,* AMUE, Paris, September / October 1990. The poll, taken in all 12 of the then European Community Member States, showed that 74% of respondents in Ireland favoured a single European currency, in contrast to 61% in the EC, on average. Support for a single currency ranged from 80% in Greece to 31% in Denmark.

30. *A Review of Industrial Policy* ('Telesis Report'), Report No.64, NESC, Dublin, October 1982.

31. See reference 30.

32. *Ireland in the European Community: Performance, Prospects & Strategy*, Report No.88, NESC, Dublin, September 1989.

33. 'The Challenge of the Single European Market', *CII Newsletter*, Vol.55, No.19, 17 December 1991.
34. 'The 1989 Budget', *CII Newsletter*, Vol.50, No.4, 6 December 1988.
35. 'The 1990 Budget', *CII Newsletter*, Vol.51, No.24, 26 October 1989.
36. *Submission to the European Commission on the Communication from the Commission to the Council of Ministers & to the European Parliament: Completion of the Internal Market & Approximation of Indirect Taxes,* COM(89)260 final – Brussels, 14 June 1989, CII submission, August 1989.
37. 'The 1991 Budget', *CII Newsletter*, Vol.53, No.24, 30 October 1990.
38. 'The 1992 Budget – Submission to Government', *CII Newsletter*, Vol.55, No.16, 5 November 1991.
39. *White Paper on Enterprise Taxation,* European Commission, Brussels, 1987.
40. Power, C, *Ireland – Europe's success story of the 1990s?*, 5th Annual Corporate Finance Conference, organised by Business Research International, Dublin, 13 November 1989, published in *CII Newsletter*, Vol.52, No.1, 14 November 1989.
41. Harcourt, T, *The Celtic Tiger Keeps Earning its Stripes,* Australian Trade Commission, Sydney, 1 August 2006.

CHAPTER 14: IRELAND ON THE WORLD STAGE

1. Quigley, G, chairman, Ulster Bank, speaking at the CII Annual Conference, Dublin, 1992. Both he and Liam Connellan, CII Director General, proposed the development of a Belfast / Dublin Economic Corridor and strongly promoted that concept both in Ireland and in the USA.
2. Inter*Trade*Ireland is one of the statutory North / South Institutions established under the aegis of the North / South Ministerial Council, which came into being formally on Thursday, 2 December 1999, under the British-Irish Agreement 1998, consequent on the Good Friday Agreement, April 1998.
3. Power, C, chairman and non-executive director, Kompass Ireland Publishers Limited, 1 January 1990 to 31 December 1993, and non-executive director of Keypass Direct Information Limited (Northern Ireland), 1 September, 1990 to 31 December 1993. The Kompass Ireland appointment was widely reported in the media – *Cork Examiner*, 22 January, 1990; *Construction & Property News*, 24 January, 1990; *Irish Marketing Journal*, February, 1990; *Irish Independent*, 1 February 1990; *The Irish Times*, 1ᵗ February, 1990; *Business & Finance*, 8 February 1990.
4. Power, C, Member of the Industrial & Commercial Members Committee, CCAB-I, May 1987 to March 1992, including chairman, 1988/1989 – CCAB-I covers the island of Ireland, North & South; chair 1990/1991 of the Development Committee, ACCA Ireland, which covers the island of Ireland; Member of the Panel of the Admissions and Licensing, Disciplinary & Appeal Committees of ACCA, for the United Kingdom, Ireland, and worldwide, February 1999 to date.

5. 'Launch of All-Ireland Business Directory', by O'Malley, D, TD, Minister for Industry & Commerce, *CII Newsletter*, Vol.56, No.2, 7 April 1992; *Sunday Tribune*, 15 March 1992.

6. Power, C, *Ireland in Europe – A Strategic Response*, 8th Annual Irish Corporate Finance Conference, Business Research International, Dublin, 11 November 1991; and Power, C, 'New European Order: Ireland's Strategic Response', *Stubbs Gazette*, Vol.XCVI, No.18, 3 May 1991.

7. Power, C, 'Economic Growth & Development: Small Country Comparisons', *Business Studies for Leaving Certificate Students*, Vol.2, Part 4, School & College Publishing Limited, Dublin, 1984; and 'Strategy for a Small Nation', *CII Newsletter*, Vol.48, No.2, 17 November 1987.

8. 'German Unification – Some Consequences for Ireland', *CII Newsletter*, Vol.54, No.4, 4 December 1990.

9. Power, C, *Eastern Europe: Opportunity or Threat?*, Institute of Management Consultants, Dublin, 4 October 1990; based on 'Irish Opportunities in Eastern Europe', *CII Newsletter*, Vol.53, No.11, 17 July 1990.

10. Power, C, 'Ireland in Europe: Peripherality – Threat or Opportunity?', *Irish Exporter*, February 1991; 'A Shift to the East', LINK, April 1991.

11. O'Hagan, JW & Foley, GJ, *The Confederation of Irish Industry: The First Fifty Years 1932-1982*, CII, Dublin, 1982.

12. The LOME Convention was an Agreement between the EEC and the African, Caribbean and Pacific States.

13. In 1982, the first year of operation of the Employment Support Scheme, 90 applications for the support of additional Irish export salespersons working abroad were approved by Córas Tráchtála, with a focus on Continental Europe, the Far East and the USA.

14. The nine international bilateral associations affiliated to the CII in 1989 were the Ireland-Japan Economic Association (founded 1974), Irish-Belgian Business Association (inaugural meeting, May 1988), Irish-German Business Association (established November, 1988), Ireland-France Economic Association (elevated to the status of a Chamber of Commerce in 1989, the Bicentenary of the French Revolution), the Ireland-Spain Economic Association (founded, March 1989), the Irish-Swedish Business Association, the Ireland-Korea Business Association, the Ireland-Taiwan Business Association, and the British-Irish Industry Circle (founded, 1989).

15. *Ireland in Europe*, relationships between Ireland and countries of Western Europe – Austria, Belgium, Denmark, Finland, France, Germany, Greece, Iceland, Italy, Luxembourg, The Netherlands, Norway, Portugal, Spain, Sweden, Switzerland, and the United Kingdom – CII, Dublin, 4 July 1988.

16. Power, C, as CII Director of Economic Policy, maintained close liaison with the Embassies in Ireland or accredited to Ireland of Australia, Canada, China, Czechoslovakia, Denmark, France, Germany, Hungary, Mexico, Poland, Russia, South Africa, USA, and the United Kingdom.

17. Power, C, *Development Strategy for Success: How a Small Island Beats International Competition*, 5th Annual Corporate Finance Conference, Business Research International, Dublin, 15 November 1988.

18. Power, C, 'European Union – Why Ireland is Ideally Located', *Sligo Champion*, 15 May 1992.

19. American Chamber of Commerce Ireland, *website* http://www.amcham.ie as at 8th September, 2008.

20. Power, C, *Promoting US Trade & Investment*, US Tax & Investment seminar, organised by CII in association with Arthur Andersen, Chartered Accountants, Dublin, 30 October 1991; and *CII Newsletter*, Vol.55, No.19, 17 December 1991.

21. Power, C, *Ireland: Gateway to Europe*, (Lawyers) Bar European Group Annual Conference, Dublin, 27 March 1993.

APPENDIX I: THE CONFEDERATION OF IRISH INDUSTRY (CII)

1. O'Hagan, JW & Foley, GJ, *The Confederation of Irish Industry: The First Fifty Years 1932-1982*, CII, Dublin, 1982

2. *Annual Report*, each year from 1979 to 1992, CII, Dublin.

INDEX

See **page vii** for explanations of acronyms used.

Barbados 107
Barrett, Sylvester, TD 112
Barrington Report, the
    see Commission of Inquiry
    on Safety, Health & Welfare
    at Work
Barry, Peter, TD 128, 133
Beddy, James Patrick 16
Belgium 21, 100, 101, 102,
                151, 153, 229, 231,
                247, 248, 249
    financial services 200
Berehaven 15
Bermuda 107
Big Government' 38
black economy' 220
Boland, John, TD 116, 204
Bord na Mona 180, 193, 209,
                222, 213, 214
Bowman, Ray 73
Brady, Vincent, TD 62
BRITE 199
British Commonwealth 15
Brooks Watson Group 73
Brooks, Albert 41
Brown, Tony 222
Bruton, John, TD 36, 61, 64-65,
                81, 182
BSTAI 171, 172
Buchanan Report
    see *Regional Development in Ireland*
Budget
    1972 35, 146
    1978 51
    1982 44, 45
    1983 44, 89
    1984 189
    1986 31, 58, 97
    1987 87, 155
    1988 87
    1990 232
    1991 167

Budget & Economic Statistics 2007
    see Department of Finance,
    Budget & Economic Statistics
    2007
Building on Reality 34, 45, 55
Building on Reality 1985-1987 114, 115
Bulgaria 229
Bundesbank 240, 241
Burke, Ray, TD 62, 116
Business Expansion Scheme 82, 208
business legislation 9
    see also company law
BUSINESSEUROPE 22
Byrne, Donal 73
Byrne, Greg 207

Cadbury Ireland Ltd 73
Calleary, Sean, TD 182
Canada 11, 14, 95,
                211, 249, 250
CAP 23, 217, 218, 230
career guidance 77
Carlson, Chester 175
Cassells, Peter 71, 73
CBI 244
    Kompass UK 238
CBI NI 237
    Joint Business Council 237-238
CCI 70
Ceann Comhairle 64
CEEP 65
CEIF 220
    Annual Conference 1970 22
Celtic Tiger 1-4, 5, 10, 17,
                18, 59, 69-72, 163,
                198, 222, 233, 253
Census
    1841 2, 75
    1926 142
    1961 2
    1971 75
    1979 75
    1986 2
    1991 2

OAK TREE PRESS

is Ireland's leading business book publisher.

It develops and delivers
information, advice and resources
to entrepreneurs and managers –
and those who educate and support them.

Its print, software and web materials
are in use in Ireland, the UK, Finland,
Greece, Norway and Slovenia.

OAK TREE PRESS

19 Rutland Street
Cork, Ireland
T: + 353 21 4313855
F: + 353 21 4313496
E: info@oaktreepress.com
W: www.oaktreepress.com